Center for
Creative Leadership

The CCL Guide
to Leadership in Action

Martin Wilcox
Stephen Rush
Editors

Foreword by

Frances Hesselbein

The CCL
Guide to
Leadership
in Action

How Managers and Organizations
Can Improve the Practice of Leadership

JOSSEY-BASS
A Wiley Imprint
www.josseybass.com

Center for
Creative Leadership

leadership. learning. life.

Published by Jossey-Bass
A Wiley Imprint
989 Market Street, San Francisco, CA 94103-1741   www.josseybass.com

Jossey-Bass books and products are available through most bookstores. To contact Jossey-Bass directly call our Customer Care Department within the U.S. at 800-956-7739, outside the U.S. at 317-572-3986, or fax 317-572-4002.

Jossey-Bass also publishes its books in a variety of electronic formats. Some content that appears in print may not be available in electronic books.

Library of Congress Cataloging-in-Publication Data

The CCL guide to leadership in action : how managers and organizations can improve the practice of leadership / by Martin Wilcox, Stephen Rush, editors ; foreword by Frances Hesselbein.—1st ed.
    p. cm.
"A joint publication of the Jossey-Bass business & management series and the Center for Creative Leadership."
A collection of articles originally published in CCL's Leadership in action.
Includes bibliographical references and index.
ISBN 0-7879-7370-X (alk. paper)
1. Leadership. 2. Executive ability. 3. Creative ability in business. 4. Executives—Training of. 5. Organizational effectiveness I. Title: Center for Creative Leadership guide to leadership in action. II. Title: Guide to leadership in action. III. Wilcox, Martin. IV. Rush, Stephen, 1954- V. Center for Creative Leadership. VI. Leadership in action.
HD57.7.C39 2004
658.4'092—dc22

2004000687

Printed in the United States of America
FIRST EDITION
HB Printing   10 9 8 7 6 5 4 3 2 1

A Joint Publication of

The Jossey-Bass

Business & Management Series

and

The Center for Creative Leadership

Contents

Foreword

Leaders everywhere will welcome this definitive guide on how to examine their own leadership philosophy, performance, and present effectiveness against the enormous challenges and opportunities that confront organizations of the future.

Fortunately, the opportunities for leaders to grow are greater than even the most formidable challenges that are part of their daily lives. Once you have read and put into practice what the knowledge community at the Center for Creative Leadership (CCL) has to say about creating healthy leaders and organizations, you can measure your own results. You can look at your own performance in providing significant leadership development opportunities for people across your organization. And with a new understanding of "what to do differently on Monday morning," you will be ready for the next challenge—dealing with change—in a period of the most massive change since the American Revolution.

As I read the powerful chapters in this book, leading change comes through as an imperative for leaders in all three sectors that I believe are necessary for a healthy society: a public sector of effective governments, a private sector of effective businesses, and a social sector of effective community organizations. This imperative requires a focus on, and an eagerness to embrace, innovation that will lead to new dimensions of performance and will give courage to the newest leader as well as the most experienced agent of change.

"Culture" is one of the most discussed and most poorly defined aspects in leadership dialogue across the sectors. In this guide you find clear direction. Working across cultures is an indispensable skill for leaders living, working, and leading in our rapidly changing universe with rich and complex diversity rapidly increasing and enriching our changing cultural landscapes. All of us who lead in any organization in any sector need to see this as an enormous opportunity to build the richly diverse, inclusive, viable enterprise. The messages on culture are a great gift.

Much has been written about coaching. It may well be the most talked about component of current leadership development initiatives. The feedback and coaching chapter helps us understand and define this support for planning and delivering a newly energized and effective leadership performance for ourselves and everyone on our team.

With all the headlines today about failing organizations and their failed leaders, there is a new urgency in all three sectors, and a new interest in building the healthy organization with superior leadership development. This guide from CCL leads the way in providing impressive help in designing the leadership development opportunities for individuals at all levels of the organization, including those in the pipeline.

This remarkable book will help you and the other leaders you work with redefine the future; build healthy, diverse, and inclusive organizations; and develop effective leaders of quality, character, and courage to lead the organization to new levels of viability, service, and significance.

New York, New York   Frances Hesselbein
February 2004

Preface:
Ideas into Action

Welcome to *The CCL Guide to Leadership in Action*. It is the aim of this book to help you, as a manager, improve your leadership and your organization, and we believe the quality of the articles offered here speaks for itself. We thought you might be interested, though, in what's behind the articles.

They were originally published in *Leadership in Action*, a bimonthly magazine that draws on the work of the Center for Creative Leadership. As an international educational institution, CCL has the mission of advancing the understanding, practice, and development of leadership for the benefit of society worldwide. Its faculty, numbering more than one hundred, carries out a range of activities including extensive research, open-enrollment programs, custom interventions, instrument development and application, and coaching.

Since CCL's founding in 1970 this work has followed a simple principle: ideas into action. That principle informs many aspects of this book, but two deserve special mention. First, the content of the articles is a product of CCL's practice as a knowledge community, a practice that takes a systematic approach to transforming ideas into action. Second, the presentation of the articles reflects what we believe is necessary for you to put the ideas contained there into your practice.

Practical Content

The ideas-into-action process at CCL is driven by the CCL faculty. In essence, the faculty takes promising ideas about leadership, tests them through research with managers and executives in a variety of organizations, puts the ideas that prove out into the most practical terms, and then disseminates them in various formats.

The ideas come from a number of sources. Most originate in CCL's research and educational activities, but many (as the interviews in this book suggest) are generated outside CCL, as the faculty draws on the work of other experts in the fields of leadership and organizational thinking. Whatever their source, however, the ideas are put through this action-oriented process.

Over the years CCL has thus produced a great deal of practical knowledge, and it continues to do so today. But just as important as the amount of knowledge produced is the fact that the knowledge is shared. Unlike the typical university department, professional association, or consultant organization, the CCL faculty is not essentially a collection of individual experts, although the individual credentials of the faculty are impressive; rather, as a knowledge community, its members hold a common philosophy of how leadership can be developed. They work together to understand and generate practical responses to today's leadership and organizational challenges.

What is this philosophy? It begins with the recognition that every person is capable of improving his or her leadership effectiveness. Further, we believe that an organization or community as a whole can enhance its leadership capability by developing the ways in which people throughout the organization or community connect to address their collective challenges.

Thus, in its educational work with individuals, CCL pays particular attention to the development of self-understanding and interpersonal competency. Feedback-rich experiences in a supportive learning environment are an effective way to promote self-understanding and motivate personal development. Among the learning formats that CCL provides are numerous vehicles for feedback, including 360-degree assessments, psychological instruments, and experiential exercises and simulations. CCL demonstrates a supportive learning environment by allowing people to decide with whom they will share their feedback and learning and by encouraging them to identify how their own hopes and dreams can be aligned with those of others to build effective organizations and communities.

The educational work of CCL also recognizes that effective leadership requires continual learning and development from a wide range of work and life experiences. Although individuals are ultimately responsible for their own learning, organizations and communities can enhance leader development by providing and encouraging participation in a variety of work and life experiences that offer assessment, challenge, and support.

CCL's work with groups and organizations focuses on leadership as a collective or shared process. Leadership processes can be improved not just through the development of individual members of a group or organization but also through collective learning and community development. Experiences that promote dialogue among group and organization members and that facilitate new ways of working together are effective approaches for enhancing leadership in organizations and addressing complex organizational and community challenges.

CCL also acknowledges that the understanding, practice, and development of leadership are subject to cultural influences. Thus the faculty is working to better understand how beliefs and practices need to be augmented to work effectively in various cultural contexts.

Straightforward Presentation

The articles offered here, because they are a product of the CCL knowledge community, are an expression of this philosophy. In order to disseminate this content in a way that is true to the ideas-into-action principle, a systematic effort has been made to ensure that the articles are straightforward and usable in their presentation.

Each article considers an organizational situation that leaders face today and helps you deal with this challenge in two ways. First, it offers an overview that orients you to the situation, and, second, it provides guidelines for action. Not only do these guidelines supply suggestions for taking immediate action, but they also lay the groundwork for future action because they have been chosen to contribute to your ability to learn from your experience as you apply them. We believe that the consistent approach to the presentation of the articles will help you incorporate the ideas contained in them into your practice.

In addition to their focus on specific organizational situations, the articles offered here have a general practical goal. They aim to expand your leadership resources.

It is sometimes overlooked that how you understand leadership has a profound effect on how you practice it—and how you develop. If you view leadership in the conventional way, as a set of characteristics—or behaviors—that you need in order to influence people to follow you, then you will probably focus on your own individual resources when confronted with an organizational challenge.

If, however, you think of leadership as a collective process, one that individuals with particular skills can facilitate but that must fundamentally involve many members of the organization, then you may well be able to access far greater resources. Many of the things you do will be the same, but you will have some additional, perhaps crucial, options.

Conclusion

We believe this book offers a distinct value: the benefit of CCL's efforts as a unique knowledge community with a well-defined educational philosophy that guides the development of products to help people learn from their own experience about how to improve leadership.

You can learn more about the authors who represent this community in the contributors list that follows this preface. For those who would like to learn more about CCL's educational philosophy and methods, we recommend taking a look at another recently published book—the second edition of *The Center for Creative Leadership Handbook of Leadership Development*.

Greensboro, North Carolina   Martin Wilcox
February 2004   Director of Publications, CCL
                                          Editor, *Leadership in Action*

                                                      Stephen Rush
                              Managing Editor, *Leadership in Action*

Acknowledgments

We would like to thank all the people who have contributed articles to *Leadership in Action* over the years, both those whom we were able to include in this book and those who provided the many other fine pieces we weren't able to include. They are too numerous to list here but they are the soul of this book.

We would also like to thank the people who have provided guidance and support in the production of *LiA:* Wilfred Drath, Joanne Ferguson, Mary Garrett, Phyllis Hawkins, Jennifer Hines, Marcia Horowitz, Ross Horowitz, Lily Kelly-Radford, Sara King, Susan Lewis, Kelly Lombardino, Elspeth MacHattie, Karen Mayworth, Tom McCarthy, Cynthia McCauley, Sarah Miller, Marianne Moorhead, Deborah Nasitka, Alice Rowan, Marian Ruderman, Byron Schneider, Pete Scisco, Kathe Sweeney, Ellen Van Velsor, Jo-Ann Wasserman, and Frank Welsch. Your help has always been appreciated.

List of Contributors

John Alexander is president of the Center for Creative Leadership.

Paige Bader, a doctoral student at George Mason University, was an intern at CCL during 2002. She holds an M.A. degree from George Mason University.

Vidula Bal, a senior research associate at CCL in San Diego, holds a Ph.D. degree from the University of Texas at Austin.

David Baldwin, a senior program associate at CCL in San Diego, holds an M.S. degree from Illinois State University.

Katherine Beatty, a program manager at CCL in Colorado Springs, holds a Ph.D. degree from Saint Louis University.

David Berke, a senior program associate at CCL in San Diego, holds an M.B.A. degree from the University of Southern California and an M.A. degree from the State University of New York at Stony Brook.

Raoul J. Buron, formerly the director of feedback and coaching at CCL, is vice president, chief learning officer, with Prudential Financial in Newark, New Jersey. He holds a Ph.D. degree from the University of Southern California.

Allan Calarco, a program manager at CCL in Brussels, Belgium, holds an M.S. degree from Shippensburg University.

David Campbell, the H. Smith Richardson Senior Fellow at CCL in Colorado Springs, holds a Ph.D. degree from the University of Minnesota.

Keith A. Caver, formerly group director of custom solutions for North America, at CCL in Greensboro, holds an M.S. degree from the Air Force Institute of Technology.

Craig Chappelow, senior manager, assessment and development resources, at CCL in Greensboro, holds an M.Ed. degree from the University of Vermont.

Jay A. Conger, a professor of organizational behavior at the London Business School and senior research scientist at the Center for Effective Organizations at the University of Southern California, was CCL's H. Smith Richardson Jr. Visiting Fellow for 2000.

Wilfred H. Drath, a senior fellow and an R&D director for leadership systems and strategies at CCL in Greensboro, holds a B.A. degree from the University of Georgia.

Christopher Ernst, a senior associate at CCL in Greensboro, holds a Ph.D. degree from North Carolina State University.

Robert C. Ginnett, a senior fellow at CCL in Colorado Springs, holds a Ph.D. degree from Yale University.

Kelly Hannum, a research associate at CCL in Greensboro, holds a Ph.D. degree from the University of North Carolina at Greensboro.

Wayne Hart, a feedback and coaching manager at CCL in San Diego, holds a Ph.D. degree from the Fielding Institute in Santa Barbara, California.

Michael H. Hoppe, a senior program and research associate at CCL in Greensboro, holds an M.S. degree from the University of Munich, Germany, and a Ph.D. degree from the University of North Carolina at Chapel Hill.

Kim Kanaga, director of CCL's Greensboro campus, holds a Ph.D. degree from Michigan State University.

Karen Kirkland, a senior program associate at CCL in San Diego, holds a Ph.D. degree from the University of Missouri.

Gene Klann, a senior program associate at CCL in Greensboro, holds a Ph.D. degree from the Free University of Brussels.

Michael E. Kossler, a senior enterprise associate in the custom solutions group at CCL in Greensboro, holds an M.A. degree from the University of Akron and an M.M. degree from Aquinas College.

Jean Brittain Leslie, senior manager, assessment and development, at CCL in Greensboro, holds an M.A. degree from the University of North Carolina at Greensboro.

Ancella B. Livers, a program manager at CCL in Greensboro, holds a Ph.D. degree from Carnegie Mellon University.

Dana McDonald-Mann, formerly senior program associate at CCL, is a vice president in leadership development at Wachovia Corporation in Charlotte, North Carolina. She holds a Ph.D. degree from the University of Maryland, College Park.

Sharon McDowell-Larsen, a program associate at CCL in Colorado Springs, holds a Ph.D. degree from the University of Nebraska–Lincoln.

Patricia J. Ohlott, a senior associate at CCL in Greensboro, holds a B.A. degree from Yale University and has completed graduate work at Duke University.

Sonya Prestridge, formerly a senior program associate in the custom solutions group at CCL in Greensboro, is retired and living in Durham, North Carolina. She holds a Ph.D. degree from the University of North Carolina at Chapel Hill.

Don W. Prince, open enrollment manager for CCL in Brussels, Belgium, holds degrees from the University of North Texas and Southwestern Seminary.

Laura Quinn, formerly a senior program and research associate at CCL in Colorado Springs, is an associate professor in the communications department at the University of Colorado at Colorado Springs. She holds a Ph.D. degree from the University of Texas at Austin.

Marian N. Ruderman, an R&D Director for context of difference, at CCL in Greensboro, holds a Ph.D. degree from the University of Michigan.

Stephen Rush is the managing editor of *Leadership in Action*.

Valerie I. Sessa, formerly a research scientist at CCL in Greensboro, is an assistant professor of industrial and organizational psychology at Montclair State University in Upper Montclair, New Jersey. She holds a Ph.D. degree from New York University.

Davida Sharpe, an enterprise design associate, is based in Nashville, Tennessee. She holds an M.S. degree from North Carolina A&T State University.

Judith L. Steed, a research associate at CCL in Colorado Springs, holds an M.S. degree from Virginia Polytechnic Institute and State University.

Jodi J. Taylor, formerly a vice president of CCL, is managing partner for US Leadership Services, Whitehead Mann LLC. She holds a Ph.D. degree from the University of Texas at Austin.

Stephanie Trovas, marketing strategy manager with CCL in Colorado Springs, holds an M.B.A. degree from the University of Colorado at Colorado Springs.

Sloan R. Weitzel, formerly a product manager for online digital services at CCL in Greensboro, holds an M.B.A. degree from Duke University.

The CCL Guide
to Leadership in Action

Part I

Creating Healthy Leaders

Chapter One

Skills for Leaders

Probably the most discussed and thoroughly researched question among people concerned with leadership is this: What skills (or behaviors or personal attributes) are necessary for a leader to be effective? Thousands of skill lists have been assembled, frequently as part of a definition of leadership, and this continues to be a fundamental question. What is significant, as this chapter illustrates, is how these lists increasingly focus on skills that allow leaders to enhance the effectiveness of others.

◆ ◆ ◆

Making the Connection: Leadership Skills and Emotional Intelligence

Marian N. Ruderman, Kelly Hannum,
Jean Brittain Leslie, and Judith L. Steed

Stuart is a senior manager at a well-known pharmaceutical company. He is brilliant, and everyone who knows him believes he has the potential to achieve great things. His primary strength is strategic thinking; colleagues say he has an uncanny ability to predict and plan for the future. As Stuart has advanced in the organization, however, his dark side has become increasingly apparent: he often lashes out at people, and he is unable to build relationships based on trust. Stuart knows he is intelligent and tends to use that knowledge to belittle or demean his co-workers. Realizing that Stuart has extraordinary skills and much to offer the company in terms of vision and strategy, some of his colleagues have tried to help him work past his flaws. But they're beginning to conclude that it's a hopeless cause; Stuart stubbornly refuses to change his style, and his arrogant modus operandi has offended so many people that Stuart's career may no longer be salvageable.

Every company probably has someone like Stuart—a senior manager whose IQ approaches the genius level but who seems clueless when it comes to dealing with other people. These types of managers may be prone to getting angry easily and verbally attacking co-workers, often come across as lacking compassion and empathy, and usually find it difficult to get others to cooperate with them and their agendas. The Stuarts of the world make you wonder how people so smart can be so incapable of understanding themselves and others.

What Stuart is lacking is *emotional intelligence*. There may be little hope of salvaging Stuart's career, but there is good news for managers who are similarly deficient in emotional intelligence capacities but willing to try to change their ways: emotional intelligence can be developed and enhanced.

Dealing with Emotions

In articles published in 1990, psychologists Jack Mayer of the University of New Hampshire and Peter Salovey of Yale University coined the term *emotional intelligence*, referring to the constellation of abilities through which people deal with their own emotions and those of others. Mayer and Salovey later went on to define emotional intelligence as the ability to perceive emotional information and use it to guide thought and actions; they distinguished it from cognitive intelligence, which is what determines whether people will be successful in school and is measured through IQ tests.

The concept of emotional intelligence was popularized by psychologist Daniel Goleman in his books *Emotional Intelligence* and *Working with Emotional Intelligence*, among other writings. Goleman broadened the notion of emotional intelligence to include an array of noncognitive abilities that help people adapt to all aspects of life. He focused on four basic competencies—self-awareness, social awareness, self-management, and social skills—that influence the way people handle themselves and their relationships with others. He argued that these human competencies play a bigger role than cognitive intelligence in determining success in life and in the workplace.

Mayer, Salovey, and Goleman were not the first to recognize the significance of the attributes now collectively called emotional intelligence. For years before, managers, educators, human resource professionals, and others had seen evidence that these attributes—known then by more generic, colloquial terms such as *people skills*—seemed to play an important role in separating the average from the first-rate performers. Like Goleman, many of these observers believed these skills were more important than intellect or technical skills in determining success.

Throughout CCL's more than thirty-year history, one of its primary approaches to leadership development has been to help managers and executives to understand themselves and others better, to increase their self-awareness, self-management, and interpersonal skills—in other words, to expand their emotional intelligence, although CCL has not used that term. CCL has done this through a range of programs, simulations, publications, and tools—including Benchmarks, a 360-degree assessment instrument that measures leaders' strengths and development needs as compared with those of other leaders. Although CCL and others have long believed that people's levels of emotional competency are related to their effectiveness as leaders, little had been done to scientifically examine and document whether specific elements of emotional intelligence are linked to specific behaviors associated with leadership effectiveness and ineffectiveness—and if they are, how they are linked. With this goal, CCL designed and conducted a study that correlated Benchmarks results with scores from an assessment instrument through which people gauge their own emotional intelligence abilities. Although the findings are not sufficient to state conclusively that leaders with high levels of emotional intelligence are better leaders, they do show that there are clear and basic connections between the higher ranges of emotional intelligence and the possession of skills and abilities associated with leadership excellence. Knowing and understanding these connections can give managers and executives additional ammunition in their efforts to enhance their leadership performance.

Note

To explore whether specific behaviors associated with leadership effectiveness are connected to particular elements of emotional intelligence, CCL designed and conducted a study in which 302 managers took part. The managers, who were participants in CCL's Leadership Development Program, were assessed through Benchmarks, a 360-degree feedback instrument that gives managers insights into how their bosses, peers, direct reports, and they themselves perceive their leadership strengths and development needs. The managers also completed the BarOn Emotional Quotient Inventory (EQ-i), with which people assess themselves on fifteen components of emotional intelligence. The BarOn EQ-i was developed through nineteen years of research conducted around the world by clinical psychologist Reuven Bar-On and is published by Multi-Health Systems of North Tonawanda, New York. The results from Benchmarks and the BarOn EQ-i were correlated to reveal associations between leadership skills, perspectives, and derailment factors and aspects of emotional intelligence.

The senior-level managers in the study averaged just under forty-three years old. Seventy-three percent were male, 81 percent were white, and 90 percent had a minimum of a bachelor's degree.

Strongest Links

The study comparing Benchmarks results with scores from the BarOn Emotional Quotient Inventory, an assessment of emotional intelligence, found that ten of the sixteen skills and perspectives assessed by Benchmarks were strongly associated with one or more emotional intelligence measures. In other words, higher levels of certain emotional intelligence components appear to be connected to better performance in those ten areas. Benchmarks is also designed to identify potential problem areas that can contribute to derailment, which occurs when a manager who has previously been seen as successful and full of potential for continued advancement is instead fired, demoted, or held on a career plateau. Associations were also found between two of these career-threatening flaws and certain aspects of emotional intelligence.

Let's look first at the connections between emotional intelligence and leadership skills and perspectives:

Participative management. Of all the skills and perspectives measured by Benchmarks, participative management had the highest number of meaningful correlations with measures of emotional intelligence. The essence of participative management is getting buy-in from colleagues at the beginning of an initiative by involving them, engaging them through listening and communicating, influencing them in the decision-making process, and building consensus. It is an important relationship-building skill, especially in today's management environment, in which organizations value interdependency within and between groups. Depending on the Benchmarks rater (boss, peer, or direct report), scores in participative management were related to the emotional intelligence abilities of social responsibility (being a cooperative, contributing, and constructive member of one's social group), happiness (feeling satisfied with and deriving pleasure from life), interpersonal relationship (establishing and maintaining mutually satisfying relationships), impulse control (resisting impulsive behavior), emotional self-awareness (being in touch with one's own feelings), and empathy (understanding and appreciating the feelings of others). These correlations suggest that managers who are perceived as being skilled at listening to others and gaining their input before implementing change are likely also to see themselves as satisfied with life and good at cooperating, fostering relationships, controlling impulses, and understanding their own and others' emotions.

Putting people at ease. People who are warm and have a good sense of humor are often able to make others feel at ease, relaxed, and comfortable in their presence. The connections between this skill and emotional intelligence qualities also varied according to who did the rating. The assessments by managers' direct reports indicated that the ability to put people at ease was related to impulse control, which suggests that not overreacting in difficult situations and avoiding knee-jerk responses such as quick anger go a long way toward making people feel relaxed. The assessments by bosses indicated that managers' ability to put others at ease was tied to the managers' own sense of happiness, suggesting that a manager's disposition is a determinant of how comfortable people feel in his or her presence.

Self-awareness. Managers who were seen by their bosses, peers, and direct reports as having an accurate picture of their strengths and weaknesses and as being willing to improve gave themselves high ratings on the emotional intelligence abilities of impulse control and stress tolerance (withstanding adverse events and stressful situations without falling apart). This suggests that managers who are aware that they may easily explode into anger or become anxious in the face of difficult situations are likely to be perceived as lacking in self-awareness. The assessments by managers' direct reports indicated that self-awareness is also related to social responsibility.

Balance between personal life and work. Managers who had demonstrated to their bosses that they were adept at balancing their work priorities with their personal lives so that neither was neglected gave themselves high ratings in the emotional intelligence abilities of social responsibility, impulse control, and empathy. This suggests that if you give your boss the impression that you are a whole person with a well-rounded life, you're more likely to believe in your abilities to contribute to a group, resist impulsive actions, and understand the emotions of others. Ratings on work-life balance from direct reports were also associated with impulse control.

Straightforwardness and composure. From all rater perspectives, the leadership skills of remaining steadfast and calm during crises, relying on facts, and being able to recover from mistakes were related to impulse control. Direct reports' ratings of their managers' straightforwardness and composure were also associated with stress tolerance, social responsibility, and optimism (the ability to maintain a positive attitude even in the face of adversity), and bosses' ratings of managers' resolve and poise were related to managers' own sense of happiness.

Building and mending relationships. Bosses' assessments of managers' abilities to develop and maintain solid working relationships with people inside and outside their organizations and to negotiate work-related problems without alienating people were linked to impulse control, and direct reports' ratings were associated with stress tolerance. These connections make sense: managers who are prone to explosive outbursts and an inability to control hostility don't do much to help their relationships with their bosses, and problematic relationships with direct reports often cause stress for managers, or conversely, managers' inability to cope with stress and adversity often results in poor relationships with the people they supervise.

Doing whatever it takes. The leadership abilities of being perseverant and staying focused in the face of obstacles, of being action oriented and taking charge, and of taking a stand on one's own if required and at the same time being open to learning from others were associated by managers' bosses and direct reports with the emotional intelligence component of independence. People who rate themselves highly on independence see themselves as being self-directed and self-controlled in their thinking and actions and as being free of emotional dependency. Additionally, bosses' assessments of managers' ability to do whatever it takes were connected with assertiveness—expressing feelings, beliefs, and thoughts in a constructive way—and direct reports' ratings on this leadership skill were connected with optimism. So it appears that managers who are good at doing whatever it takes are more likely to be self-reliant, autonomous, and persistent and positive, even when they encounter adversity.

Decisiveness. Managers said by their direct reports to prefer quick, unhesitating, and approximate actions over slow and precise moves gave themselves high marks on the emotional intelligence quality of independence. This indicates that managers who characterize themselves as independent thinkers and as being self-directed and self-controlled in their actions are more likely to be seen as decisive by the people who work for them.

Confronting problem employees. Peers' assessments of the degree to which managers were able to deal with difficult workers decisively and fairly were tied to the emotional intelligence measure of assertiveness. This indicates that being able to express one's feelings, beliefs, and thoughts in a constructive way is helpful in handling employees whose performance isn't up to par.

Change management. Direct reports' ratings of their managers' effectiveness at implementing strategies to facilitate organizational change initiatives and overcome resistance to change were connected with the emotional intelligence ability of social responsibility. Peers' assessments of managers' change management skills were linked to the emotional intelligence measure of interpersonal relationship. Thus it appears that managers who are cooperative members of their social groups and who are adept at building and sustaining working relationships characterized by intimacy and affection are likely to also be good at leading change by example, involving others in change initiatives, and adjusting to changing situations.

Fast Track to Nowhere

The second section of Benchmarks is designed to identify potential problem areas that can contribute to career derailment. The study found associations between two of these career-threatening flaws and certain aspects of emotional intelligence.

Problems with interpersonal relationships. The connections between managers' difficulties in developing good working relations with others and managers' self-assessments of their emotional intelligence abilities were some of the most striking found in the study. From all three rater perspectives, managers who were seen as having problems with interpersonal relationships—a career flaw characterized by insensitivity, arrogance, impatience, authoritarianism, volatility, and other negative traits and behaviors—scored low on the emotional intelligence ability of impulse control. Interpersonal relationship ratings from direct reports and peers were related to stress tolerance, ratings from direct reports were associated with social responsibility, and bosses' assessments were connected with empathy. These results suggest that no matter how strong their intellectual or technical skills, managers who care little about being cooperative and contributing members of their groups, who can't handle pressure, who easily explode and take their frustrations out on others, and who don't understand or appreciate the feelings of others may be setting themselves up for derailment.

Difficulty changing or adapting. Direct reports' ratings of their managers' resistance to change and ability to learn from mistakes were related to the emotional intelligence measures of stress tolerance and impulse control. A possible explanation for this connection is that managers who have a hard time with change often have a limited comfort zone. When they are forced outside that zone, it sets off anger and resentment, which in turn produces stress.

Points to Ponder

Four principal themes stand out from the relationships found between leadership abilities and emotional intelligence and between derailment characteristics and emotional intelligence:

- As organizations realize that the command-and-control, hierarchical model of leadership is no longer effective, they are increasingly moving toward a more participative management style. It appears that managers can more easily embrace this change and adapt to this style when they have certain emotional intelligence abilities—forming good working relationships, being cooperative and constructive members of a group, controlling anger and other impulses, and in general being pleasant to be around. Co-workers view managers with these characteristics as being effective in the participative style.

• Being centered and grounded is a valuable quality for managers. It's important for managers to give the impression that they are in control of themselves, understand themselves, and know their own strengths and weaknesses. The degree to which managers are perceived as being self-aware, straightforward, and composed and as having balance between their personal and work lives is based largely on how they react under pressure and in difficult situations. If they fall apart or flare up with anger, their leadership abilities are liable to be questioned; if they are imperturbable and resist flying off the handle, their managerial skills are likely to be confirmed.

• A willingness and ability to take action is key to effective leadership. Decisiveness and doing whatever it takes to achieve a goal are associated with independence in thought and actions. Managers who are independent do not ignore the opinions of others but are also not dependent on such input. This self-reliance helps them think strategically, make good decisions, and persevere in the face of obstacles.

• Organizations are placing increased value on interpersonal relationships, and managers who don't handle their emotions well, who lack understanding of themselves and others, and who are abrasive or abusive make others feel uncomfortable. That increases their chances of derailing.

What You Can Do

Emotional intelligence can be developed and enhanced, although doing so takes a lot of effort. Managers who are in danger of derailing because of poor interpersonal relationships are particularly good candidates for working on their emotional intelligence. In general, assessment and feedback instruments such as Benchmarks are good ways to begin improving emotional intelligence, followed by goal setting and a developmental experience that may take the form of classroom training, job assignments, simulations, coaching, or learning from a role model. Managers should identify and address any obstacles to their goals, practice new behaviors in a supportive environment, and review and reassess their behavioral changes to help lock in what they have learned.

More specifically, organizations today value managers who can put the needs of the group ahead of their personal needs—in other words, who have the emotional intelligence capacity of social responsibility. One way to develop this ability may be to involve yourself in the community through charities, nonprofit organizations, and other worthy causes. Devoting time and energy to such groups can help you see beyond your own concerns and improve your ability to be a valued member of a group. Another way to develop social responsibility is to review your individual work goals, then consider them from the perspectives of your team and organization. Ask yourself whether your individual goals facilitate and are aligned with the group and organizational goals, and what you can do to contribute positively to the larger goals.

The ability to handle stress is related to a range of leadership skills and derailment factors. Managers who are lacking in these related characteristics may want to consider stress management training. Be careful, however, to choose a program or workshop that is well designed and has a record of good results. Some of the better programs include assessment, feedback, modeling and practice of new skills, and ongoing support to keep people from lapsing back to their old ways.

Finally, the emotional intelligence ability of impulse control was related to ratings on eight Benchmarks scales. The manifestations of poor impulse control—such as aggression, hostility, irresponsibility, and frustration—are highly conspicuous to colleagues, so learning to restrain impulsive behavior can do a lot to improve a manager's interactions at work. If you have problems with impulse control, you might want to consider coaching as a way to develop composure, patience, self-awareness, adaptability, and coolness under fire. A coach can help you pinpoint your hot buttons and learn how to respond more effectively in situations of conflict or adversity.

◆ ◆ ◆

Through a New Lens:
A Talk with Margaret J. Wheatley

John Alexander

Margaret J. Wheatley writes, teaches, and speaks about radically new ideas for organizing and leading in chaotic times. She is president of the Berkana Institute, a global leadership foundation supporting life-affirming leaders around the world. Wheatley works to create organizations, communities, and systems that are worthy of human habitation and in which people are seen as the blessing, not the problem. She has written two award-winning books: *Leadership and the New Science* and *A Simpler Way* (with Myron Kellner-Rogers). Her latest book is the just-published *Turning to One Another: Simple Conversations to Restore Hope to the Future*. Her articles and work can be accessed at www.margaretwheatley.com.

I met with her during the third annual Friends of the Center Leadership Conference in Kansas City, Missouri, at midyear of 2001. Here are excerpts from the interview:

JA: I would like to focus on the understanding of leadership and the role of the leader in organizations. You have talked about the importance of trust in the leader, so let's start there.

MW: What's interesting to me about this question of trust is that it is a very reciprocal relationship. People need to trust their leader and need to feel that their leader trusts them. One of the biggest stumbling blocks in moving toward more participation and dealing with more diversity is that leaders have not been taught to trust people. Leaders always think about the people in their organization who are untrustworthy. These people kind of mesmerize the leaders with their presence.

JA: *Still, you can reach a tipping point at which these people can have an influence on everybody else and a kind of malaise develops.*

MW: For me this is always an indication that the organization or part of the organization is not walking its talk. In a strongly cohesive, principle-centered work organization, rumors can't spread, because people won't believe them. How do people evaluate whether what they hear is true? It's based on their experience with the organization and with its leaders. So trust is the solution to stopping the incessant flow of rumors and gossip. I have been saying for years that we don't appreciate how much order we can get from good values.

JA: *If you had to give a leader of an organization one bit of advice, would it be to look not only at his or her own values but also the values of the organization?*

MW: I would say that the leader should spend a lot of time creating the identity of the organization—what its values are, what its mission is, what its purpose is, and how is everyone in the organization going to act together as one. These are agreements on how people are going to work together.

JA: *So part of that philosophy would be living the values, not only in the positive sense but also in the sense that if the values are violated then disciplinary action is taken. People who violate the values are spoken to, and if there is a repetition of the behavior they are asked to leave.*

MW: That's right. You can get a whole team or a whole group to hold one another accountable. It isn't the sole responsibility of the leader to notice who is breaking the values and who needs to be fired. In fact, a team can regulate itself in a much more immediate way than a leader can. A leader does sometimes have to step in in cases of true deviants or people who are out to sabotage the organization. Otherwise, I am seeing teams that call each other to account for their behavior. So even that responsibility moves off the shoulders of the leader.

JA: *You have talked about how the leader can no longer be seen as a lone player in an organization.*

MW: The World Wide Web, which is the best example of a self-organized network, has shown us that it is impossible to see or know all that you think you are supposed to know. So we need to realize that we need many more eyes and ears interpreting the information we receive. But people can do that only in a cohesive organization, and the only way to form a cohesive organization is to pay attention to the identity first.

JA: *You have also talked about passion and creativity coming from within the individual in a spontaneous way and your belief that individuals will give true support only to that which they have created. With costs what they are today, almost anything creative that people do seems to have an expensive technology component attached to it. When it comes to creativity and the funding of technology to enable creativity, how do you balance the desire to let a hundred flowers bloom with the need to prioritize and pick only certain flowers?*

MW: In the old model, leaders said they were going to reward creativity, took everyone's suggestions, then paid bonuses to the people who came up with the solutions that the leaders thought were best. In my experience, when you get people together as a unit or team to figure out the most effective response to the question of balancing creativity and funding, they are far more realistic. I find that people in groups are more capable of making intelligent decisions and putting intelligent restrictions on their creativity. When you get a team together to figure out a solution to a problem and you say it can't cost more than this and it can't take longer than this, people get creative within those parameters. They also make much more holistic decisions that account for many more factors. What I do see as a problem is that every time organizations and leaders spend a lot of money creating a solution and then trying to impose it, they spend even more money trying to get people to accept the structure that was imposed. They spend not only money but also an enormous amount of time trying to mop up from the consequences.

JA: *How do you organize around the work without people saying, "I don't know what I'm being held accountable for; I don't know where to go to get a decision made"?*

MW: For me, one of the big questions is, "How do you lead in that work?" Let's assume that the work will be networked, because that's the natural form of organizing. I accept that that is our future. I also accept that for many hundreds if not thousands of years we have been struggling under a form of power relationships and hierarchy that has not prepared us to deal with a networked world. But how do you create very effective localized units that have great levels of autonomy yet are connected to the whole through their identity? What is the information that people should report to each other across the local unit? I don't know the answers to these questions yet.

JA: *What does one say to a leader of a publicly held company whose stock price and quarterly numbers are scrutinized on a daily or even hourly basis?*

MW: There are no solutions for effective leadership within this current insanity of playing companies as if they were poker chips. What has to change is the whole game.

I am looking at companies that are buying themselves back; that is a small but significant trend. Some leaders are just trying to get back the space in which they can think long-term. I'm waiting for the time when a group of powerful CEOs will get together and start to push back against this ridiculous way of life.

JA: *HR professionals with whom we work at CCL are being pressed to figure out how to develop people faster to get them to a higher level of performance. Do you have any advice for them?*

MW: It is an impossibility. If you look at any good company's approach to development, it is long-term; it includes a real focus on the values of the company and developing real business capacity. You cannot fool employees that you are actually developing them if you are only thinking, "OK, here's the next thing you have to learn, but we are not really thinking about you as a long-term resource for the company."

Many companies need to understand that if they are not in development for the long term, they should not even be thinking about it. We are experiencing a vast implosion of all kinds of highly structured organizations. Look at what is going on in religious institutions—they are suffering from the weight of their past and their inability to move according to the needs. It's happening in the military, which can't continue to use its old structures and be effective. It's happening in public schools, health care, and government.

JA: *What do these organizations and sectors need to do?*

MW: My own desire is to support those systems that are really inventing the *new*. They include the dot-coms, which will come back with the next way to use the Internet. They include the people changing how schooling is done in their communities, the people choosing alternative health care and other ways of getting past the big bureaucracies of medicine.

JA: *What about the dot-com phenomenon, though? There was, and to a certain extent still is, a tremendous amount of wide-open, fast-paced experimentation and innovation, and yet it appears that the great majority of these companies crashed and burned partly because they didn't have any kind of structure, plan, strategy, bottom line, or development.*

MW: I would expect that when they come back they will have learned that you can't operate at that pace without any kind of grounding. They were the first experiment. What is going on now is just part of a redefining of the way the world works and how organizations are structured. I have been looking at what happens to human motivation and human energy when there is a whole new frontier such as the dot-coms. What the Web has given us is a whole new frontier for creativity. We need to hear both sides. The traditionalists and the dot-coms need to learn what can be transferred from the old to the new, and what there is in the new that hopefully could reinvigorate some of the old.

JA: *CCL is in the business of helping adults learn, grow, and change. How does one learn in this environment, in which there is pressure not only to develop faster but also to learn on the fly?*

MW: We do have to acknowledge the pace at which people now need to learn. We know that learning accelerates when the things that people are studying are relevant. We also know that if people are learning alongside colleagues they will learn better and faster.

However, it also takes time to integrate learning and to find its deeper meaning. We can support people through more sporadic learning—rather than a five-day program, for instance, it might be two days, then you go back to the workplace and apply and think about what you have learned, and then you go back to the program.

JA: *If the workplace supports that sort of thing.*

MW: Right. If the workplace doesn't support that approach, I don't know what the motivation would be except for a sense of individual learning and achievement—or seeing that maybe you should leave that workplace.

JA: *What about the current focus on action learning—the idea that people learn mainly by doing and that working on projects is the principal vehicle for learning?*

MW: I think action learning is good, but the one thing that is missing from action learning in this country is an appreciation of reflection and taking the time to think. Sometimes action learning seems to be more about just making sure that people are working, that their work doesn't slip. When I teach in other cultures I can feel that people want to be thoughtful in a way that is no longer true in the United States. People want the theory behind something and want to understand the logic behind an argument. When I speak in another country I can't make a broad statement without getting called—"Why are you saying that?" or, "That seems inconsistent with what you said before." Most American audiences don't challenge the underlying integrity of the argument. That has made me aware that we have just become sloppy thinkers. We think, "Well, maybe this will work and maybe it won't," and we either accept it because we like the speaker or trainer or we don't. We are not doing well as a nation of organizations; we are not doing well at successfully changing and in developing curiosity and people who want to learn—even though curiosity is a natural function. We are not doing well at motivating people. I think we need to start thinking again. I don't know where the leadership for that is going to come from.

JA: *You have founded a research institute; we have a long research tradition at CCL and now are focusing on that even more. But it is difficult, we have found, to support an aggressive research agenda in this arena. People want to see the results of the research but they are not always willing to fund it early on. How can we make the case for good, solid, validated research on behavior and human interaction and even organizational structure?*

MW: The history of research findings in the United States is not a pretty picture. We have had consistent research to support solutions such as empowerment and self-managed work teams since the 1940s, and it still hasn't convinced people that if they are really sincere about productivity they should move to self-management. We ignore that employees are motivated not by money but by achievement, recognition, and good relationships.

At one level, I think that what we are up against is a deep anti-intellectualism in America. [Education activist and author] Parker Palmer often says that the crisis we face is not caused by a lack of data; it is a spiritual crisis. It is a failure to have the will to make the changes that the data indicate should be made.

JA: That parallels a comment that I heard [organizational behavior expert] Chris Argyris make. He stated that despite all the research and all the books on management, very few people have been successful in applying the ideas from the research. How can an individual leader apply an idea and make it work?

MW: With an individual and with small to medium-size organizations you create a culture in which you can move the theory into action. That requires experimenting and learning from the experiments. It requires an absolute commitment to a chosen path—"We are going to become *this* kind of organization, have *these* values, and go into *these* markets." Then it means learning how to do all that.

JA: So you advocate experimentation, taking smaller steps and learning from those.

MW: I propose that the steps can be bigger, but the process should be seen as one of continuous learning. You have to assume at the beginning that whatever you try is not going to be quite right. You will go for what you think might work best and then you will have to reflect on it. Then you will try something else and reflect on that again.

I am not describing a fantasy world. What seems to be happening with this great speed-up is that we try something, and if it doesn't work, we don't reflect on it, we just try something else and something else again, et cetera. We haven't realized that our experience is the best teacher for how to succeed and achieving the outcome. We are living in a time of accelerating stupidity.

JA: *Could you cite any examples of individuals or organizations that are working well in the ways you describe?*

MW: I really liked [former Harley-Davidson chairman and CEO] Rich Teerlink's book, *More Than a Motorcycle: The Leadership Journey at Harley-Davidson*, about the transformation of the company in the 1990s. He and his coauthor, [consultant] Lee Ozley, tell the whole story. They talk about the failures, the times of reflection, the high involvement of everyone, and the moments of doubt—the moments when they had done absolutely the wrong thing and had to recover. It was the first true story of organizational change that I ever read. The other book that contains a lot of great stories and cases is *The New Pioneers: The Men and Women Who Are Transforming the Workplace and the Marketplace*, by Thomas Petzinger. There are lots of examples of self-organizing systems within corporations. There are exemplary schools. In fact, there are exemplars in every industry—there are always courageous people who are trying to involve the community, to involve the whole system, to get people focused on a goal and working toward it, and to keep changing— not changing the goal but changing the structures that get you to the goal. There are many examples, but most of us are not paying attention to these teachers in our midst because we are still so preoccupied with responding to an immediate demand or pressure.

Crisis management used to be an unusual phenomenon; now, that's all there is. We have got to wake up and realize what we have created, then exert will and some compassion to help one another within the organization change. Until we pull Wall Street off the backs of corporate leaders, I don't expect much. Until we pull state legislatures off the backs of schools, I don't expect a lot of change. Right now, we are driving our culture in a destructive direction by trying to apply big sticks to whatever problem comes up. I think we are in a period where we are actually reversing and forgetting any-thing we have learned about better ways to lead and manage. It is command-and-control-squared as we get more fearful that we don't know how to create outcomes. We don't know how to create good health care or good public schools, and we just apply bigger sticks to those inside of those organizations rather than trying to rethink the whole structure.

Cheerful, I'm not. But I am hopeful that enough people will wake up and realize that in our current situation we can't create high organizational performance, and we certainly can't create or-ganizations with integrity and a sense of social accountability. We can't even create a sense of the whole system and how we are af-fecting it. If we continue in this way, we will just drive people faster and faster into nowhere.

◆ ◆ ◆

Redefining Accountability: A Talk with Peter Block

Stephen Rush

Author, consultant, and speaker Peter Block believes that to be-come truly service driven, organizations must move beyond efforts that produce only cosmetic change and instead must create ac-countability at all levels by placing control close to the core work. Block, who helped spark interest in empowerment with his 1987 book *The Empowered Manager: Positive Political Skills at Work*, was one of the keynote speakers at the third annual Friends of the Cen-ter Leadership Conference. His current work focuses on ways to bring service and accountability to organizations and communities.

Block, whose recently updated book *Flawless Consulting: A Guide to Getting Your Expertise Used* is the top-selling consulting book of all time, is a partner in Designed Learning, a training com-pany that offers consulting skills workshops. His other best-selling book, the 1993 *Stewardship: Choosing Service Over Self-Interest*, is about being accountable for the outcomes of an organization without acting to control or take care of others, which puts the focus on individual and team ownership and responsibility. Block has received several national awards for his contributions in the field of training and development. He is on the board of directors of the Association for Quality and Participation and is the founder of the association's School for Managing and Leading Change, which teaches teams from the private and public sectors how to redesign their organizations.

I recently interviewed Block by telephone. The following are excerpts from the interview:

SR: Your session at the Friends of the Center Leadership Conference will be about the quest for accountability. Can you explain briefly what your ideas about accountability mean for leaders and their organizations?

PB: It's like we're caught between two worlds. The existing world, which you can call the default culture, the culture without our intention, has accountability as something that individuals need to be held to. We have this basic feeling that if we don't hold people accountable they won't be, that if you give people freedom they won't use it in service of something else. This treats accountability as a form of compliance, a willingness to deliver on promises made to a boss. The alternative is to view accountability, first of all, as a choice to care for the well-being of the whole, which is to balance the deep individualism of this culture. The second thing is that one is accountable to peers more than to bosses. The essence is that people choose accountability; they aren't held accountable. If you think of it in that way, maybe it's possible to create a culture of accountability that doesn't have to be enforced or coerced or driven. If you start with that as your goal, then you say, "What would a change effort look like in that context?" Because change in the current context is that we have to hold people accountable: "I'm accountable to my boss, and I'm accountable individually for what I deliver." That leads into whole notions about driving change, installing change, leading change—most of which doesn't work. It's inefficient, or it's a struggle. We have all these myths that people hate change, they resist change. We have change agents to over-come resistance to change. All of that grows out of the context that people do not wish to be accountable and will not act on behalf of the well-being of the whole if left to their own devices.

SR: Why must accountability be freely chosen rather than imposed or coerced?

PB: I'll only care for what I own. And I will only really care for what I've helped create. It gives me an emotional stake in the future if I feel the future is mine to create rather than yours or theirs to cre-ate. And most of us defend against the future created by others and against the idea that someone else knows what's best and we don't. A lot of evidence we have about high-performing teams, about the whole quality movement, where self-inspection suddenly became possible, shows that improvement was done by working teams in-stead of by third-party experts. We placed the word *self* in front of *management*, and something important shifted. Change by consent and chosen by employees is a radical thought, and it goes against the stream of management literature from the last fifty years or so.

SR: Are there some specific things that an organization can do to nurture accountability, and what are the ultimate benefits to the organi-zation if it does?

PB: You nurture it by changing your mind about control and re-alizing it's most effective when it is self-imposed. Most organizations, if they want to create real accountability, have to get involved in employee involvement, empowerment. The benefit is that you get members who care—about customers and about each other. In the long run you might even get democracy, which is a form of self-government that we've forgotten about, if we ever had it.

SR: What are some of the pitfalls that organizations and leaders face, and what types of mistakes do they make in trying to establish a culture of accountability?

PB: The biggest pitfall is that nobody is asking for it. Employ-ees are not demanding it; in fact they have too often given up on the possibility. Instead they have chosen safety. The price of accountability is to live with anxiety. The cost of our freedom is to be anxious, to realize that the future is in our hands and no one except God is going to take care of us. That's a heavy responsibility that most of us can only carry once in a while. So you don't do this for the sake of the employees, you do it for the sake of the whole, the team, the organization, the community. The mistake we make is that we think we're going to install and legislate improvements. Right now, state legislators are trying to create students who are accountable for learning. They're passing laws with the idea that if you raise the standards and threaten people with high-stakes testing, that will increase learning. There's no evidence that it does that; we've been trying that for twenty years and been disappointed with the results. So this whole mind-set of putting accountability in the context of having to induce it fails. All you do is create compliance at a deeper level and more resistance.

SR: Let's say the CEO of a Fortune 500 company resigns under pressure. The company's performance has lagged for several years, and the stock is at a three-year low. The shareholders are getting restless. Employee morale and productivity are low. What qualities should the board of directors look for in a new CEO, and what can the new CEO do to turn the company around?

PB: The first thing is to have the members of the board of directors look at their own contribution to the problem. Nobody they hire is going to help that much unless they change their minds about what is important. It all begins with the question of purpose: What's the purpose of this institution? If it's to deliver stock price, results in weeks instead of years, then it doesn't matter whom they hire. Because when they hired this last CEO they thought they were making a good decision. What makes them think they'll make a better one next time? They also probably forced out the wrong person. Maybe they should have reconstituted themselves.

Look at these CEOs of companies whose stock prices have fallen drastically in the past six months. Did these CEOs suddenly have a lapse in performance, did something happen in those six months? Did they drink fluoride in the water or did they lose attention or did they go through an emotional slump and go off Prozac or something? Institutional performance is dependent on something larger than the CEO and more important than the faddishness of stock price. It's a question of purpose, and the people at the top need to confront this even if it is risky. Shareholder value as the number one purpose is a narrow purpose that's not very sustainable.

SR: You're one of the people who first brought attention to the idea of empowerment, beginning with your book The Empowered Manager. *How did your concepts of empowerment evolve, and has your thinking on the subject changed since then?*

PB: I thought I was writing a book about political systems at work and about trying to find a humane form of politics. When I finished the book and read it, I had not used the word *empowerment* anywhere in the book. And I said, "This isn't about political stuff; it's about empowerment." At that time *empowerment* was a dirty word. It smacked of collectivism, of communism, of socialism. And nobody used it. But after I read the book I gulped and said, "Political skill is too small a god to worship." So I went back and redid the book and reframed it and renamed it. By accident the book came out when the wave was starting to build, so I kind of named something that was about to happen.

What I didn't get at the time was that I thought when bosses opened the door, employees would walk through it. But they didn't; they stood outside the office and said, "Why have you opened the door?" I have a much deeper appreciation now that the audience creates the performance, that followers create leaders, and employees create institutions. I have a deeper appreciation of how it's the employees who have to decide what they want in their lives. They can't just keep looking for management to be more accommodating and sensitive. The whole attention on leadership I think is totally misguided. It's a self-defeating focus that just treats the illness with the disease.

SR: Considering that, what do you think the biggest challenge facing leaders and managers is today, and what skills are the most important for them to have?

PB: The biggest challenge is to shrink their notion of leadership back to a manageable perspective, discover some humility, and realize that they are not the cause or creators of the universe. I would have leaders say, "Let me be a social architect; let me convene and bring people together in different ways, and then let me join them." The one thing that is needed from the boss is to know the business and figure out where it's headed, and bosses can do that because they have a wider perspective. Most of our "great leaders" are not really great leaders; they're just great businessmen. They may know something profound about software or finance. But they are not role models for leaders. We need to get over the notion that just because you're rich means you're right.

In some ways the not-for-profit and the public sectors know more about organizing and mobilizing action on meager resources than the business sector will ever dream of, and yet we think business is the one we're going to learn from. Business leaders would benefit from spending a year running a not-for-profit organization. Run a church, be a city manager, run a school system, and then you'll understand something about what leadership really is about.

SR: One of the buzzwords lately has been e-leadership, the idea that old approaches to leadership must change as technology rapidly alters the business landscape. Do you agree with that, and how do your concepts of empowerment, accountability, and partnership fit in with e-leadership?

PB: I think e-commerce is changing the distribution system and allowing businesses to have much more leverage as a result. But I think that as soon as the dot-com companies get large enough, we're still going to have the same mind-set; they're just going to re-create the leadership they thought they were arguing against. This generation of e-leaders—the only difference is now they're in charge where before they worked for somebody.

We've been in a heated romance with e-commerce because it seemed to offer a lottery kind of wealth. It's the idea that "with four people I can build a $100 million business that will be valued at $100 billion, and I can do it in my garage." I think that by the time this article is published, the myth of that will be buried even further.

People forgot about this little thing called profit, making money the old-fashioned way.

What makes the new economy attractive is the start-up quality of it. But every business when it starts up is much more of a collective effort, where everybody's in it together and survival is at stake. And those are always the best times of your life: starting a career, starting a marriage, starting a life. You always learn the most when you're creating something. I think the e-world is interesting and technologically amazing, but so are special effects on a movie screen.

SR: Do you find that leaders who are exposed to your ideas are mostly receptive to them, or do you encounter a lot of resistance and a refusal to break from the traditional way of doing things?

PB: Nobody argues with the ideas; everybody thinks they're too idealistic, though. The question I have is: When did common sense become so radical that we brand it as idealistic?

It takes enormous courage to change your way of operating. You go through a period of enormous vulnerability, moments of great unpredictability when the future seems foggy instead of clear. All of us get anxious when we do that; it takes courage, and it's a conversation about faith, about hope, about some kind of reason for doing it that's a little more compelling than one of economics. If you want you can buy the Hallmark Cards version of life, that life is a symphony. But no one has experienced it that way, no one has grown into adulthood without suffering or being wounded. And if you ask people what were the most important learning experiences of their lives, they were those times of great vulnerability, when they didn't know what the hell was happening. So if you talk about a learning organization, you're talking about stress.

Everybody wants to drive fear out of the workplace, but where are you going to send it? You can't eliminate that part of life. And in some ways that's what gives us strength, gives us meaning. It's the same with institutions: they can't grow and develop without crisis and without anxiety.

SR: What developments in leadership development training do you see on the horizon?

PB: Right now it is moving away from a human system and being driven more toward commerce, toward training leaders in finance and the implications of the new economy. The people side of leadership training is even more lip service than it was. I think we're in a recession when it comes to any real leadership training.

What I think is going to emerge is a shift toward deeper humanistic learning for leaders. I'm doing a training program now, and one of the tenets is "You will learn nothing here that you can use in the next week." That takes a burden off the participants. It's like, "Let's just think for a change." In most places thinking is called lost production. And when you ask people to think, they say, "This is fun; I haven't done it in a while." I think philosophy and the humanities are going to be the center of what leadership training is headed toward.

◆ ◆ ◆

Nine Keys to Good Leadership

David Campbell

What characteristics are needed to be a successful leader? That's a broad question, but it's one that leaders—whether they're in charge of a small group such as a committee or an entire organization such as a corporation—need to contemplate. Effective leadership is crucial to the success of any enterprise, and understanding and emulating the features of a good leader can improve one's chances of success in a leadership role.

Working from knowledge gained during thirty years of experience with CCL's research and training programs—especially noting recurring themes that appeared in program participants' personal and psychological assessment data as well as a host of studies, projects, conferences, and discussions with leaders—I derived a list of nine essential leadership components. Then, using the same accumulated

CCL experience as well as leadership competencies identified by various organizations, I developed lists of adjectives that describe each of the nine characteristics of successful leaders.

The components and adjectives represent universals in leadership performance, so they are applicable in virtually any setting, whether it be a corporation, governmental agency, nonprofit organization, educational institution, military unit, hospital, or symphony orchestra. They are also applicable across a range of functions within a single organization, such as operations, finance, marketing, human resources, and information systems. Some components might be more applicable in some settings than in others, and some components might be more applicable than others at specific times—for instance, during a crisis. But over the long run, each component is relevant in most organizations at most times and for leaders at all levels and of all ages.

The nine leadership components and their corresponding descriptive adjectives form the basis of a new self-scored assessment tool, the Campbell Leadership Descriptor. The descriptor is designed to help leaders identify their leadership strengths and weaknesses, evaluate the implications of their ratings, and develop an action plan for improvement. Using a simple questionnaire that takes thirty to forty-five minutes to complete, leaders rate themselves on a scale of 1 to 4 on each of the descriptive adjectives. The leaders also rate two other leaders they have known—one of whom they regard as a *good* leader and the other as a *poor* leader—on each of the adjectives. The resulting ratings enable leaders to compare themselves with models of those they perceive to be good and poor leaders, based on universally relevant characteristics.

Following is a brief look at the nine major leadership components and their corresponding defining adjectives. The first six components cover the *major tasks* of organizational leadership that must be present and well executed if the organization and its members are to thrive. These tasks are typically accomplished by the organization's leaders, either directly or through delegation. The remaining three components represent the *personal* characteristics needed for successful leadership. These characteristics cannot be delegated; effective leaders must have the characteristics themselves or be able to develop them.

Vision. How effectively do you establish the general tone and direction of your organization? Leaders who are successful as visionaries in today's global economy are described as *farsighted* (they see the big picture in developing a vision for the future); *enterprising* (they enjoy taking on new projects and programs); *persuasive* (they present new ideas in ways that create buy-in); *resourceful* (they use existing resources to create successful new ventures); and *having a global view* (they think beyond national and cultural boundaries).

Management. Effective leaders set specific goals and know how to focus resources on achieving those goals. When it comes to their management skills these leaders are characterized by being *dedicated* (they are determined to succeed and willing to make personal sacrifices in pursuit of their vision); *delegating* (they effectively assign responsibility and appropriate authority to others); *dependable* (they perform as promised and meet deadlines); *focused* (they set clear work priorities for themselves and others); and *systematic* (they develop systems and procedures for efficiently organizing people and resources).

Empowerment. The ability to select and develop subordinates who are committed to the organization's goals is one of the keys to good leadership. Leaders who are effective at empowerment are *encouraging* (they help others achieve more than they thought they were capable of); *mentoring* (they provide challenging assignments and related coaching); *perceptive* (they recognize talent early and provide opportunities for growth); *supportive* (they help others deal with difficult personal situations); and *trusting* (they see the best in others and are not suspicious of differences).

Diplomacy. The ability to forge coalitions with important people inside and outside the organization—including superiors, peers, subordinates, customers, stakeholders, and outside decision makers—helps leaders achieve their organizational agendas. Leaders who are politically adroit are described as *diplomatic* (they understand the political nuances of important decisions and readily involve those who will be affected); *tactful* (they gain goodwill by not being offensive, even when disagreeing); *trusted* (others are confident that the leader will be a fair mediator of any conflict); *well connected* (they know a wide range of people who can help get things done); and *culturally sensitive* (they develop teamwork among people of different cultures, races, and religions).

Feedback. Observing and listening carefully to employees, team members, clients, and customers and sharing the resulting information in a way that all involved find beneficial is an important element of effective leadership. Leaders who are proficient at creating and delivering feedback are *good coaches* (they give constructive, beneficial evaluations at the individual level); *good teachers* (they communicate information that individuals and groups require to perform well); *candid and honest* (they don't suppress information that might be personally embarrassing); *good listeners* (they are open and responsive to the ideas of others); and *numerically astute* (they organize data in informative ways to reveal trends in individual and organizational performance).

Entrepreneurialism. The ability to find new opportunities, such as increased revenue or expanded markets, through projects, programs, and policies is one of the hallmarks of successful leadership. Leaders who are adept at creating new endeavors are *adventuresome* (they are willing to take risks on promising but unproven methods); *creative* (they think independently and come up with novel ideas); *durable* (they persist in the face of criticism and are hard to discourage); *good fund raisers* (they can secure the necessary financing for new projects); and *globally innovative* (they enjoy the challenge of creating new programs and projects in different cultures).

Personal style. CCL's research on derailment strongly suggests that for leaders to excel they must have an effective personal style, one that sets an overall organizational tone of competence, optimism, integrity, and inspiration. Such leaders are seen as being *credible* (they are believable, ethical, and trustworthy); *experienced* (they are skilled at and knowledgeable about the organization's core activities); *visible role models* (they understand the symbolic value of personal visibility); *optimistic* (they are upbeat and see many positive possibilities); and *good at providing an effective global leadership image* across cultural categories and national borders.

Personal energy. The physical demands of leadership—long hours, extensive travel, conflict, and stressful decisions—require leaders to have a disciplined, wholesome lifestyle that provides energy and durability. Such leaders are *balanced* (they adapt well to conflicting personal and work demands); *energetic* (they are active and constantly on the go); *physically fit* (they are in good health and durable); *publicly impressive* (they present an appealing, energizing leadership image); and *internationally resilient* (they readily adapt to other cultures and are comfortable crossing time zones and eating unfamiliar foods).

Multicultural awareness. Leaders today need to be experienced at and comfortable with managing individuals and organizations across a wide range of geographic, demographic, and cultural borders. The five descriptors of leaders who are multiculturally aware are drawn from the other leadership components—that is, each of these descriptors is used twice. Multiculturally aware leaders are noted for *having a global view* and for being *culturally sensitive, globally innovative, good at providing an effective global leadership image,* and *internationally resilient.* There are a number of ways that leaders can become more multiculturally aware, such as by seeking opportunities to work, travel, and attend conferences in other countries; studying other languages; and learning the histories of other countries.

The experience with the Campbell Leadership Descriptor thus far has been that people who fill out the instrument soon realize that virtually all good leaders have a few flaws and all poor leaders have some virtues. However, by providing a detailed description of the flaws and virtues of both a good leader and a poor leader, the descriptor makes leadership performance more understandable and offers a way to focus attention on possible developmental activities for improvement—even for good leaders.

Chapter Two

How to Deal with Change

Change is probably the greatest challenge that leaders face—whether it is a sudden and unexpected calamity or the predictable, day-to-day shifting of standards, values, and processes that contributes to conflict between individuals and groups. This chapter covers how to handle change and how to develop the adaptability and resilience necessary to do so.

◆ ◆ ◆

Leading Transition: A Talk with William Bridges

John Alexander

For more than twenty years William Bridges has been helping people understand change and take effective action in its wake. He has done this by authoring an impressive series of books (see sidebar at end of interview), developing a popular range of training programs, consulting with hundreds of companies, and speaking to diverse groups around the world.

His success in this work has been widely acknowledged. For instance, in 1993 the *Wall Street Journal* listed him among the top ten executive development consultants in the United States.

One of the reasons for this success is that his practical message, for both individuals and organizations, is backed by a set of clear and related ideas. At the center of this framework is a distinction between change and transition: change is a shift in the external world, whereas transition is an internal process that people go through in response to that shift. Given this, Bridges makes the observation that transition involves three distinct phases: endings (where a loss occurs and people must let go of the old and seek closure), a neutral zone (where people feel the chaos of change but have nothing yet to replace the loss), and beginnings (where people gain new understandings, values, attitudes, and identities). And given this, he develops many insights into how organizational change (and the accompanying transition) can be managed effectively. For instance, successful transitions, according to Bridges, must begin in endings.

Recently, William Bridges visited our Greensboro campus and met with me to discuss his ideas from a leadership perspective. This interview presents a part of that talk.

JA: *In your work, you talk about a neutral zone: a time of transition in organizations when the old is decommissioned but the new isn't yet in people's minds and hearts. It is usually a period of great anxiety. What can leaders do to help with that?*

WB: When I talk with executives about managing transitions, I like to emphasize the two C's and the four P's.

The two C's are *connection* and *concern*. When people are in transition, they feel abandoned very, very easily. The leader must maintain a connection with them.

This is partly literal. A leader who goes off on an extended trip during a transition contributes to the feeling of abandonment. But it is also psychological. People must feel that the leader sees them, that he or she knows what they are going through.

At the same time, the concern of the leader must also be evident. He or she must not only see what people are going through but also clearly care about it.

The four P's are *purpose* (Why was it necessary to do this? What would have happened if we didn't?), *picture* (How is it going to look, feel, work?), a *plan* (Step by step, how do we roll this out? What do we do on Tuesday?), and *parts* (What roles can people play in this?). I think the leader must address each of these.

There is always a purpose behind change, but frequently it is not discernible to people in the organization. This may be because it has not been explained to people in terms that mean something to them or it may not have been explained at all. The leader needs to clearly explain the purpose behind a new beginning.

The picture is sometimes an evolving thing; part of the leader's task is to get the people involved in filling in the picture. Consequently, the leader doesn't want to be too detailed about it at first.

Some people really respond to the picture, and once they have it in their heads, they will move ahead. But other people require more details about the specific steps that they personally will need to take. Leaders tend to be picture oriented, but they shouldn't ignore those who need a plan.

Finally, people need to be given two parts to play. One involves their role in the new scheme of things once the change has taken place. The other, which is equally important, is the role they will play in the transition. Leaders need to see that people feel involved in the planning and implementation of change. It is true that people implementing something get a kind of investment in it that they don't have if they are not involved.

Another thing that is really important for leaders to remember is how far ahead of the followers they are. They have typically been wrestling with these issues for months and months—even years— while many of their followers probably haven't questioned some of the things that ultimately will have to be changed. So there is quite a mismatch as to where people are in the transition process.

Of course, all the way through transition, you have different people at different places. Some people move through fast; some people move through slowly. So I think this role of leading the human side of change is an underestimated piece of leadership.

JA: What are some of the signs of a difficult transition? And what are some of the pitfalls that leaders face in such a situation?

WB: Often a leader is so impatient with people in transition that he or she becomes frightening, and people think, "Don't tell the leader that!" And thus the leader gets a very distorted impression about where people actually are.

And I often see leaders who think, "We have to end this initiative [or policy or whatever], but if we don't say it is over, we won't offend the people who want to hold onto it." That kind of thinking is understandable, but it's ultimately self-defeating. People need to know what is over and what isn't. They may make some choices on the basis of that. Some decide that this isn't the place they signed up with and they need to move on. Others decide this isn't the place they signed up with but it is kind of interesting—maybe they'll stay on awhile. That sorting process has to be allowed to go on.

JA: *There is so much to sort today. You often hear that changes are coming more rapidly now than they did even just a few years ago. Do you agree with that? Is change happening more rapidly today?*

WB: I think there are certainly differences between today and the past. One is that the people who are in transition feel less secure in the rest of their lives than they did twenty years ago. Families are in transition more. So sources of solidity that people had in their lives often feel a little shaky or a little more questionable.

Is there more change? Yes, I think there is, but I don't think that is the whole story. One of the important parts of the story is that modern communication puts us in immediate contact with every change almost instantaneously. When there was an earthquake in Turkey, we all knew about it virtually as it happened. So the interconnectedness that we have and the rapidity with which information moves means that changes that used to be filtered out by time and distance aren't filtered out anymore. We are exposed to a great deal more change than in previous times, and we have lost our buffers.

JA: *I think leaders can do some buffering.*

WB: I think you're right. Sometimes leaders can say, "I am really not worrying about that one too much. I am putting my attention over here." It can be a relief to know that we don't have yet another high-priority item that is dropped on our plate to deal with this week.

JA: *In your work you have made the point that change has to make sense to people. How do leaders help things make sense?*

WB: There are a lot of kinds of sense that people can make of a situation. One of them is business sense. I think that a leader can help people see the connections between new external situations and the well-being of the institution. Making such connections is natural to a leader but not to many of the people who do the day-to-day work. A leader should also make it clear how the connections are important to the things that people care about.

JA: *You work with a lot of leaders. What is the one thing that they don't do now, that if they did do, you think would make things better?*

WB: I think the one thing that I see them failing to do is to think through the implications of change at the level on which people work and in matters with which they are concerned. They talk strategically; they talk organizationally. But the people that they are trying to lead are operating at a much more concrete level—they are concerned with getting something done by the end of the day or with failing to get a raise this year. Leaders talk about becoming a world-class organization and fail to carry that down to the level of attitude and behavior where an actual person can recognize himself or herself. It's a question of altitude, I suppose. Leaders are operating at a different altitude, and it makes for a huge gap in communication.

JA: *Looking at it from the other side, what do you find that leaders are doing well?*

WB: I think the good news is that most of them really care about their organization and the people who work in it. I certainly meet a lot of leaders who are really admirable in the amount of anguish and concern they have about the impact of things on people. But that isn't always translated into a form that people can see, appreciate, understand, and believe.

JA: Do you have a definition of leadership that you use in your work?

WB: I don't think a lot in terms of a thing called *leadership*. I really think a lot in terms of what somebody can do to help people come to terms with a change.

JA: What about the people you work with? Do they think a lot about being leaders or of a larger process of leadership?

WB: They sometimes do—although I think they are more likely to be lost, embedded, in the actual issues of what they have to do: "This merger is breaking down; we need to pull it back. What happens when we are trying to integrate a group that hasn't been part of us before?" I think most leaders don't think much about leadership per se. They think about the challenges that they actually face. People who observe what leaders do extrapolate out of their actions something they call leadership.

To tell you the truth, and I hope this isn't the wrong place to say it, I sometimes wonder if leadership is as useful a concept as we once thought it was.

JA: I think this is the right place to say it. At CCL, if we didn't question the value of the concept of leadership, I don't think our work would be as useful as it is. Of course, despite its difficulties, we continue to think that there is something important, albeit often very complex, to which the word refers.

WB: I admire your courage in this. It's difficult work.

JA: Let me shift our focus here. You have a background in American literature. Until 1974 you were a professor at Mills College. Is that experience useful to you now that you have made the transition to your current work? Do you ever go back for the things that literature has taught you?

WB: Some of it has been my North Star. My reading of and my appreciation of writers like Emerson, Thoreau, and Whitman (who are among my favorites in American literature), with their emphasis on speaking your own truth, trusting that a sequence of things has a shape to it even if you can't perceive the shape, and having faith that your own voice is the one that is right to speak with rather than some other voice, have been central to everything that I have done. It was such a funny experience twenty-six or twenty-seven years ago to be struggling to publish one of my first articles and having my wife say to me, "You don't sound like you. Why don't you write in your own voice?" Emerson talks over and over again about this—tell me what you believe, what is true for you? I think I was very slow to believe that. I sometimes look at the management books that get pumped out, seemingly by the millions, some of them about leadership, and I think these are not human beings talking. They are not talking about things that human beings care about. They are talking about something that a business school somewhere has identified as a subject to be taught. So I am humanistic, I guess, in the broadest sense.

JA: Some people believe that cultural figures—say a poet like Whitman—can be seen as a kind of leader.

WB: You could say that. But I happen to be one who resists, at least mentally, the notion of extending the idea of leadership so broadly to cover so many positive qualities and positive behaviors that everything becomes leadership. I think we lose something when we attenuate the idea of leadership to the point that it covers everything.

JA: Do you see that happening in organizations?

WB: I see it happening not so much in organizations as I see it happening in books about leadership in organizations. There are writers who say that everything is leadership. Everybody needs to be a leader. I think everybody needs to exercise initiative, everybody needs to take responsibility, everybody needs to produce results—but that to me doesn't add up to being a leader.

JA: What writers or thinkers out there today do you think are particularly good on leadership?

WB: You know there are a couple of people that I especially look forward to a book from. One is Peter Drucker. What I appreciate from him is not so much his insight into organizations as his ability to draw on so broad a storehouse to teach about organizations. I just always learn something.

The other is Charles Handy. I like his, for want of a better term, *humanism*; he can do justice on the one hand to the most hard-nosed profit-and-loss concerns and on the other hand to the place of the heart in the workplace. He has that kind of a grasp that he is able to connect those two things. That is something that I think leaders need too—to be able to be the conduit of the energy running between those two things. With Handy's work, I find myself underlining and doing things way beyond what I do with most books. So I guess Drucker and Handy are personal heroes of mine.

It seems as if these days when you read about organizations in the popular press, it is financial concerns that are given by far the most attention. We're hearing mostly from financial analysts. They seem to know everything, and they seem to pretty much dictate everything. It is almost as if leaders are Gulliver-like figures with this army of analysts around them telling them what to do, what not to do: "Yeah, you had a good quarter, but it wasn't good enough."

I just wonder about the human side of the equation. Of course, it's always there under the surface, and if you look into organizations very long and very hard, it's going to be there. But now more than ever it seems to be masked to me by these other forces—financial, global, technological—and there is this sense that people in leadership positions have a very narrow window in which to operate, in which to be successful. If they are almost not immediately successful in a very short period of time, unless they have a very patient board, they are out. There is sort of a sense that somehow there has been a disgrace—you know, they just didn't perform and they are out. Then someone else comes in, and by gosh, not always but sometimes, things improve. You just wonder how healthy this really is and what it really means. I think the pendulum is certainly swinging that way—mergers and acquisitions, lawyers, the high-flyers, the M&A specialists, and the analysts seem to be controlling what goes on in organizations.

I think if leaders in general took a stronger stand, the power of analysts might be moderated, and organizations would find it easier to address a range of neglected but crucial concerns.

JA: One of those concerns that occurs to me is trust. Let's end by talking about that. You've done a lot of thinking about what some call the new employment contract. At one time there was a tacit agreement that if a person were loyal to the company he or she would be guaranteed lifetime employment. The company trusted the employee to be loyal, and the employee trusted the company to provide a stable job. This kind of agreement is clearly no longer possible. Do you have a notion of what the new contract would be in the sense of how people would redevelop trust for their organizations and vice versa?

WB: There is a book about this by Robert Bruce Shaw which I think is pretty good. It's called *Trust in the Balance: Building Successful Organizations on Results, Integrity, and Concern.* It was published in 1997 by Jossey-Bass. I recommend that people take a look at it.

The fact is, most of the leaders who talk about regaining trust don't really want to do what it would take, or perhaps they experience themselves as unable to do what it would take. I think it takes a degree of transparency in the process that decisions are reached by. It takes sharing the real information about the organizational situation, and very often leaders say, "Well, we can't let shareholders know that." But they are really just scared of operating in an open environment where people see clearly what is going on. For such leaders, I think the idea of regaining trust is illusory.

I don't know any shortcut to trust—other than saying what you will do and doing what you say, showing some definite concern for people, and showing that you see what they are dealing with. I am almost embarrassed saying things like that because it is very simple stuff. Yet when somebody comes in and says, "You know, we are having a little problem with loyalty here and we want to know how to regain it," you say about three sentences, and you realize that they don't want to do any of the stuff that would be necessary to regain the loyalty. Furthermore, they have really destroyed it to the point where it can't be regained. I don't mean to say you can't get commitment from people. I think in most organizations the better direction to go is away from trying to rebuild loyalty into reconstituting the organization on the basis of commitment. I certainly see the two as quite different. Commitment is dedication to an undertaking, to a person, to a team, to an outcome: "I will do that. I am committed to that." Loyalty suggests to me the notion of being a vassal, as in the Middle Ages, and we have killed the vassals.

Books by William Bridges

Transitions: Making Sense of Life's Changes. Reading, Mass.: Addison-Wesley, 1980.

Surviving Corporate Transition: Rational Management in a World of Mergers, Layoffs, Start-Ups, Takeovers, Divestitures, Deregulation, and New Technologies. New York: William Bridges and Associates, 1990.

Managing Transitions: Making the Most of Change. Reading, Mass.: Addison-Wesley, 1991.

The Character of Organizations: Using Jungian Types in Organizational Development. Palo Alto, Calif.: Consulting Psychologists Press, 1992.

JobShift: How to Prosper in a Workplace Without Jobs. Reading, Mass.: Addison-Wesley, 1994.

Creating You & Co.: Learn to Think Like the CEO of Your Own Career. Reading, Mass.: Addison-Wesley, 1997.

The Way of Transition: Embracing Life's Most Difficult Moments. Cambridge, Mass.: Da Capo Press, 2001.

◆ ◆ ◆

Getting a Grip on Conflict

Davida Sharpe

In organizations, conflict is inevitable. Discord is a natural by-product of today's turbulent business environment, with its multiple pressures, rapid and complex change, fierce competition, mergers and acquisitions, and employee turnover. Conflict is so prevalent that executives estimate they spend nearly 20 percent of their time dealing with it.

Consequently, the ability to manage conflict has become a critical skill for leaders to add to their repertoire. CCL has found that this ability plays a major role in determining whether executives who have reached at least the general manager level and who are considered by their superiors to be likely candidates for further promotion will continue to be successful or will derail. (Derailed executives are those who, despite their perceived high potential for advancement, impressive track records, and solidly established leadership positions, are fired, demoted, or held on a career plateau.)

The essential skill of managing conflict doesn't come easily, however. Conflict can occur at various levels—between or among direct reports or team members, between a boss and one or more direct reports, or between an executive and his or her boss or upper management as a whole, to name a few. One of the factors that make managing conflict difficult is that individual perceptions of and experiences with a conflict can be dramatically different for the people on opposing sides of that conflict. A situation or event might create conflict for you but not for the person or people with whom you perceive yourself to be butting heads. Different individuals can view the same set of circumstances in different ways—usually owing to their different personalities, experiences, beliefs, and opinions, as well as other internal and external factors.

In this article you will learn first what conflict is and some specific forms it can take. Then you will see that conflict need not have negative results—*if* it is managed properly. Finally, you will learn the steps you can take to develop the interpersonal and collaborative skills needed to manage conflict successfully and help keep your career on track.

What Is Conflict?

Conflict is a state of disharmony between incompatible or antithetical people, ideas, or interests. Sometimes it is an internal turmoil

that results from the opposition or concurrence of mutually exclu-
sive impulses, desires, or tendencies. In either case, conflict inevitably causes a struggle.

Many incidents of conflict, however, are classic examples of perception versus reality. Many personal and situational factors influence the way that each individual experiences differences and
disagreements. On any given day, people in organizations face potential conflict arising from ideas, goals, results, emotions, relationships, and personality differences. But one person's state of conflict
is another person's healthy, stimulating, productive work situation.

People tend to superimpose their own personalities, frames, and
judgments on an event, and that largely determines their conclusions about whether the event has created conflict and, if so, the
degree of conflict experienced. Some people, for example, are able
to detach themselves from the strong emotional responses that can
be elicited by conflict; others tend to be swept up in and influenced
by the emotions associated with conflict. Interestingly, despite the
fact that conflict may not be recognized by each of the parties involved, it is usually plainly evident to outside observers.

Consider the following illustration of how conflict can be interpreted variously by different individuals.

Jack is the director of new products for a manufacturing company.
At a meeting of company executives, he presents a proposal for a
new product. He and his team worked long and hard on the details
of the proposal. Sandra, the company's marketing director, raises her
voice in opposition to developing and launching the new product,
citing the competitive landscape of the industry and a lack of consumer demand. A spirited exchange follows between the two, leaving a clear impression among the others attending the meeting that
Jack and Sandra are in conflict—and not just over the proposed
new product.

Sandra, although she knows she disagrees on the new product
issue, isn't really cognizant that she is in conflict with Jack. She believes her opposing view will help everyone analyze the situation ra-

tionally and could avert an unwise move by the company. She has always viewed dissent as a way to increase objectivity and believes that only through debates such as the one between her and Jack can issues be clarified. In addition, she thinks that in situations such as this the focus should be on the issues at hand—not on people's feelings.

Jack has the opposite view of what occurred in the meeting. He sees Sandra's opposition to the new product as a conflict—in fact, as a personal attack against him. He has always operated according to his belief that maintaining harmony is extremely important to the working process and that dissent is usually just for the sake of argument and is counterproductive. In addition, he thinks that in situations such as the one at the meeting, people's feelings should be the primary concern, even more important than the issues at hand.

It's clear that Jack, because of his personality, his outlook on how business should be conducted, and his commitment to a proposed new product to which his team has already devoted a lot of time and effort, holds a perspective about the exchange that is different from Sandra's. Although the conflict and resultant struggle are as plain as day to him, Sandra believes she merely presented all the evidence so the organization can make the best and most rational decision on whether to proceed with the new product.

The lesson is that the first key to managing conflict effectively is recognizing that regardless of the objective realities of a situation, the person or people on one side may view it as a conflict whereas the other party may not.

Poles Apart

A number of characteristics have been found to mark the difference between executives who continue to be considered for promotion and those who derail. Part of the profile of successful executives is that they find ways to use their interpersonal and collaborative skills to manage conflict effectively. In stark contrast, the profile of executives who went off the track includes the following characteristics:

- They did not resolve conflict among their direct reports.
- They were unprofessional about their disagreements with upper management.
- They had unresolved interpersonal conflicts with their immediate superiors.

What do these contrasting types of leaders—the conflict-savvy and the conflict-challenged—look like in the real world? Stories related by participants in CCL's research provide portraits of each. First, let's look at comments about leaders who have problems with conflict:

> People were always quitting or requesting transfers. [The manager] was dictatorial, overly protective of the group and of her own ideas, which she forced onto the group. She tried to isolate the team from the other departments and the outside world, cutting all links.

> [The manager] often berated employees verbally and had to have the final word. He behaved this way with subordinates, but frequently caved when interacting with more senior managers. He was not supportive and didn't challenge situations when it could have created conflict with superiors.

Now contrast the following statements about leaders who successfully managed conflict:

> There was a lot of chaos and confusion on the part of the team about priorities and objectives. It all came to a head during a team meeting at which people were essentially rising up in revolt. The leader came back into the meeting the next morning and accepted full responsibility for the situation. He laid out in a very specific and confident way exactly what the team was going to do and why. He significantly reduced the number of initiatives, clarified the game plan, and expressed confidence in his ability—and more importantly, in the team's ability—to accomplish the game plan. The team pulled to-

gether and accomplished much good work. Confidence grew, the leader grew, and the team moved forward.

[The manager] had a deep belief that working democratically would benefit all workers. She was honest, collaborative, and open to new ideas. She was a great supporter of people and people's ideas. She made herself accessible to everyone in the company. She was extremely ethical and dependable.

Positive Versus Negative

Executives can and should manage conflict, but it's unlikely that conflict can be eradicated—nor should it be. Robert Townsend, who turned around then-struggling Avis after he became CEO of that rental car company in 1962 and who authored the seminal management book *Up the Organization: How to Keep the Organization from Stifling People and Strangling Profits,* perhaps put it best when he wrote: "A good manager doesn't try to eliminate conflict; he tries to keep it from wasting the energies of his people. If you're the boss and your people fight you openly when they think that you are wrong—that's healthy."

When conflict is managed appropriately and effectively, there are positive outcomes; the conflict itself becomes *constructive.* Conversely, when conflict is not managed appropriately and effectively, the results are negative; the conflict becomes *destructive.* Let's look at some specifics of how both sides of the coin play out.

When conflict is managed effectively:

- Effort is increased because differences motivate each side to work harder to make its point.
- Feelings are dealt with openly rather than being suppressed or ignored; the latter only builds resentment.
- More information is circulated, which leads to better decisions—even if the information is not what everyone wants to hear.

- Disagreements are not frowned upon or squelched; such acceptance of conflict stimulates critical thinking and learning in an organization.

- The organization becomes an open forum for diverse ideas and perspectives, which stimulates creativity and innovation.

When conflict is not managed effectively:

- Productivity erodes because disagreements and clashes use up everyone's energy.

- Communication decreases because people no longer speak up for fear of a fight.

- Contentiousness leads to bruised feelings and torn relationships.

- Workplace stress rises as conflict takes an emotional and physical toll on people.

- Cooperation declines as teams divide into factions and cliques, each lobbying for its own viewpoint.

Common Ground

In essence, managing conflict involves reaching agreements—even if they are agreements to disagree. Executives who are skilled at managing conflict are able to settle disputes equitably, in the process finding common ground between the parties in dispute and getting cooperation from them. It's a tough job, especially when conflicts are so deep-rooted that they appear irresolvable. But it's a job that executives must accomplish if they want to develop effective interpersonal relationships, increase productivity and decrease stress in the workplace, boost their ability to make good decisions, and keep their careers on track.

Before you can manage a conflict effectively, you need to address four questions:

- What are your own attitudes toward conflict?
- What is the precise situation that is linked to the conflict?
- How do other people view the situation?
- What conflicting responses are others expressing?

By following the process outlined in the rest of this article, you will be able to answer these questions effectively and learn to better manage conflict. The process has four steps: (1) increase your personal awareness, (2) understand the perspectives of others, (3) create and implement an action plan, and (4) evaluate the action plan.

In each stage of the process, you will discover a little more about the causes of conflict, your reactions to it, and solutions to help you manage it.

Personal Awareness

The initial step in managing conflict is increasing self-awareness of its causes. You first need to examine the way you respond to events and situations and understand how your responses cause you to perceive events and situations as conflict. Two components—triggers and coping mechanisms—are key to understanding how events and situations cause conflict for you.

Triggers are events or situations that produce immediate emotional or thought responses. These responses can cause you to act as though you are in conflict. Triggers are hot buttons—things that set you off. For example, being criticized in public by your boss might trigger anger and humiliation in you. By becoming aware of your triggers, you can heighten your awareness of the events, situations, and people that cause conflict in your life and can identify the thoughts, feelings, and behaviors associated with those triggers. This in turn enables you to work toward managing conflict internally so you can better control your behavior and respond to situations in a more effective manner.

The second component of personal awareness of the causes of conflict is *coping mechanisms*. These are the consistent patterns of action and reaction that you use to deal with conflict. If these mechanisms cause you to *avoid* dealing with conflict when it would be preferable to *manage* the conflict, they are ineffective. Following are some examples of ineffective coping mechanisms:

Complaining. You express your frustration to everyone except the person with whom you are in conflict. For instance, you might come home from work each day and make your aggravations the dominant topic of conversation.

Daydreaming. Your thoughts consistently turn to wishing to be free of the person or situation that is causing conflict for you.

Obsessing. You dwell on the motives of the person with whom you are in conflict, or endlessly plan strategies to deal with the person or situation.

Vilifying. You talk about the person behind his or her back and try to recruit people to your side of the conflict.

Getting depressed. You feel helpless and imagine that nothing will improve your situation.

The best way to identify the types of triggers that initiate conflict for you and the ineffective coping mechanisms you may be using in the face of conflict is to look back on clear, unambiguous examples of conflict that occurred in your past. What were the events or situations that sparked the conflicts, and what were your subsequent thoughts, feelings, and behaviors? Did you respond to the conflicts by trying to avoid or escalate them? Once you can answer these questions, you'll be ready to move to the next step of learning to manage conflict effectively.

Other Perspectives

Developing a better understanding of the thoughts, feelings, and behaviors of other individuals involved is key to managing and resolving conflict because it is the only way you can clearly separate facts from opinions and assumptions.

Seeing things from the perspective of others involves suspending judgment, asking questions to enlarge your perspective, and validating the perspective of others. Don't jump to conclusions about the perspective of others; instead try to quiet your own thoughts and feelings so you can come to terms with perspectives other than your own. Ask yourself objective, clarifying questions about the conflict-causing event or situation and its aftermath. Force yourself to explore different perspectives and to generate multiple possible reasons why the other person holds a particular point of view. This does not mean you have to adopt or agree with the perspective of the other person. The object is only to understand it.

Validating the perspective of others involves moving beyond *sympathizing* with other people to *empathizing* with them—an ability shown by the most successful managers. When you sympathize with someone you recognize and have compassion for his or her situation, motives, and feelings. When you empathize with someone you identify with and have a deep understanding of his or her situation, motives, and feelings. You show the other person that his or her perspective is important to you, and you can communicate that point of view with as much passion as you can your own. This additional level of understanding puts you in a far better position to manage conflict successfully.

The Action Plan

Creating and implementing a specific plan of action will help to lower your anxiety level as you work to manage conflict. To create a purposeful plan, carry out these steps:

- Identify the person with whom you are in conflict.
- Describe the source of the conflict and the situation or event that led to the conflict. Define the triggers of the conflict.
- Describe the other person's behavior during the situation or event that led to the conflict. Use verbs and cite the other person's specific statements and body language.

- Describe the impact that the situation or event had on you. Identify your reactive thoughts, feelings, and behaviors.

- Set a date for a meeting with the person with whom you are in conflict, and choose a neutral location.

- Establish clear objectives for the meeting. Rather than settle for nothing less than a personal victory, be prepared to do some bargaining. Ask yourself what points both you and the other person might be willing to concede to reach a mutually beneficial solution to the conflict.

After you have created your action plan, you are ready to implement it. During the meeting, it's important to focus on issues in which both sides can find common ground and to seek a solution that is as win-win as possible. Giving in on some points will show respect for the other person's position and reduce the possibility of raising further conflict.

Instead of immediately bursting forth with feedback, it may be helpful to break the ice and establish a rapport by first having a conversation. This sets the stage for a collaborative discussion. From there, communication should be clear and focused on the problem at hand. Explain your position and your reasons for holding it, and ask the other person to do the same. Describe how you view the other person's behaviors associated with the conflict and their impact on you and others. As you do this, try just to state the facts rather than pass judgment. For instance, instead of saying, "You were wrong in what you did," say, "You interrupted me three times, and I felt discounted."

Be specific about how you would like to resolve the conflict and what you are prepared to give up to do so. Above all, express yourself openly and honestly, and be conscious of the effects of your words and body language. Finally, ask for feedback about what you have said, and carefully listen to and consider that feedback.

Evaluation

After you have implemented your action plan, it is likely that the conflict will have been resolved. However, there is an important final step to the process of managing conflict that leaders often overlook. Reviewing your experience of conflict and evaluating your action plan are essential to your learning process and the ongoing development of your ability to manage conflict effectively.

You might start by asking yourself what you intended to do, what actually happened, and what you would do differently. Keeping a personal journal is a helpful way to ask and answer these questions and to track, analyze, and understand the ways you experience and handle conflict, so you can modify your behaviors as needed and manage conflict at its earliest stages. Such a journal might include factual descriptions of the events or situations and the people involved; a chronicle of your thoughts, feelings, and behaviors during conflicts, including what you might have wanted to do as opposed to what you actually did; and reflections on the larger meaning of the experiences, including any patterns seen in the events and your reactions to them, insights gained, and your overall progress in managing conflict.

In organizations where conflicts are often never resolved and hostilities consistently remain open, turnover and absenteeism tend to be high and motivation, morale, quality, and productivity tend to be low. In most organizations, executives are expected to be active in managing conflicts toward resolutions that satisfy everyone involved. Executives who develop the important interpersonal-relationship skill of managing conflict effectively not only give themselves a better chance of furthering their own careers but also give their organizations a better chance of surviving and thriving in today's competitive business environment.

◆ ◆ ◆

After the Storm: Leading in the Wake of a Crisis

Gene Klann

Recent years have provided many unwelcome opportunities to learn how to be an effective leader during a crisis. The attacks on the World Trade Center and the Pentagon on September 11, 2001, left the leaders of the companies and military departments that occupied those buildings in a state of shock. They struggled to cope with the devastating loss of life suffered by their organizations and somehow regroup and carry on. Soon after, a series of exposures to anthrax spores delivered through the mail resulted in the deaths of four workers and tested the resilience of the leadership of the U.S. Postal Service as well as the media organizations and governmental offices that had been targeted. Then a nonlethal but still chaos-inducing crisis emerged as a procession of companies was linked to accounting and fraud scandals of mammoth proportions, sending the offending organizations into free fall and America's trust in corporate leadership into the tank. And in October 2002 a sniper spree cast a pall of terror and anxiety over the Washington, D.C., region for three weeks as law enforcement, governmental, and school officials tried to infuse perseverance, hope, and calm through their leadership.

In each case the effectiveness of the leaders embroiled in the crisis was sometimes crystal clear, sometimes painfully lacking or even nonexistent. But much was learned about providing leadership during a crisis, and a consensus emerged that good leaders naturally and rightfully turn their attention to the human side of the crisis—to the emotional and physical needs and concerns of their followers. A crisis can strike any company at any time, and there are many eventualities aside from the types of crises seen in the recent past that can land organizations in trouble—financial catastrophes; problems that threaten the public image of a company or product; and disasters that pose a danger to consumers, employees, the community, or the environment.

In any such event the three key approaches for leaders are to communicate fully and honestly, to set an example of consistency, and to be present, visible, and totally involved in the situation and attempts to mitigate it. In these ways leaders can offer those they lead constructive means for dealing with fear, stress, grief, and anxiety; for maintaining focus and productivity; and for picking themselves up and moving forward with renewed strength.

Building to Last

But what happens after a crisis is over? Are there steps leaders can take to ensure that the organization and its employees establish a daily routine that does not passively fall back on practices that during the crisis were found to feed uncertainty, fear, panic, and a lack of trust but instead builds on new insights, strengths, responsibilities, and cooperation to enhance cohesion, balance, focus, productivity, and readiness to meet challenges? The goal of leadership after a crisis is to rebuild and strengthen relationships and to learn from the experience to be better prepared for any future crisis. Leaders who view the period of recovery after a crisis as an opportunity and an impetus to develop a better routine can help their organizations emerge stronger and more purposeful.

The first challenge for leaders is more difficult than it may sound: recognizing when the crisis has passed. A crisis may end, but it doesn't just fade away; the ensuing period of repair, recovery, and healing is likely to be long term, difficult, and painful—physically, emotionally, and financially. However, a number of signs can help leaders recognize when the immediate crisis is over:

- The news media have dropped coverage of the story or are no longer giving it high visibility.

- The organization and its employees are slowly returning to something approaching normalcy.
- The number of inquiries about the crisis from outside the organization—from customers, suppliers, shareholders, the community, and employees' families, for instance—has dropped considerably.
- Internal rumors and employees' anxiety levels have returned to normal.

One of the most important things for leaders to do after a crisis is to assure employees that the likelihood of an identical crisis occurring is very low. This reduces employees' anxiety and increases their morale and productivity. Leaders can accomplish this in a number of ways. First, they should talk with the employees personally and be open to questions; this behavior can have a therapeutic and calming effect. Second, leaders should oversee a comprehensive update of company operations, rules, and regulations, with the aim of preventing a similar crisis, and should share these measures with the employees. The update can address improved crisis assessment procedures, including those designed for early warning and detection, and better methods of communication among leaders and employees. The latter deserve special attention. Just as clear and continuing communication is essential to preparing for a crisis and leading during a crisis, keeping the lines of communication open and reviewing and rebuilding the organization's communication strategies after a crisis help the organization and everyone in it learn from the experience and be better able to deal effectively with any future crisis.

Causes and Effects

One of the biggest challenges for leaders after a crisis is determining all the causes of the crisis. If this is not done well or at all, the likelihood of the crisis reoccurring increases.

Determining all the causes and effects of a crisis and informing employees of the findings are key to bolstering the employees' emotions and behavior and the organization's recovery overall. When a crisis is over, people naturally want to know what happened, why it happened, what it means for them and for the organization, and what is being done to make sure it won't happen again.

A crisis seldom has a single cause, and finding out all the causes requires good and complete information, diligent research, and intuitive thinking. It also requires consulting every source of information, no matter how seemingly insignificant or unrelated. Sources may include customer feedback, production reports, safety data, and employee complaints and suggestions. The information-gathering process should begin as soon as possible after the crisis is contained.

Similarly, leaders should closely scrutinize the effects of the crisis. Some effects will be plainly evident in the immediate aftermath of the crisis, but it's highly likely that other effects will emerge as time passes and the dust settles—and the effects that are at first hidden may have even more severe consequences than the primary effects. Secondary effects may include financial costs, emotional consequences, and fallout from the community.

Leaders should review how they, their employees, and the organization overall reacted during the crisis and any lingering effects. The best way to begin this review is to assess the emotional state of the workforce. Some employees will still be emotionally distressed, and leaders need to address these employees' needs and find ways to help them cope with their fear, pain, and stress.

One way for leaders to do this is simply to walk around, listen to employees, and be available to offer encouragement and support. This personal approach not only strengthens communication lines but also builds the relationships that are essential to dealing effectively with any future crisis. Leaders should also consider making counseling available and endorsing and underwriting support and discussion groups that could meet during working hours.

Next, leaders should review how the organization overall reacted during the crisis. One way to do this is through a process similar to the U.S. Army's After Action Review. Previous attempts by corporations to assimilate this process have met with mixed success. The key is to treat the crisis review process not as a one-time postmortem but as an ongoing organizational learning practice and a disciplined approach to improving performance over time.

During the crisis review process the people who were most closely involved in the crisis record their impressions and recollections of the organization's response to the crisis—what went well and what didn't go well or could have gone better. Looking at the bigger picture, the review participants should determine not only what was learned but also when and how the organization will apply what was learned. The crisis review can be carried out by a large group or by several smaller groups; in the Army's experience, smaller groups work best because reviewers are more likely to share sensitive information in small groups than in large groups.

The information and conclusions gathered during a crisis review can be grouped into two categories: *validations* and *lessons learned*. The former are reinforcements of the things that worked well; the latter are reflections on the things that didn't work well or that the organization did not do but should have done.

A crisis review should not be intended to cast blame or to find and penalize anyone who may have had a hand in creating the crisis or in failing to react to it appropriately. The main focus of a crisis review should be to learn from the crisis—not to determine responsibility, accountability, or guilt. If an organization is inclined to determine who, if anyone, was responsible for the crisis, it should undertake additional procedures separate from the crisis review, such as a formal internal inquiry or an outside legal action. For some crises, determining who was responsible and bringing the guilty party or parties to justice is not only appropriate but mandatory because it may be the only way for employees and others who feel they have been victimized by the culpable individual or individuals to heal.

Call to Action

The next step for leaders after a crisis is to incorporate the findings of the crisis review into an organizational crisis action plan. Again, special emphasis should be placed on communication before, during, and after the crisis. The lessons drawn from the crisis review can be used to update and improve the organization's crisis communication tactics, such as responding quickly when a disaster occurs, managing the organization's messages during a crisis, establishing a policy for dealing with the media, monitoring news coverage, and defining how and to whom employees should report a potential crisis situation.

The information and lessons unearthed during the crisis review process can also be used to draw up the what-if scenarios that are part of an effective crisis action plan and to write the final organizational report on the crisis. Employees should be briefed on the report and trained on how the crisis action plan works and their role in it; these steps not only fulfill the requisite of communication but also boost employees' confidence in their leadership as they see that crisis prevention and planning are priorities.

Aside from the crisis action plan, leaders should eliminate or change organizational procedures, policies, and regulations that were found to be inadequate during the crisis.

Values Added

Additional elements that leaders should review and revise after a crisis are the organization's vision and values. How did they fare during the crisis? Did they help or hinder the organization in weathering the storm? Did the organization and its leaders live up to their values during the crisis or jettison them in the struggle to survive?

Leaders may find it necessary to realign or redefine the organization's values and vision to make them more potent or relevant not only during times of crisis but also when everything is operating normally. Values may have to be reworded to make them stronger (an obvious example is an increased emphasis on employee safety), new values may need to be added, and obsolete values may need to be eliminated. If values that were found to be irrelevant or were ignored during the crisis are not altered or cut, they pose the risk of becoming a joke among the employees and threatening the leadership's credibility.

Because effective postcrisis leadership involves focusing on the human side of the situation, attention must also be paid to personal values. The high-pressure environment of a crisis can stress or damage relationships, and these need to be rebuilt and strengthened. Again, communication is the foundation on which the relationship restoration process is built, and establishing an atmosphere in which people feel safe talking about their feelings and in which a premium is placed on forgiveness is key.

Working Plans

The final piece of the postcrisis puzzle for leaders is attending to the organization's operational needs. In many cases a significant clean-up effort is required—recovery, repair and rebuilding, and reorganizing. Human resource issues also need to be addressed; personnel voids may need to be filled by promoting current employees or hiring replacement workers.

Operational concerns after a crisis inevitably involve the financial repercussions, such as the costs of cleaning up, salvaging, rebuilding, managing public relations, and working overtime. Sometimes the potential for litigation poses the most far-reaching implications for an organization's finances—a follow-up lawsuit can place the organization in a crisis situation far worse than the one it has just endured—and leaders need to stay thoroughly apprised and attuned on the legal front.

Image Counts

When leaders fail to handle a crisis adeptly and sensitively—and sometimes even when they do the best job possible—organizational damage, problems, and challenges will inevitably result. The organization's reputation may be hurt, stock values may plunge, key employees may leave, and lawsuits may loom.

Organizations live and die by their reputations, so it's essential that leaders develop a strategy to restore the organizational reputation after a crisis. The best way to do this is to implement a concerted public relations campaign focusing on employees, shareholders, the media, the community, and public interest groups. By reestablishing the organization's reputation, by affirming a sense of security and well-being, leaders can reduce the emotional impact of the crisis and strengthen the connection between the organization and its employees and stakeholders. If leaders can accomplish this, they will have taken a big step toward helping the organization emerge from a crisis not only intact but also with a better and more effective foundation.

◆ ◆ ◆

Adaptability: What It Takes to Be a Quick-Change Artist

Paige Bader and Allan Calarco

Metathesiophobia. That's the tongue-tying word for the *fear of change*—a fear that most people, if they are honest with themselves, will admit to having experienced. Change, even when it's relatively minor and even when the individual wants a change, can be unsettling and unnerving—and as a result intimidating. And with fear usually come stress and resistance.

For leaders, fearing and resisting change and balking at venturing into the unknown can be their own, their followers', and their organizations' undoing. It's a truism of today's business environment that the only thing that remains the same is change—and change is more copious, rapid, and complex than ever before. Mergers and acquisitions, corporate restructurings, downsizings, increasing globalization, and market upheavals are just a few of the dramatic transitions that leaders and their organizations must deal with at an unprecedented level. Another source of transition is the ephemerality of technology, with increasingly rapid rates of obsolescence and replacement requiring individuals and organizations to engage in a constant learning process. In addition, the people who make up organizations, work groups, and teams often shift at a breakneck pace. Institutional loyalty is hardly what it used to be (the Bureau of National Affairs recently reported that employee turnover is occurring at the highest rate in nearly twenty years), and it's common for people in organizations to be quickly shuttled in and out of different assignments. Managers' ability to deal with this type of change—losing well-known team members and working with new and unfamiliar colleagues—has a profound impact on organizational effectiveness and productivity.

Feeling the Heat

Statistics bear out the prevalence, increasing scope, and sometimes devastating effects of change in the business world. Of the one hundred largest U.S. companies at the beginning of the twentieth century, only sixteen exist today. And according to government figures, in the past decade in the United States more than 450,000 companies went under, more than 24 million jobs were lost, nearly half of all companies were restructured, more than 80,000 firms were acquired or merged, and more than 700,000 organizations sought bankruptcy protection.

Leaders are well aware of how important change—and the way they and their colleagues react to change—has become to their effectiveness and the success of their organizations. In a recent survey conducted by Ernst & Young and Cap Gemini Ernst & Young, eighty-six executives identified the top three threats that they and their organizations will face in the next two years. The executives cited regulatory changes (38 percent), competitive dynamics (29 percent), and market uncertainty (19 percent). All these concerns are related to transition.

Managers who participate in CCL's The Looking Glass Experience leadership development program indicate that change is omnipresent in today's organizations. Most of these managers say they have been through not just one but multiple acquisitions, mergers, reorganizations, or other significant organizational changes during their careers. They indicate that the pace and degree of change continue to spiral upward.

But recognizing that change inevitably exists is not the same as dealing with it effectively. Even though organizations rise or fall based largely on their ability to react to, manage, control, and introduce change, many managers have little or no understanding of or training in navigating the process of change.

Research conducted by CCL has identified ten flaws that can contribute to derailment—that is, to a manager who has previously been seen as successful and full of potential for continued advancement instead being fired, demoted, or held on a career plateau. Of these ten flaws, *the inability to develop or adapt* was the most frequently cited reason for derailment among North American managers. Conversely, the most frequently cited success factor for North American managers was *the ability to develop or adapt*.

If leaders don't consider their own adaptability and the adaptability of their subordinates, new initiatives can be halted or stifled before they are given a chance, or simply left to die on the vine. When a fresh vision emanates from an organization's top leadership, for instance, managers and their teams are expected to embrace the vision and move it toward implementation as quickly as possible. To understand and get on board with the new vision and to inspire subordinates to do the same, managers need to be adaptable.

During times of change and uncertainty, adaptability is required to foster progress and to help the organization and its members remain effective and productive. It's not enough for leaders to be adaptable themselves, however; they also must be able to recognize adaptability in their employees. This skill helps leaders choose people who are most suited to doing work involving change and who can motivate and act as role models for others during the transition period that accompanies any new initiative.

So it's clear that adaptability is crucial to leaders' effectiveness and success. This probably doesn't strike you as revelatory news. (After all, the subject of change is prominent on many people's radar screens; Spencer Johnson's book *Who Moved My Cheese?* about the inevitability of change and the need to adapt to the unexpected, is the top-selling business book of all time.) Yet even though the importance of adaptability in leaders is now widely regarded as a given, not much is known about what adaptability actually looks like. Until now, little research has been done on the specific behaviors that constitute adaptability. If leaders can gain insight into what these behaviors are, it will help them not only recognize but also take the first steps toward developing adaptability in themselves and others.

Under the Microscope

To clarify what it means to be adaptable, and to describe what adaptability looks like, CCL is conducting research in collaboration with George Mason University and the U.S. Army.

Note

Managing change is one of the biggest challenges faced by leaders today, yet there is little understanding of what adaptability looks like. To begin to clear up this problem, CCL is conducting research in association with George Mason University and the U.S. Army. The research is taking place during selected sessions of CCL's The Looking Glass Experience leadership development program.

In this five-day program designed for experienced managers, participants develop the ability to recognize opportunities and avoid pitfalls, gain a more complete view of their strengths and weaknesses in the context of the organization, and set goals that can help them navigate complex leadership situations. A major part of the program is a business simulation in which participants operate a fictional glass company. The simulation so closely parallels real life that participants invariably find that their performances mirror the behaviors they exhibit in their actual jobs.

The simulation includes a period of significant change, and as part of the research into adaptability, observers rate program partic-

Adaptability is a term that is thrown around a lot without a concrete definition or understanding of what it is. By explicitly identifying and describing the behaviors that make up adaptability, the research should help leaders approach adaptability in a more practical way and provide a foundation for recognizing and developing the skill in themselves and others.

The study thus far has been focusing on three main components of adaptability: cognitive, dispositional (personality related), and emotional. Following is a look at the behaviors that signify proficiency in each adaptive component.

Cognitive

Adaptability requires effective interpretation of change, and the first step is acknowledging that change has occurred. Successful

ipants on eleven dimensions of adaptability during this transitional time. Also, in the week before the program, participants are measured on three behavioral elements that may predict adaptability during a period of change—optimism, emotional intelligence, and metacognition (thinking about thinking). The study is looking into relationships between these three elements and ratings on the eleven dimensions of adaptability. It is also trying to ascertain whether some behaviors are more important than others to overall adaptability—for instance, whether it is more important to acknowledge the emotions of others than to be realistically optimistic.

The experience of one manager during a recent Looking Glass Experience exemplifies just how traumatic change can be for some people. The manager had been so adversely affected by change in his organization that when it became clear during the simulation that there were going to be changes, he refused to participate further. He took his laptop computer into the hallway and didn't return until two hours later, after the simulation was over.

adapters then address key aspects of the change—for example, how a new vision will create new markets, competitors, and organizational roles. Identifying how the change will affect the way the organization functions is also important.

The ability to formulate alternative strategies is another aspect of cognitive adaptability. Leaders who are adaptable are able to let go of old roles and ideas, identify and embrace new roles, and come up with new tactics and action plans that address the implications of the change. Specifically, their language often shifts from past tense ("We used to do this . . .") to future tense ("Now we will do this . . .").

Cognitive adaptability also involves divergent thinking—for instance, contemplating a totally new direction that turns the change into an advantage, or acknowledging and putting to use the skills of new members of a team. Finally, cognitive adapters are good at spanning boundaries—they consider the implications of the change for others in the organization and communicate this information to the various organizational units and top management.

Dispositional

The ability to remain optimistic—but at the same time realistic— is one of the linchpins of adaptability. Successful adapters approach change not as a threat but as an opportunity. They take the attitude that they can continue to be effective in the new environment. Optimism also appears to boost managers' self-confidence in their ability to be effective during times of change.

It's debatable whether optimism can be developed, but next time you are in a situation of change, try identifying something that is positive about the situation and building on it. Make a list of the opportunities presented by the change and communicate those opportunities to others in the organization.

Personality-related adaptability also entails remaining highly involved during times of change—not "checking out" emotionally or physically, but staying excited and energetic, consistently and usefully contributing to brainstorming on new strategies, and successfully integrating into a new team or working across new organizational boundaries.

Leaders who are adept at the dispositional aspects of adaptability also encourage others in the organization or team to go with the flow of change. They elicit contributions from others, sincerely commend others for their innovative contributions, and make formal introductions of those who are new to the organization or team as a way of acknowledging that change has occurred and new group dynamics will emerge.

Emotional

It's all right for managers to admit resistance to change—in fact it's preferable, because emotions that are denied will eventually resurface and have to be dealt with. Resistance to change is natural; recognition and awareness of change are the keys to the emotional element of adaptability. Conceding your resistance to a change enables others in the organization to help you cope with the change. At the same time, it's important not to let emotions get the best of you, but to maintain a balance, and to remain on task.

Addressing the emotions of others is a large part of the emotional component of adaptability. Managers should encourage others to express their emotions about a change—whether those feelings are positive or negative—and should not be critical of the expression of such emotions. One way to do this is to take thirty minutes each day for an organizational or group discussion and (with the aid of a flip chart) let everyone express his or her thoughts and feelings about the change that is occurring and the effect it is having.

Opportunity Knocks

Adaptability is not changing for changing's sake—it is responding to environmental factors in a way that has functional, effective results. Nor is adaptability easy. Staying positive and overcoming the fear and resistance that naturally accompany change can be difficult.

In addition, a manager's cognitive adaptability won't be recognizable or influential if it is not expressly stated, so it's important for managers to communicate any new ideas or strategies they have to deal with a change. And even highly adaptive managers will be stifled if they are surrounded by colleagues who are stalwartly resistant to change and who discourage the expression of ideas and emotions related to change.

But the more positive experiences you have with change, the more you will become comfortable with and skilled at adaptability. So it's important not to shy away from change but instead take it on and look for the opportunities within it. For change, scary as it may seem, offers a chance to develop and progress not only on the organizational but also on the individual level.

No Change Is Small Change

People's natural discomfort with and resistance to change—even change that may seem insignificant to others—was succinctly described by syndicated columnist Ellen Goodman in her 1979 book, *Turning Points:* "We cling to even the minor routines with an odd tenacity. We're upset when the waitress who usually brings us coffee in the breakfast shop near the office suddenly quits, and are disoriented if the drugstore or the cleaner's in the neighborhood closes.... We each have a litany of holiday rituals and everyday habits that we hold on to, and we often greet radical innovations with the enthusiasm of a baby meeting a new sitter."

Everyone can think of examples of the extent to which some people carry their aversion to change—some of these examples border on the absurd—and the sometimes crippling repercussions of refusing to or being unable to change. There are a number of tales, for example, about proprietors of traditional barbershops who steadfastly declined to adjust their enterprises during the 1960s trend toward unisex styling salons. As a result they watched their businesses go under. (There is a lot to be said for appreciating heritage, but clinging to tradition isn't worth much if it threatens survival.)

Alternative-medicine guru and author Caroline Myss has said that some people would rather die than change. In one extreme example of stubbornness toward change, a woman who was a confirmed lover of M&M's candies was shocked and infuriated when manufacturer Mars, Inc. conducted a nationwide survey in 1995 to determine whether to add a new color to M&M's. Believing that what wasn't broke shouldn't be fixed and that her favorite candy would never be the same, the woman sent letters of protest to Mars. But "blue" won out in the vote over "no change" (as well as "pink" and "purple"), and the woman has since refused to open another bag of M&M's. Because of her obsession with having things stay the same, she has forgone what used to be her favorite comfort food.

Chapter Three

How to Work Across Cultures

The challenge of leading people who come from different cultures arises from several organizational situations—for instance, you may be working as an expatriate, managing international projects, or working entirely at home but dealing with the growing diversity of the workforce. All these require you to interact effectively with people whose values and standards of behavior are not the same as yours, and to help them interact with one another. This chapter will contribute to your ability to do that.

◆ ◆ ◆

Getting the Message:
How to Feel Your Way with Other Cultures

Don W. Prince and Michael H. Hoppe

During a visit to a foreign country, distant city, or even another company, cultural differences can seem colorful, exotic, and appealing. But when the time spent in another culture is longer than a visit, or when you work and conduct business with people of other cultures, your cultural biases can emerge with more force. The disregard for time that seemed so delightful on the island vacation feels very different on Monday morning in the office when the clock is ticking. A modest, deferential manner that was appealing in one cultural context may strike you as passive and ineffectual in a conference room.

These experiences feel unfamiliar because we are looking through the lens of our own cultural expectations. Unconsciously we expect other people to think, feel, and act the way we do. When they don't conform to our expectations, we put our own interpretations on their behavior. But when you're working across cultures, interpretation often becomes misinterpretation. You run the risk of negatively judging the words and actions of people of other cultures or incorrectly assigning motives to unfamiliar behavior because you're viewing an experience from the limited perspective of your own culture.

The discomfort you feel when cultural boundaries collide can be used to your benefit by alerting you to cultural differences. In your interactions with other people, be aware that cultural differences may be coming into play when you experience feelings such as confusion, anxiety, frustration, misunderstanding, tension, impatience, irritation, or anger.

Keeping Your Feet on the Ground

When you feel uncomfortable, it's natural to retreat from that discomfort. After all, you probably feel you are most effective as a manager when you are operating from a familiar place, where you can draw confidence from and make decisions based on past experience. From our work at CCL, we have coined the phrase *jump-back response* to describe this desire to retreat. To be more effective when communicating across cultures, resist your jump-back response. Stay with the uncomfortable experience and learn from it. Compare the unexpected and discomforting behaviors you experience when communicating across cultures against your knowledge of your cultural expectations.

Why doesn't she just say yes or no? In one culture an indirect answer may signal indecisiveness, whereas in another culture it may signal deference and respect.

Why is he always staring at me like that? In one culture staring may signal aggressiveness or intimidation, whereas in another culture direct eye contact may show attention and esteem.

Why does he have to get right in my face whenever he talks to me? In one culture the halo of personal space and privacy may be much smaller than it is in another culture.

Why doesn't she tell me if she doesn't understand something? In one culture asking questions may be accepted as an effective tool for communication, but in another culture questioning superiors may signal insolence.

Why does he sit there smiling when I'm talking about his performance problems? In one culture smiling during a discussion about performance problems may signal contempt and disinterest, whereas in another culture a smile may reflect sincerity and attention.

Why does he make a joke out of everything? In one culture a glib nature may signal a lack of confidence or seriousness, but in another culture it may be a sign of deference.

Time to Change Your Style?

When you work with people of other cultures, you should expect that differences will surface, recognize those cultural differences by the discomfort they produce, and anticipate that those differences will create a need for more thoughtful and deliberate communication. Don't assume that your own cultural customs are correct and superior to others or take the attitude that the other person has to change his or her ways. Be alert to the need to modify your communication style when

- Another person's behavior makes you uncomfortable.
- Another person's response or reaction seems inappropriate or confusing.
- You assume that you're right and the other person is wrong.
- You stereotype and denigrate another cultural group.
- You ignore or exclude someone because understanding and making yourself understood seem too difficult.

It's important to make changes in your communication patterns quickly once you recognize that changes are necessary. A person from another culture is likely to be forgiving the first and second times you make a mistake, but if you persist you will appear ignorant, insensitive, dismissive, or disrespectful.

Consider, for example, the use of *why* questions as a way to get more information. In some cultures, such as that of the United States, it's completely acceptable to ask, "Why did you do the job this way?" In other cultures, Japan's, for example, the same question is considered rude because it puts the other person on the defensive. In this case you can change your communication behavior: "That's an interesting approach you took to the problem. Tell me a little more about it." This gives the other person a chance to share more information with you without risk. Other simple changes that you can make after recognizing different cultural behaviors include learning how to make the correct greeting (a handshake? a bow? a hug?), when to offer your business card (before or after the other person does?), and when and how to question superiors.

It's Not So Easy Anymore

When you listen to people who have the same cultural background and native language as you do, you can usually get the gist of their meaning without special effort. You can easily understand their words and "read" their body language and tone of voice. You can make assumptions that are valuable shortcuts to understanding.

When you listen to people from other cultures, your task is more difficult. You can't make the same assumptions. Effective cross-cultural communication requires an extra measure of awareness and attention. To focus on the other person's message, keep the following questions in mind each time you communicate across cultures:

- What do I know about this person's culture?
- Do I take the time to focus on a person from another culture, so I can understand where he or she is "coming from"?
- Do I pay attention to a person's words and body language?

- Do I listen for feelings and unvoiced questions?
- Do I clarify and confirm what I have heard?
- Do I check to make sure the other person has fully understood what I said?

Look for Nonverbal Communication

Whether you're talking to someone from your own culture or someone with a different cultural perspective, much of the message is relayed through nonverbal cues. When communicating across cultures, it's important not only to hear what the other person is saying but also to observe what that person's body language (facial expressions, hand gestures, eye contact, tone of voice) is saying.

Keep in mind, however, that like spoken language, nonverbal expressions such as eye contact and body position have different meanings in different cultures. A clenched fist, a slouched posture, an open hand, or a smile can tell us how to understand a communication only if we have a cultural context for defining the body language.

Even silence can communicate. In some cultures, remaining silent after someone has spoken shows respectful contemplation and consideration of the person's words. If your culture doesn't allow for such conversational pauses, resist filling these gaps with additional explanations and alternative wording.

Also remember that body language is a two-way medium—your own gestures and facial expressions can have unintended messages when you are communicating with someone from another culture. Although your words may say otherwise, your body can communicate boredom, defiance, persuasion, or condescension.

How can you interpret, or "hear," all of that body language if you're not familiar with the other culture? Keep your eyes open for patterns of behavior among various cultural groups. Ask a trusted person from the cultural group. Read up on the business customs of other cultures, and pull information from the Internet (travel sites can be especially helpful in describing cultural customs).

A Little Self-Reflection Helps

Another good place to start is with a look at your own body language. Ask someone to videotape a presentation that you give at your organization, or observe yourself in a mirror. Ask yourself:

- What do my nonverbal communications look like?
- How might I be perceived by someone with a different cultural background?
- Do I match the stereotype of people from my country?
- How can I check if I suspect that my body language is being misinterpreted by someone from another culture?

Body Language Varies by Culture

Body language is not a universal language. If you experience unexpected behavior when you are trying to communicate in a cross-cultural setting, it's likely that the other person's culture is different from yours and that you are unfamiliar with the cultural context behind the behavior.

> A manager is conducting an annual performance review with one of his direct reports. He begins the session by discussing all the areas in which the employee's performance met or exceeded goals. The employee listens attentively, with a serious and thoughtful expression. But when the manager begins to discuss weaknesses and problem areas, the employee starts smiling. The sterner the manager's tone, the broader the employee grins. The employee doesn't comment on anything the manager says or defend or explain himself. The manager becomes angry because he believes the employee is mocking him and treating the evaluation as a joke.

Sustained eye contact means respect and attentiveness in some cultures but is a rude invasion of privacy in others. A gesture that denotes enthusiastic approval in some cultures is an insult in others. In this case the employee's smile was not a sign of mockery but an expression of deep embarrassment and shame. The manager's angry feelings toward the employee's behavior signal that there may be a miscommunication because of cultural differences.

> Frank and Nick leave the office to go to lunch together. When they get into the elevator, Nick stands one foot away from Frank even though the elevator is otherwise empty. When Frank moves a couple of steps away, Nick moves closer to him so that they are almost touching.

Every culture has its own standards about how much personal space feels right and comfortable. From Frank's cultural perspective, physical closeness is an expression of intimacy and feels completely inappropriate in a business relationship. In Nick's cultural view, such closeness is natural behavior. Putting more distance between himself and Frank would show that they don't know or don't like each other.

> John goes to the airport to meet Yuri's plane. The two men have talked several times on the phone but have met only once before. When Yuri spots John in the baggage area, he enthusiastically embraces him and kisses him on both cheeks. John feels uncomfortable and hopes nobody he knows has witnessed this greeting.

Every culture has its own unwritten rules about touching. In John's culture the only acceptable touching in business relationships is a handshake. In Yuri's culture bear hugs and kisses are an acceptable and even expected form of greeting, no matter what the relationship is and regardless of gender.

> When Hong Mei presents her proposal at the meeting, Vincent reacts strongly. He pounds on the table and questions her in a loud voice. When Hong Mei casts her eyes down in embarrassment, Vincent seems to get more excited. He leans across the table and jabs his hand toward her face.

Every culture has its own ideas about what kind of emotional expression is acceptable and right. In Hong Mei's culture emotional reserve and restraint are cherished and expected. In Vincent's culture feelings are freely expressed in loud voices, expansive gestures, grimaces, groans, and exclamations. Anything less conveys coldness and disengagement.

> Susan travels to London for a meeting with Gillian and Philip. She wants to make a good impression and to indicate that she is happy to be working with them, so she nods and smiles at their comments and observations.

Even the most innocent gestures can be misconstrued. Susan thinks her smiles and nods indicate attentiveness and express her happiness at being part of the team. Gillian and Philip come from a cultural background in which attentiveness and sincerity are marked by a reserved demeanor. Susan's behavior indicates to them that she is insincere, superficial, and unprofessional.

Just as spoken words can be misunderstood during a cross-cultural encounter, so too can nonverbal behavior. If a behavior upsets you beyond what seems appropriate, that's a good sign that cultures are colliding, not communicating. Ask questions to make sure you understand the meaning of behavior that seems out of place.

New World, New Lenses

Managers can no longer afford to view the world—an increasingly connected world—through a single cultural lens. Instead, an expanded cultural horizon is becoming increasingly essential to effective leadership. Teams, work groups, communities, and organizations become more diverse every day. Adding new lenses to your cultural viewpoint not only increases your awareness of other cultures and your effectiveness in working with people from other cultures but also develops your understanding of your own cultural conditioning.

There are many personal and leadership benefits of an expanded cultural horizon, and their effects are powerful. You can appreciate different ways—perhaps better ways—of accomplishing goals. You can gain insight into your own behavior. You can discover "out of the box" ways to communicate clearly and effectively. And you can become more comfortable in suspending your judgment, which fosters a more creative work environment.

Cultural differences arise in all levels of an organization and affect all leaders, from the project team to the executive suite. As you become more aware of those differences and more skilled at communicating across cultures, you'll become a better manager and a more effective leader.

Practical Note

There are three practical rules for ensuring better cross-cultural communications:

1. *Capture.* To avoid misunderstandings, injured feelings, and confusion, focus fully on the conversation. Capture what is said and refer to your knowledge about other cultures to derive meaning.

2. *Clarify.* If you aren't completely sure you have understood what the other person is saying, look for nonverbal cues to explain the message. Alternatively, you can ask a knowledgeable insider to check your understanding.

3. *Confirm.* To make sure the other person has understood you, give him or her an opportunity to paraphrase or clarify what you have said. You might want to write down your message or schedule a short follow-up conversation to repeat, in a different way, your original message.

Suggested Reading

Dresser, N. *Multicultural Manners: New Rules of Etiquette for a Changing Society.* New York: Wiley, 1996.

Gannon, M. J. *Understanding Global Cultures: Metaphorical Journeys Through Seventeen Countries.* Thousand Oaks, Calif.: Sage, 1994.

Harris, P. R., and Moran, R. T. *Managing Cultural Differences.* Houston: Gulf, 1996.

Storti, C. *Figuring Foreigners Out: A Practical Guide.* Yarmouth, Maine: Intercultural Press, 1998.

Wilson, M. S., Hoppe, M. H., and Sayles, L. R. *Managing Across Cultures: A Learning Framework.* Greensboro, N.C.: Center for Creative Leadership, 1996.

◆ ◆ ◆

Global Managing: Mastering the Spin of a Complex World

Christopher Ernst

As a high-level manager at a U.S.-based manufacturing company, Matthew leads a number of teams. He has just been asked by his boss to turn over responsibility for one of those teams to someone else and take on a different task—managing a new plant in Frankfurt, Germany. The factory was recently acquired in a merger and there's a lot riding on its success, so Matthew views his selection to manage it as a vote of confidence and another feather in his cap.

He starts to imagine what his life would be like as an expatriate. But reality stops him short—after all, his boss didn't ask him to move to Frankfurt. He didn't even ask him to spend a lot of time there. Instead, the boss wants Matthew to continue to manage his domestic teams as he always has and at the same time use the tools of technology—e-mail, videoconferencing, faxes, and the like—to connect with and direct his new team in Germany. The boss says Matthew needs to meet face-to-face with his people in Germany only occasionally.

Matthew believes that although his new task will mean some additional work and an increase in the scope of his job, he'll be able to manage his new team in much the same way he has managed his domestic teams. But he's in for a shock. He is about to take on a job that is not only bigger but far more complex.

Global managers are faced with a range of new challenges. They must become integrators of performance results, business acumen, social patterns, and perpetual technological advances, not only in their home bases but around the world. They need to acquire a new set of skills to effectively meet these complex challenges.

For many organizations, succeeding in the global economy has risen to the top of their agendas, and global managers are increasingly being asked to lead the way. And yet, because the global economy has come of age relatively recently, many managers find themselves in Matthew's situation—thrust into a global leadership role in which their skills don't match the requirements of the job.

What are those requirements? Are the skills required for success in managing a global operation completely different from those needed to effectively manage a domestic operation, or do they overlap? And what can organizations and leaders do to develop the skills needed to excel in a global context? CCL research work with a group of managers produced some insights that go a long way toward answering these and other questions (see note on page 84).

Grave New World?

For global managers to get a firm grasp of the challenges they face, they must first develop a realistic picture of the new, expanded, and diverse environment in which they operate and how it differs from the relatively homogeneous setting of the domestic manager.

Note

In an effort to learn whether managers with global responsibilities and those with purely domestic responsibilities need different types of knowledge and capabilities to be effective, CCL recently conducted a study of 214 managers from thirty-nine countries working in thirty countries around the world. The managers' companies represented four industries and had corporate headquarters in Sweden, Switzerland, and the United States. Half the managers had local responsibility (they directed operations within the borders of one country), and half had global responsibility (they directed operations in multiple countries and across various cultures).

The managers completed a number of questionnaires comprising nearly 1,000 items, and each manager's boss completed a questionnaire about the manager's job effectiveness. CCL researchers then conducted a series of correlational analyses and found that there is one set of capabilities that all managers need to be seen as effective by their bosses whether their work is global or local in scope. These are the essential capabilities—core business knowledge; the ability to cope with pressure; and the ability to manage people, action, and information. More important to the objectives of the research, CCL also identified four pivotal capabilities that are uniquely related to the effectiveness of global managers.

In the 1997 best-seller *One World, Ready or Not: The Manic Logic of Global Capitalism*, political writer William Greider provides a lucid and vivid description of the crucible in which novice global managers find themselves. It is a world in which managers are required to process, integrate, and make decisions based on huge amounts of disparate information; negotiate with governments that have very different notions of how business should be done; interact with a complex web of organizational relationships in multiple and diverse countries; recruit and develop the best talent from anywhere in the world; and develop strategic alliances—even with competitors that operate within different models of capitalist systems. Stir all of these ingredients together and one gets a sense of the ambiguity and stress inherent in globally complex work.

Through its research, CCL has identified several dimensions across which the global manager must work simultaneously—even if, like Matthew, the manager spends the majority of his or her career behind a desk at the home office.

Geographic distance. Global managers must be able to deal with the inconveniences of time differences and the practical and psychological difficulties of not always being able to see the people with whom they work.

National infrastructures. Global managers must negotiate multiple and sometimes antithetical variations in political and economic systems, regulatory and legal frameworks, and civic and labor practices.

Cultural expectations. Global managers must familiarize themselves and comply with a wide range of sometimes startling expectations in regard to behavior—their own and that of their colleagues, employees, customers, suppliers, and distributors—and the ways in which work should be done.

The complexity faced by global managers grows exponentially with the number of countries, cultures, and time zones in which they work. During teleconferences, for instance, each participant could well be in a different time zone. A global manager at a meeting in Tokyo must be aware not only of Japanese exchange rates, corporate culture, laws, investment policy, and labor unions but also of the infrastructures of each other nation in which his or her company does business. When a global manager gets off a plane or sends an e-mail message, a different set of cultural expectations awaits at the arrival gate or the recipient's computer monitor. Constantly confronted with such Byzantine situations, it's no wonder that global managers can often be reduced to conducting reality checks—asking themselves, "Where am I?" or, "Who is that sitting across the table from me?" rather than the most critical question: "What do I need to do to be effective in this context?"

What these managers need to sort out the massive and manifold input of a complicated world is more than just a firm command of the *essential capabilities* that are required of all managers to be effective, whether their work is global or local in scope. They must also learn to nurture and attain four *pivotal capabilities* that are uniquely related to the effectiveness of global managers.

Turn, Turn, Turn

Think of the axis on which a globe rotates. Just as the globe spins on its axis, the global manager adapts to fluid, complex situations by using the pivotal capabilities—*international business knowledge, cultural adaptability, perspective taking,* and *innovation.* The pivotal capabilities are the global manager's axis—the knowledge, motivation, and skills needed to be effective and adaptable amid the complexity of the global marketplace. Global managers who develop the pivotal capabilities are less likely to become immobilized by that complexity.

International Business Knowledge

To be effective, global managers must have a solid understanding of how business is conducted in each country and culture where they have responsibilities. On the big-picture level, international business knowledge means having a thorough grasp of your organization's core business and how to leverage that business within and across each country where your organization has markets, vendors, resources, and manufacturing operations. On the grassroots level, it means knowing the laws, histories, and customs of each of those countries.

Gaining international business knowledge involves taking classes, reading books, and talking with experts. Being sophisticated in the realm of international business not only gives global managers the savoir faire to behave appropriately and stay out of trouble but also guides them in developing a broad, long-range strategy and keeps them aware of how decisions at one location affect possibilities and outcomes at others.

But intellectual knowledge goes only so far. No matter how prestigious a manager's education and how thorough the data the manager receives from the organization's information technology, human resources, and legal departments, such knowledge is of limited value if the manager can't use it to adjust personal behavior to various business contexts and to help co-workers do the same. To capitalize on international business knowledge, global managers must also pay attention to the other pivotal capabilities.

Cultural Adaptability

Global managers must act on their knowledge of cultural differences and use that knowledge to help them interact effectively with people from different cultures. A large part of cultural adaptability is being able to deal with the stress and the perceptions of eccentricity and strangeness that can arise from global complexity.

For instance, a U.S. global manager who faces an important deadline on a project in Mexico may notice during a teleconference that the team members in Mexico seem unconcerned as they deliver an overdue status report. Cultural adaptability would allow the manager not only to know that Mexican business tends to be conducted under a different time orientation than is common in the United States—in Mexico, people take precedence over schedules—but to act on that knowledge in an appropriate way. Similarly, cultural adaptability would allow a female global manager in Europe who is negotiating with a Saudi Arabian to use her knowledge of the role of hierarchy, class status, and gender in Saudi culture and to adjust her words and actions accordingly.

In an article published nearly twenty years ago in the journal *International Studies of Management and Organization*, Indrei Ratiu of the global business school INSEAD, which has campuses in France and Singapore, was one of the first to examine the role of cultural adaptability in determining the success of global managers, or *internationalists*.

One characteristic of successful internationalists, wrote Ratiu, is that they begin with general knowledge, or prototypes, of cultures when they first start dealing with those cultures. As they get to know people from those cultures as *individuals*, however, successful internationalists are able to let go of or adjust elements of their prototypes and gain a less stereotypical knowledge of the cultures and their people. Unsuccessful internationalists either don't start off with prototypes (and as a result interpret everything based on their own mental frameworks) or are unable to discard their prototypes despite evidence culled from their interrelationships with people from other cultures that ought to dispel preconceptions.

Managers who are culturally adaptable, then, sign on to the notion that logic and truth are relative. In her book *International Dimensions of Organizational Behavior*, Nancy Adler, a professor of organizational behavior at McGill University in Montreal, wrote that "in approaching cross-cultural situations, effective business people . . . assume differences until similarity is proven. They recognize that all behavior makes sense through the eyes of the person behaving and that logic and rationale are culturally relative."

This view can create tension for global managers, however, especially if they tend to approach the business world as a nuts-and-bolts environment of budget sheets and Pareto charts. To ease this tension, global managers need to develop the next pivotal capability.

Perspective Taking

Everyone has a personal perspective—images of and beliefs about what things are and should be. But not everyone is adept at taking the perspectives of others—seeing and understanding their views of what things are and should be.

There are several idioms that give a sense of what is meant by perspective taking: *Walk a mile in my shoes. I know where you're com-*

ing from. I see what you mean. All of these show that there is a large element of empathy in perspective taking. In the case of global managers it is *cultural* empathy—knowing, understanding, and acting in accordance with the deeply held values and beliefs of people from other cultures.

Imagine that you and a friend are hiking up a steep, wooded slope. As you near the summit, you both stop to catch your breath and look back at the view. Your friend says she can see a town over the treetops. But she is ten yards ahead of you, and you can see only the trees. Because you and your friend are standing in different places, you literally have different points of view. To see what your friend sees, you must move to where she is standing, and vice versa.

Of course, walking up or down a hill to see the view from a different perspective is easy. Understanding how to act, communicate, and lead while taking into account the perspectives of colleagues, direct reports, and customers from other cultures is not so easy.

Whether the context is global or is confined to a single culture, the processes and behaviors involved in perspective taking are largely the same: listening to and absorbing information skillfully, recognizing that other people's views of a situation may be different from yours, understanding that other people's assumptions about what things are and should be may be different from yours, and accepting the limitations of your own point of view.

Yet implementing these processes and practicing these behaviors can be especially difficult for managers operating in a global context, because they do not have the luxury of working from a single, commonly understood cultural framework. The frame of reference held by each individual with whom global managers deal, and which they must strive to understand, changes from culture to culture.

An example of how fundamentally different cultural perspectives can be was offered by Erica Goode in her August 8, 2000, *New York Times* article "How Culture Molds Habits of Thought," which reported on a study of U.S. and Japanese managers who were asked to look at the same picture and describe it. The U.S. managers tended to talk about the people in the picture, whereas the

Japanese managers were more interested in the setting of the picture. The study underscored how two people looking at the same thing will often focus on different aspects of it because of their cultural perspectives.

Developing the ability to distinguish the moods, temperaments, and intentions of people from other cultures requires a concerted effort, especially in the virtual environment in which global managers typically work. Global managers who interpret and label the behaviors of others based on their own cognitive and interpersonal frameworks will be more likely to make mistakes about others' motivations, and their own actions and reactions will be liable to leave other people shaking their heads. However, global managers who learn to take the perspective of others and to reorganize their own sense-making frameworks will grow to see multiple perspectives as not incompatible but as all having potential for contributing to solid managerial decisions and actions. Such managers will make sense to, rather than confound, the people from other cultures with whom they work.

Global managers who add the final pivotal capability— innovation—to the first three will have the tools not only to understand and adapt to the complexity of the global business environment but also to capitalize on that very complexity to achieve success for themselves, their teams, and their organizations.

Innovation

For global managers, the role of innovator is integral to the other pivotal capabilities. Only through skill in innovation can global managers take their knowledge of international business, understanding of cultural differences, and ability to experience the perspectives of others and leverage them to create something new—a new policy, procedure, product, service, or practice—that is greater than the sum of its parts.

In this respect, innovation is the most essential of the pivotal capabilities. It takes managers beyond merely managing the complexity of global operations to turning that complexity to their advantage.

Building skill as an innovator is a step-by-step process of gathering information, learning to listen and pay attention, letting go of the need to always be *right*, and seeking out useful combinations.

Examples of skill in innovation can be found in the realm of music. In the 1960s the Beatles' George Harrison developed an interest in Indian culture, religion, and music. It wasn't just a passing fancy; he took lessons from sitar virtuoso Ravi Shankar and immersed himself in the culture and traditions of India. The knowledge Harrison gained, his cultural adaptability, and his willingness and ability to take a different perspective led him to write and record songs that transcended both the rock and classical Indian genres—they were an entirely new type of music that was neither Eastern nor Western. Similarly, Paul Simon became captivated by the stirring harmonies of the a cappella group Ladysmith Black Mambazo during a visit to South Africa in the mid-1980s and incorporated their traditional sounds into his album *Graceland*, which fused a number of styles into a completely new one. The innovations of both Harrison and Simon are credited with creating and popularizing what is now called *world music*, which is not a *type* of music in the traditional sense, like blues or jazz, but is rather a hybrid of any number of combinations of musical styles from around the globe.

An example of innovative skill in a business context is found in the story of a British manager assigned to set up a manufacturing plant in an impoverished area of Africa. He had hoped to recruit a reliable and loyal workforce, but many employees weren't showing up for work. In an attempt to solve the problem he began offering free lunches to workers. But absenteeism continued to be rampant and was severely cutting into the bottom line. Unwilling to reconcile himself to a constantly revolving workforce, the manager brought into play his pivotal capability of perspective taking by talking with the local tribal leaders to try to get a handle on the problem. He learned that the workers didn't feel justified in coming to the factory and being fed while their families were left hungry at home. The manager innovated by serving lunch each day to work-ers *and* their families. The cost was more than offset by the fact that absenteeism all but disappeared.

Seeking the New

As a set, the pivotal capabilities provide the knowledge, motiva-tion, and skills that global managers need to master the spin of a complex world. Developing these capabilities requires continually seeking out new and varied experiences that challenge your current perspectives and offer new ones. There are many possibilities for such experiences, but here are some that have proven effective for global managers:

- Study new languages, not primarily to gain fluency but rather to become familiar with their syntaxes and structures. This can be a powerful way to understand and appreciate how people from other cultures think.
- Make a habit of arriving a day or two before a business meet-ing in a country you have never visited before. Hitting the streets, interacting with merchants, and tasting the local cui-sine are simple yet effective ways to orient yourself to other cultures and their people.
- Read the literature and listen to the music that are popular in a country you're getting ready to visit. This gives you a deeper and richer understanding of the culture than you can get from skimming a guidebook.
- Host foreign visitors in your home, and get to know people in your own country who are of different ethnicities or religions.
- Read as much of the international business press as time allows.

As globalization becomes the norm and advances in informa-tion technology become even more rapid, the world of international business will become only more complex. Developing the pivotal capabilities and establishing a synergy among them will enable global managers to stretch to meet this challenge, and increase their chances of achieving success for themselves and their organizations.

◆ ◆ ◆

One Prescription for Working Across Cultures

Craig Chappelow

For me, the best part of working in the field of leadership and leadership development has been the opportunity to travel to other countries to work with clients. As much as I would like to prepare for every possible subtle cultural difference I encounter, however, the reality is that I travel on short notice. So I have adopted a simple dictum that I apply when I'm visiting and working in other countries. It's stolen from the medical profession: *First, do no harm.* It boils down to using basic manners and a bit of self-awareness to monitor my behavior—for instance, whether I'm being too loud or hogging people's personal space. (Both are my tendencies.)

There are a number of resources that I use to get a quick overview of the basic do's and don'ts in encounters with other cultures. I particularly like the *Culture Shock!* series of books from Graphic Arts Center Publishing Company; they teach me just enough to not offend. For anyone considering spending time in France, I enthusiastically recommend Polly Platt's *French or Foe*, in which you learn, among other things, why *not* to smile at a French shopkeeper.

But very little of our important learning comes from reading books. Most significant learning results from experiencing key events (which in my case generally means screwing things up). I try to gain as much knowledge as I can from such events and to never repeat a mistake. Here's a look at some of the key events I have experienced in my travels—some were elementary and many were embarrassing, but all were educational.

Watch What You Eat

Table manners vary wildly from place to place, and you'll often encounter some quirky edibles. At a dinner party in Australia, one of the dessert courses was a rectangular piece of nougat. After unwrapping the outer foil, I discovered a second, thinner layer of white paper covering the candy.

I painstakingly removed each bit of the paper, even though it was disintegrating in my fingers. Finally my host said, "G'wan, Craig, eat the paper. It's made of rice." I looked up to see that I was the only one at the table with a neat pile of crispy pieces of paper next to my plate.

Traditional Approach

Taking a genuine interest in other people's heritage can go a long way. I once asked a Saudi businessman if there were still Bedouins in his country. I remembered reading about them in Leon Uris's book *The Haj*, and I was intrigued by the idea of twentieth-century nomads. The businessman was surprised but pleased when I asked. It turned out he was descended from a Bedouin family, and he proceeded to happily tell me stories about his family's tribe.

Eager to Please

One benefit of traveling is that I have learned to extend to visitors to the United States the same hospitality I have received around the world.

During a trip to New Zealand, a co-worker and I stopped at a store to ask for directions to a tourist attraction in a distant town. The woman in the store immediately called a relative in the town to get directions. Later my colleague and I got off track and stopped to ask a farmer for directions. He insisted that we come into his barn to see his newborn calves.

That night we were still driving way out in the country, and by that time we were starving. We managed to find a restaurant, only to discover it was closed for the night. But the maitre d' unlocked the door and let us in. The cook had gone home, but the maitre d' went into the kitchen and emerged a few minutes later with a giant bowl of French fries and garlic bread. He said it was the only thing he knew how to cook. To us it was ambrosia.

Riding Shotgun

On my first visit to Australia I jumped in the back seat of an airport taxi. I told the cabby where I wanted to go but he just sat there, looking at me in the rearview mirror. Finally he said, "Well, are you going to come ride up front or just sit in back like an American?" I was a little puzzled (not to mention jet-lagged) but moved to the front seat.

Steer Clear

I've noticed that there are wide variations among cultures in people's need for personal space. The English, for instance, tend to need a lot of it. One of the funniest scenes in the movie *The Full Monty* is the one in which the jobless steelworkers pulsate to a disco beat in the unemployment line. Even as they break into spontaneous dance, each one maintains an invisible but precise bubble of space around himself. I've learned that when I get on an elevator in London and everyone backs away, it isn't a reflection on my hygiene.

Keep Moving

In a remote public market in the Guatemalan highlands, I found myself packed in among hundreds of locals shouldering their way through the narrow rows between the stalls, where everything from cornmeal to kittens was for sale. When I slowed down a little to look more closely at something, I felt myself being propelled forward by a hand in the small of my back. Behind me a tiny woman was politely but firmly keeping me moving through the crowd. I noticed this was a frequent practice among the locals.

Bad Hair Day

I awoke early in my hotel in Shanghai, with an entire Sunday to do as I pleased. My body was still on U.S. time, and I was wide-awake at 4 A.M. At 6 I decided to take a walk and find some breakfast. Even though it was early, the streets were already crowded. I stopped to rest and watched a surreal scene: white-clad senior citizens doing aerobics to big-band music. As I sat on the edge of a concrete planter, an ancient man came and plopped down right next to me, so close that our legs were touching. He knew a little English and struck up a conversation. Another man came and sat on my other side. He began rubbing his hand up and down my arm, laughing. As I recoiled he pointed at the hair on my arm and then at his arm, which was hairless. I felt a little as though I belonged in the primate house.

Accidental Cheapskate

One thing I always do before going to a new country is to familiarize myself with the currency and the exchange rate. One time at a gift shop in Ireland, I was behind an American couple who apparently hadn't bothered to do so. They were holding up the line as they engaged in a loud conversation about the difficulties of keeping track of *foreign* money.

Even if you think you know the currency, you have to stay on your toes. At a beer garden in Cologne, Germany, a group of young women approached the table where a colleague and I sat. One of the women held a menacing pair of scissors. The women spoke to us in German and pointed to one of their group who was wearing a red skirt with a grid pattern on the front. When they realized we were American, they explained in English that the woman was getting married the next day and it was a tradition to sell squares of the betrothed's skirt to raise money for a wedding gift. Being a good sport—after all, what choice did I have?—I gave what I believed to be two five-mark coins and used the shears to cut off a square. After the women had moved on, my colleague gently pointed out that I had given not two five-mark coins but two five-pfennig coins—worth about a nickel.

Messing with Texas

During a dinner in France with a dozen European participants in a leadership development program, the conversation turned to President George Bush, who was new on the job. The Europeans immediately launched into jokes about Bush, most of which ridiculed his intellectual capacity. At first I took offense, thinking they were ganging up on me. But soon I was cracking up along with them. The jokes weren't all that funny, but it's hard not to laugh when you hear French, German, and Italian versions of a Texas accent. Later, one of the participants gave me something of a compliment when he told me I wasn't too uptight—for an American.

I like to think that these and similar experiences have widened my awareness of other cultures to the extent that I really am doing no harm. My ultimate goal is to gain a deeper understanding and acceptance of the nuances of a few specific cultures. Just don't walk up behind me and rub my arm.

Chapter Four

Feedback and Coaching

Helpful feedback is essential for effective performance and for continuing development. As a leader, you need to know how to provide it to the people you work with and how to get it for yourself. This chapter lays out guidelines for both of these important activities.

◆ ◆ ◆

Leadership Through Feedback:
Helping Subordinates Succeed

Raoul J. Buron and Dana McDonald-Mann

Effective feedback provides the information people need to build on their strengths and overcome weaknesses. Without it, the probability is that people will not identify their best skills and that weaknesses and errors will become ingrained through practice and repetition.

To succeed in your leadership role, you must learn how to make feedback a part of developing your subordinates to their full potential. More than that, you must learn how to provide effective feedback that is empowering, not damaging; that is constructive, not debilitating. The purpose of this article is to show you when and how to give effective feedback to subordinates.

When to Give Feedback to Subordinates

Giving feedback is not the same as holding an annual performance review. It's true that honest feedback is an essential ingredient of a formal review process, but the benefits of feedback occur when feedback is an ongoing process, not a one-shot deal. Your goal is to create a relationship with your employees that allows you to give honest feedback about behavior and performance without putting them on the defensive. Timing is critical. You should give feedback regularly, at the moment it is needed, when development opportunities arise, and when an employee needs to modify behavior to improve performance.

Frequently

Because the benefits of feedback accrue over time, you should give feedback often. This gives you the best chance of reinforcing positive behavior and of influencing change in unacceptable behavior. By frequently giving feedback, you will find it's easier to focus on a specific behavior. Giving frequent feedback also helps you develop a less formal approach to delivering your message. This kind of feedback need take only a minute.

> Lucy, the logic of your argument in that meeting was very persuasive. You had my complete attention. I noticed that others were asking different kinds of questions at the end of your presentation than they were asking at the beginning. Your presentation moved me from skepticism to enthusiasm. Judging from the body language around the room, I think others shared that feeling.

In a Timely Manner

There's little value to dredging up a behavior that occurred six months earlier. Whether you want to reinforce or correct an employee's behavior, it's important to speak to the employee when the experience is fresh. If a subordinate's actions threaten the success of a task, now is the time to talk. You want to help your employee improve before another project derails.

> Jake, you haven't kept your team informed of its progress on a timely basis. As a result, a project milestone was missed, and I've had to move the completion date back two months. I am having doubts as to whether you can manage this team. Already this delay will negatively impact product introduction and sales.

Giving timely and frequent feedback lets you observe more of your subordinates' behavior. Too often, managers notice and comment only on extreme behavior—the truly outstanding performance or the truly dreadful gaffe. But almost everything an employee does falls between these extremes. Look for and give feedback on those more usual behaviors.

For Development

Making employees aware of potential opportunities for success and providing constructive steps they can take to achieve those goals are key motivations for providing effective feedback to subordinates. Help your subordinates look to the future by guiding them to the actions they need to take to succeed.

Let's take the case of Angela. You believe she would be a good person to manage the new branch office. She has most of the skills she needs to succeed there, and you can help her find resources so she can learn what she doesn't know. You want to let her know about this opportunity and to see whether it fits in with her personal career goals.

> Angela, your performance over the last several months, which we've talked about before, shows me that you've developed quite an array of skills. We're in need of a manager for the new branch office, and I think you would be the right choice for that position. Now, to be honest, there are a couple of areas that would be completely new

to you. But the company has some excellent training opportunities that would help you build your skills, and we would make the time available to you to acquire that training. In addition, Bobbi Towers, who has managed our San Antonio branch since it opened two years ago, has agreed to be a mentor to whoever agrees to this assignment, and to help that person in whatever way is needed. Can you tell me if this kind of assignment fits in with your personal career plans?

For Solving Performance Problems

If you are planning a feedback session to address a performance problem, don't deliver your feedback in the hall, off the cuff, or on the run. Your feedback session should be scheduled, private, focused, and structured. You know, perhaps from personal experience, how tense and unpleasant such feedback sessions can be. If you deliver timely feedback on an ongoing basis, the relationship and trust you build with an employee can alleviate some of that pressure. But you must also think about what the employee's thoughts and reactions might be to your feedback. Timely and frequent feedback goes a long way toward creating an environment of trust in which you can deal with these reactions.

Larry, for example, is the kind of results-oriented manager that you value, but his style is abrasive to some. Now two of the people who report to him have resigned, both citing his abrupt, critical behavior as the reason. You have no doubt that this behavior is limiting his effectiveness as a manager. You do not know if he is aware of what he is doing to make his direct reports feel intimidated and inadequate. You do not know if he would be willing to modify his behavior. You have in mind a series of steps that could help him if he does want to work on that behavior, and you have scheduled a time to talk with him about this performance issue.

Larry, two of your direct reports have resigned. Both of them said during their exit interviews that they were intimidated by your style of management. The fact that two people have left indicates to me that perhaps you're not aware of the impact your behavior is having on your subordinates. I will say right now that we value your contributions to the company. I think you can contribute even more by passing on some of the passion you have for the job to the people under you. To do that, you need to appreciate the different ways in which people accept information and learn. If you're willing to accept that changes in your management style might achieve better results from your staff, the company is willing to send you through a leadership program to help you reach that goal.

How to Give Feedback to Subordinates

Creating or seizing an opportunity to give feedback to an employee is your first task. Next, you have to make your feedback effective. Compassionate and honest feedback from you will help your subordinates develop goals, make and reinforce positive changes, raise their self-confidence, and feel motivated to take action.

Be Specific

To increase the quality and effectiveness of the feedback you give, we recommend using the three-step process that we teach and practice at CCL: the situation-behavior-impact model. SBI is a simple feedback structure that keeps your comments relevant and focused to maximize their effectiveness. When following this model, you describe the situation in which you observed the employee, the behavior you observed, and the impact of that behavior on you and others present in that situation.

> Jim, I saw that presentation you made to the Excelsior group [situation]. I liked how you picked up on their questions. I noticed that you were able to move out of your prepared presentation to address their concerns without missing a beat [behavior]. They were all nodding their heads in agreement when you answered that question

about the delivery time frame. You made me confident that you were in control of all the material and information. Joel Smythe told me afterward that our company seems to have a much better understanding of Excelsior's situation than anyone else on their short list [impact].

Keep It Simple

You may be accustomed to moving quickly to the impact or effect of a subordinate's behavior or action in an attempt to find a solution. But if you want to encourage real development among your subordinates, slow down. Reduce your feedback to its essential elements. Re-create the situation in your mind, and describe it ("I'm glad you came to the staff meeting yesterday"). Describe the subordinate's behavior in that situation, without embellishment ("During the meeting you kept looking at your watch"). Make your comments as direct as possible, and stick to the impact that the behavior had on you ("You made me feel that you didn't think our discussion was important"). Directness enforces honest feedback. Don't get ahead of yourself. Remember to go through each SBI step.

Avoid Interpretations

In keeping your message simple, not only do you keep it direct and honest but you limit it to the impact of the subordinate's behavior. When you observe troublesome behavior, you may be tempted to go beyond describing the impact to exploring reasons for the behavior. That invites misinterpretation that can damage the trusting relationship you have worked so hard to build. Even when you are perfectly correct in your attributions and interpretations, your subordinates are responsible for changing their behavior. You have to give them choices for making changes, not excuses for avoiding changes.

How to Structure the Feedback Session

Delivering honest, direct, effective feedback is difficult. Although many feedback situations can and should be handled informally, feedback about performance or development issues may require a more structured approach. As a leader, you can take steps to make these meetings more comfortable and productive.

1.   Make an appointment in advance, and let your subordinate know the purpose of the discussion. For example, you might say that because he or she has just taken on a special project, you would like to discuss the development opportunities associated with that project. Or you might come to your subordinate just after he or she has completed a difficult project and say that you have noticed the struggles he or she had and you would like to talk about some ways to address that problem. Your goal is to give your subordinate time to think about the upcoming session and to avoid causing undue worry or anxiety.

2.   Give your subordinate a private setting for the meeting and your undivided attention. Close the door. Don't take phone calls. You want to underline the fact that this is an important conversation. You want to give the employee a safe place in which he or she can listen, think, and respond to your feedback without interruptions or distractions.

3.   Be sensitive to the imbalance of power. As manager, you have the power on your side. This is a time to deemphasize it. You might have your employee sit beside you rather than across from you. Or you might consider having the discussion in some room other than your office, in a more neutral (but still private) setting.

4.   Give your subordinate a chance to talk. After you have described the situation, behavior, and impact, ask for your employee's thoughts about what you have described. It's not uncommon for people to be unaware of the impact of their behavior. As often as not, you will hear a reaction of surprise. However your subordinate responds, even if it's a form of defensiveness, allow that response

and accept it. You might ask if the individual has heard this kind of comment about himself or herself before or has noticed this kind of impact in other situations.

5.   Offer your subordinate suggestions and support for changing the behavior in the case of a performance problem or for expanding skills in the case of professional development. Be ready to suggest constructive steps that your employee can take next.

How to Handle Feedback's Emotional Impact

By providing frequent, honest, and compassionate feedback, you help your subordinates grow and develop. You can't control how they feel about it, but you can and should use what you know about each employee to make your feedback as constructive and beneficial as it can be. You already know from your management experience that different people respond differently to information they receive about their performance. Understanding, anticipating, and mentally preparing yourself for the different ways your feedback might be received is part of the art of management.

Take into Account the Individual Situation

Suzanne has worked for you for one month. She is clearly anxious about how well she is performing in this new job. You know she has the necessary qualifications and experience, but she is coming across to colleagues and customers as hesitant and weak. You know that if she continues to withhold her ideas and avoid making decisions, she won't function well in her position.

You could give Suzanne feedback on the negative impact that her novice behavior is having, but that will probably only increase her anxiety. At this point, given your appraisal of this specific situation, you decide that Suzanne will benefit more from getting feedback on her positive behavior and assurances of your confidence in her.

Recognize That People Process Information Differently

You have just given Jeff feedback on the high number of errors his budget contains and the impact of all those mistakes. Jeff is very interested in doing well and getting ahead, and he's astonished by this information. He clearly had no idea that his work in this particular area was slipshod. But when you ask what specific actions he can take, Jeff offers only vague assertions and promises.

You could work out a plan for Jeff to begin assembling his reports earlier and to have his numbers checked by others before they are distributed. But you see that Jeff is surprised and chagrined, and you know that he would probably prefer to work out his own plan for correcting the problem. He needs time to absorb the bad news and to figure out what he needs to do differently.

In giving feedback, you will find that some subordinates understand your message instantly and move immediately into talking about all the implications and ramifications. Other subordinates need time and privacy to digest information, and hate to be put on the spot to make decisions on the basis of perceptions and suggestions that are brand-new to them. If you press such a person for a decision before he or she has had time to ponder, the result is likely to be a bad choice and a weak commitment.

These differences between people should not be taken to represent defects or weaknesses but should instead be recognized for their strong implications about how people may express themselves and how they may react to new information and novel situations.

Factor in Health, Personal, and Family Problems

Michelle is one of your most promising subordinates, and now there is a great opportunity for her to develop her skills and advance her career. You would like to put her in charge of training in a particular system at your field locations around the country. The position requires traveling two days a week. When you present this idea to her, Michelle bursts into tears.

When you give Michelle a chance to talk, you find out that she is in the process of moving her mother into a nursing home. This is a terribly difficult situation because the mother expected that Michelle would quit work to care for her. Michelle has had her eye on that training and traveling opportunity, and it seems to her a cruel fate that it has come along at the very time when she must devote extra time to her mother and can't even consider overnight trips.

Stresses and problems outside of work contribute to how people perform at work. When you know about temporary difficulties, you can adjust the timing and content of your feedback accordingly. But you must also be prepared to have unexpected information crop up in feedback situations.

Draw on Your Subordinate's Problem-Solving Abilities

Marcus has brilliant analytical and technical skills, but putting him on the sales team has not worked out well. At meetings where he must present technical information to customer teams, he is losing sales. He bombards the customers with far more information than they want or need and throws technical jargon around right and left. During those meetings his actions strike you as arrogant and insensitive. He doesn't look people in the eye. You give Marcus this specific feedback, with the idea that he, like you, will conclude that he should be removed from the sales team, even though he volunteered for that assignment.

Marcus surprises you. He is very interested in sticking with this assignment and learning to get it right. Learning how to present technical information effectively to nontechnical people is high on his personal-development agenda. He's also quite aware of the negative impact of his behavior, and he's already taking some steps to improve. He's working through a self-teaching book on presentation skills. He would like you to suggest other resources that would help him get up to speed quickly on these skills.

People who are motivated to do well in their work often can work out their own solutions to problems you bring to their atten-

Suggested Reading

Brutus, S., and Manoogian, S. "The Art of Feedback." *Leadership in Action*, 1997, *17*(3), 8–10.

Dorn, R. C. "Performance Problems: Taking Action." *Issues & Observations*, 1982, *2*(3), 6–7.

Fleenor, J. W., and Prince, J. M. *Using 360-Degree Feedback in Organizations: An Annotated Bibliography*. Greensboro, N.C.: Center for Creative Leadership, 1997.

McCauley, C. D., Moxley, R. S., and Van Velsor, E. (eds.). *The Center for Creative Leadership Handbook of Leadership Development*. San Francisco: Jossey-Bass, 1998.

Van Velsor, E., Leslie, J. B., and Fleenor, J. W. *Choosing 360: A Guide to Evaluating Multi-Rater Feedback Instruments for Management Development*. Greensboro, N.C.: Center for Creative Leadership, 1997.

tion. In giving feedback, you should give them that opportunity before telling them how you propose to fix the problem. The solution the subordinate works out will not feel like a punishment to him or her and may well suit his or her personality and style better than any solution you could devise.

Practice Makes Permanent

Like developing any other leadership skill, giving feedback to subordinates may at first feel unnatural and uncomfortable. Don't be concerned if your initial attempts are awkward. Take that first step. Give feedback often to build your confidence and to create a trusting relationship with your subordinates that you can use to provide honest feedback that delivers your message clearly.

What you cannot do is avoid giving feedback to your employees. By withholding feedback, you deprive your employees of your contributions to their development and success. If the only time you talk to them about their career goals and performance is during an annual review, you're missing hundreds of opportunities to maximize strengths and improve performance. If you remain silent when subordinates make errors or when they achieve goals, you do them, yourself, and your organization a disservice.

◆　◆　◆

Three Keys to Effective Feedback

Sloan R. Weitzel

Managers who spend a lot of time developing specific what-if scenarios about their businesses and who examine business data with the intense rigor of a scientist often use no such specifics or data when evaluating the company's most important capital: employee performance. But effective feedback requires using the same attention to detail that is used when analyzing business information.

Creating and delivering a specific message based on observed performance is key to effective feedback. You may have told a fellow manager, a co-worker, or even your boss that he is a good leader, that she communicates well, or that he needs to be more strategic. You may believe such statements are helpful feedback. But they only evaluate or interpret; they don't describe specific behavior so a person can learn and develop by repeating or avoiding that behavior.

Effective feedback should enable the receiver to walk away understanding exactly what he or she did and what impact it had on you. When the result is this specific and this direct, there is a better chance that the person getting the feedback will be motivated to begin, continue, or stop behaviors that affect performance.

Think about statements you might have made to co-workers, bosses, or subordinates about their performance. Then ask yourself: What did the person do that made you think he was a good leader? What did she say and how did she say it to make you think she communicates well? What did he do that made you conclude his thinking wasn't strategic enough?

There are a number of common mistakes that people make when giving feedback. Among them are delivering feedback that is framed in judgmental terms, that is too vague, that goes on ad nauseam, or that contains an implied threat or inappropriate humor.

You can avoid common feedback mistakes by learning how to communicate important information about performance to subordinates, peers, or superiors in a way that helps them hear what you are saying and helps them identify ways in which they can improve. During the course of giving feedback to tens of thousands of people over many years, the Center for Creative Leadership has developed a feedback technique called situation-behavior-impact, or SBI. Using this technique, you can deliver feedback that replaces personal attack, incorrect judgments, vague statements, and third-party slights with direct and objective comments on a person's actions. Hearing this kind of feedback, the recipient can more easily see what actions to take to continue and improve performance or change behavior that is ineffective or an obstacle to performance.

The SBI technique is effective because it's simple. When giving feedback you describe the situation, describe the behavior you observed, and explain the impact the behavior had on you. The following is a look at how to use each component of the SBI approach.

Capture the Situation

The first step in giving effective feedback is to capture and clarify the specific situation in which the behavior occurred. If you say, "On Tuesday, in the break room with Carol and Fred," rather than,

"A couple days ago at the office with some people," you avoid the vague comments and exaggerations that torpedo so many feedback opportunities. Describing the location and time of a behavior creates context for your feedback recipients, helping them remember clearly their thinking and behavior at the time.

Capturing the situation is only the start of your feedback session. Here are a few examples of how you might successfully describe a situation when giving feedback:

Yesterday morning, while we were inspecting the plant . . .

Last Monday, after lunch, while we were walking with Cindy to the meeting . . .

Today, first thing this morning, when you and I were talking at the coffee machine . . .

Specificity is important when recalling a situation. The more specifics and details you can use in bringing the situation to mind, the clearer your message will be.

Describe the Behavior

Describing behavior is the second step to giving effective feedback. It's also the most crucial step and the one that is most often omitted—probably because behavior can be difficult to identify and describe. The most common mistake in giving feedback is communicating judgments by using adjectives that describe the person but not the person's actions. That kind of feedback is ineffective because it doesn't give the receiver information about what behavior to stop or to continue in order to improve performance. Consider these statements:

He was rude during the meeting.

She seemed bored at her team's presentation.

He seemed pleased with the report his employees presented.

These statements describe an observer's impression or interpretation of a behavior. Now consider the following actions an observer might witness that could lead to those impressions and interpretations.

He spoke at the same time another person was speaking. (*Rude*)

She yawned, rolled her eyes, and looked out the window. (*Bored*)

He smiled and nodded his head. (*Pleased*)

The statements in this list describe the actions that led to the impressions and interpretations in the first set of statements. The focus is on the actual behavior, not on what the behavior might mean. By using the details of observed action to describe behavior, you avoid the mistake of judging behavior. By focusing on the action, not the impression, you can communicate clear facts that a person can understand and act on.

To become more adept at identifying behavior and effectively communicating what you have seen to the feedback recipient, you need to capture not only *what* people do but *how* they do it. The new CEO who stands before her company and says, "I'm excited to be your new president," will appear insincere if she has no expression on her face, speaks in a flat voice, and uses no hand gestures. When giving people feedback using SBI, it is important to capture not only *what* is said or done but also *how* it is said and done. You can capture the *how* by paying attention to three things: body language, tone of voice and speaking manner, and word choice.

Body Language

Body language is nonverbal communication and can include facial expressions, eye movement, body posture, and hand gestures. For example:

Jim was becoming increasingly irritated with Alice during their meeting. Alice frequently shook her foot, shifted in her seat numerous times, tapped her pen on the table repeatedly, and nodded her head at people as they passed by her cubicle while he was talking.

Although Alice never spoke, she sent loud and clear messages through her body language. Jim can begin to give Alice effective feedback by saying something like this:

> "Alice, during our meeting yesterday in your cubicle I noticed that you looked at your watch several times during a fifteen-minute period. You tapped your pencil loudly on the table and shifted from side to side in your seat. You also nodded your head at people as they passed by your cubicle while I was speaking."

Jim has communicated the situation and some clear instances of behavior to Alice. His approach will help Alice understand the impact of her behavior.

Tone of Voice and Speaking Manner

Tone of voice and speaking manner relate to the pitch of a person's voice, the speed and volume at which the person speaks, and the pauses used. Voice mannerisms can be hard to notice and describe for the purpose of giving effective feedback, but can be useful behavioral cues. For example:

> Jason is introducing a new product idea to a group of his peers. During his presentation he pauses on at least six different occasions, halting in midsentence. After these pauses his voice slows down considerably. He speaks in a low monotone. When people ask him questions, he suddenly speaks very fast. He ends his talk by saying, "Thank you, thank you very much," in a tone that is louder than he has used throughout the whole speech.

Jason probably created the impression that he was uncertain, nervous, and hesitant. But to say just that to him won't help him develop. Effective feedback can include a description of Jason's speaking manner. It can talk about how he presented the material—the pauses and the tone and volume of his voice:

"Jason, during your presentation yesterday you stopped several times and spoke so low that it was difficult for me to hear you. Then toward the end of your presentation, when people asked questions, you spoke faster and your voice got louder. The way you presented made me feel that you weren't well prepared or that you didn't care much about your presentation, and the way you spoke faster at the end made me feel that you were in a rush to get out of the room."

Word Choice

A person's choice of words often can be the least important component of behavior. Nevertheless, capturing the specific language a person uses during a specific situation can help you give effective feedback.

During a face-to-face team meeting with a small development group, Bob loses his temper when he learns that Fred will miss a deadline. Bob calls Fred a loser in front of the entire group. When the meeting breaks up, the team members quietly file out without speaking to one another.

If the content of a person's message has an impact on you and you want to give effective feedback, write down the speaker's words so you can remember exactly what was said:

"Bob, during the team meeting this morning you called Fred a 'loser' in front of the whole group. I was really uncomfortable that you singled out one person and used that kind of insult. After hearing that, I felt that we weren't a team at all."

Deliver the Impact

The final step in giving effective feedback is to relay the impact that the other person's behavior had on you. The impact you want to communicate is not how you think a person's behavior might affect the organization, co-workers, a program, clients, a product, or any other third party. The impact you want to focus on and communicate is your reaction to a behavior. There are two directions you can take when sharing the impact of a person's behavior.

- You can evaluate or make a judgment about the person's behavior: *"I thought you showed interest when you asked for the group's opinions."* This tactic is the most common but also the less effective of the two, because the person getting the feedback can argue with your interpretation of the behavior.

- You can acknowledge the emotional effect the person's behavior had on you: *"When you told me in the meeting that my concerns about product deadlines were 'overblown,' I felt belittled."* This approach can be more effective than the first because it truly is your reaction to someone's behavior, a reaction that only you experience. The person hearing your feedback can't easily dismiss your personal experience, so she is more likely to hear what you've said.

By communicating the personal impact a behavior has had on you, you are sharing a point of view and asking the other person to view that behavior from your perspective. That kind of sharing helps to build trust, which in turn can lead to even more effective feedback as communication is improved.

To develop your effectiveness in carrying out the impact stage of giving feedback, practice putting your feedback in these forms: When you did [behavior], I felt [impact]. When you said [behavior], I was [impact].

Here are some examples of how you might use these forms when giving feedback:

- *Peer feedback.* "Sophie, this morning in the hallway you asked for my opinion about decisions to launch our new product. You also often ask me to join the group at lunch. *That makes me feel included, part of the team.*"

- *Subordinate feedback.* "Matt, in the meeting with the new vice-president yesterday, you kept your voice at an even tone, even when she questioned your numbers. You held out your hand with your palm up several times. *I felt really at ease with your delivery.*"

- *Boss feedback.* "Karen, you have not commented once about the field reports I have completed. *I feel slighted.*"

Putting It All Together

Review the situation, behavior, and impact steps that build effective feedback, and practice them at every opportunity. You don't have to wait for a feedback situation to arise to review your skills. For example, the next time you attend a trade show and hear a compelling presentation, think about what you are experiencing that makes the presentation so valuable. Observe the speaker and take note of the situation, the speaker's behavior, and the impact that behavior is having on you. Is the speaker using hand gestures? What about tone of voice? What kinds of facial expressions is the speaker making? Are the speaker's words appropriate for the audience and the subject?

Take time to reflect on your feedback efforts. Ask yourself, Why did I pay attention to this particular behavior? What does this say about me? Perhaps you have observed behaviors that you want to develop in yourself or that you want to drop or guard against. Reflection also gives you time to understand the true nature of the impact the behavior had on you. Ask yourself, How did I feel when she talked to me in that tone of voice? What emotional response did I have when he shook my hand and said my reports showed good research and attention to detail? Reflection will help you become more concise and focused in delivering your feedback message and help you avoid traps that weaken your message.

As you become more familiar with the SBI approach and more comfortable with the delivery, your feedback skills will become increasingly effective. The people you work with—your boss, colleagues, and subordinates—will benefit from the effort you put toward helping them develop. You in turn will benefit from developing a useful skill that not only helps to raise the productivity of all the people around you but also bolsters your personal leadership skills.

Suggested Reading

Buron, R. J., and McDonald-Mann, D. *Giving Feedback to Subordinates*. Greensboro, N.C.: Center for Creative Leadership, 1999.

Kirkland, K., and Manoogian, S. *Ongoing Feedback: How to Get It, How to Use It*. Greensboro, N.C.: Center for Creative Leadership, 1998.

Stone, D., Patton, B., and Heen, S. *Difficult Conversations*. New York: Viking, 1999.

◆ ◆ ◆

A Winning Recipe for Working with a Coach

Wayne Hart and Karen Kirkland

Executive coaching is all about change—often, developmental change. When you hire a coach, you set in motion a process for effecting that change. The elements of a coaching engagement are *ongoing assessment, challenge*, and *support*. You may think that those three elements are the responsibility of the coach—after all, they are what the coach is trained and hired to do. But you will get much more benefit from coaching if you are an active participant in every aspect of the engagement.

The initial phase of a coaching engagement is an assessment—a baseline picture of your current situation and level of skills. This assessment might be designed to elicit information on how you see yourself, how others see you, who your advocates and enemies are, the dynamics and politics of your organization, your strengths that can be leveraged, and your shortcomings that can be improved.

Your coach will almost certainly have you complete written assessment instruments that provide information on your leadership style, leadership competencies and capabilities, skill at building and managing relationships, and other characteristics. The coach may ask your permission to have some of your colleagues and direct reports, as well as your boss, complete similar assessment instruments. In addition, the coach may want to interview these individuals and, in some cases, your spouse and other family members; may ask to review performance appraisals; and may want to accompany you to work to see how you interact with others, conduct meetings, and present ideas. You can veto any of these activities, of course, but all of them will help the coach create a complete picture of you fairly quickly, and accurately focus on the areas that will make the most difference in your managerial effectiveness.

Filling In

In addition to completing formal assessment exercises and activities, it's best to provide your coach with other relevant information about yourself and your world. You operate in a unique context of work and personal relationships, and your coach needs to understand you in the context of your situation.

You can bring your coach into the picture by describing:

- The industry you work in and the issues and challenges it faces;
- The organization you work for and its culture;
- Your home life and how it intersects with your work (for instance, whether you talk with your spouse about your work, whether you have an office at home, and whether you try to keep work and family life strictly separate);
- Your health habits and personal preferences.

Because executive coaching is meant to produce visible, measurable changes over a period of months, not all assessments take place at the outset of a coaching engagement. Your coach should assess your progress at intervals during the course of your working together. Decide with your coach how results will be measured. You may have your coach interview your boss, for example, to see what behavior changes your boss has observed. Your coach may ask the people who previously provided written or oral assessments to complete follow-up assessments. Or you may choose to supply some kind of self-assessment using a formal assessment instrument or a set of questions determined early on in the coaching process.

Meeting Challenges

One of your coach's jobs is to help you identify challenges and develop plans for meeting them. Challenges can be external obstacles such as limited resources or conflicting directions from within your organization. Or they can be internal factors such as your own resistance or insufficient set of skills.

Plans for overcoming obstacles are created as you work with your coach to identify developmental objectives that you can achieve by executing specific behavioral action plans. These action plans are like homework assignments—single objectives you work to meet before your next coaching session. You have an important role in collaborating with your coach to identify the obstacles, set realistic yet challenging goals, and create meaningful action plans to improve your leadership effectiveness.

With your coach's guidance, you can break the final objective into incremental goals. Perhaps the goal for one week would be to learn to structure an effective team meeting and set a clear agenda for the next meeting. After you have achieved that goal, your next task might be to deal with the issue of a group member who takes up too much time in the meetings. Achieving that goal might involve role-playing with your coach to figure out how to give constructive feedback to the group member. Most of the challenges you face will require this step-by-step approach.

Setting your targets too high or too low can subvert the coaching process. So it's critical that you tell your coach if you think the suggested goal is too easy or too difficult. Some coaches are inclined to make the incremental goals far too easy. If this happens, you must make it clear that you can handle more and that you expect to be challenged. You're not paying the coach to make you feel good—you're paying for assistance in reaching developmental goals that are important to you.

Although the ultimate developmental goal you set with your coach is likely to remain constant during the course of your coaching relationship, the challenges you take on in moving toward that goal can change according to circumstances. A task that is reasonable during a normal week, for example, may be unreasonable during a week when you're moving your elderly parents into a nursing home or you're scheduled to have oral surgery. During the course of your coaching engagement, be honest with yourself and your coach about what is realistic in terms of the tasks you can accomplish.

Developing Trust

You and your coach will work together to devise a developmental action plan that will enable you to reach your goal of improved leadership effectiveness. Your part in the process is to carry out this action plan and to complete your homework. Your coach's part is to give you support as you carry out the plan.

Your coach can support you best when you are completely honest about what you want to accomplish and what you need to reach your goal. Supply the coach with detailed information about what kind of support you find most helpful and the people to whom you can turn for support. Work with your coach to create a developmental support network.

As you and your coach work together and develop a high degree of trust, the coach will be better able to offer you many kinds of support. Different kinds of support serve different purposes—some kinds of support are more direct than others and some are more helpful in certain situations than others. Following are some examples of various supportive roles your coach can play:

Listening. Sometimes you need a sounding board for your ideas or frustrations. You may need to think out loud, explore a number of possibilities or scenarios, review events, or draw conclusions. Your coach can support you by restating what he or she has heard you say, which gives you a chance to develop a deeper understanding of the challenges you face and how you might address them. Be willing to address these issues with your coach.

Accountability. A valuable service that your coach can provide is to hold you accountable for performing your action plans. The fact that your coach counts on you to execute those plans is motivating and supportive. Reporting your progress to the coach keeps you focused.

Encouragement. During your coaching engagement, you might occasionally get discouraged. You might feel stuck or that you've taken a step backward. Such feelings are part of any kind of personal change. Your coach will know how to keep you motivated and focused on your tasks and your ultimate goal. Let your coach know what kind of encouragement works best for you.

Celebration. When you have a breakthrough in your performance, it's important to recognize that achievement. Your coach can support you when it's inappropriate for you to celebrate with direct reports, colleagues, or your boss. By talking with your coach about your successes, you can find reinforcement for further developmental tasks.

Building a Network

Your coach isn't the only source of support you can access during your developmental efforts. But your coach can, with your help, identify and create support resources among your personal and professional network—family members, for instance, or friends and colleagues with whom you like to process ideas and experiences.

Line up the support you need in advance of your developmental efforts. Telling the people you trust what you're doing and how they can best help you will maximize your chances of having a successful coaching engagement.

Chapter Five

Striking a Balance

Just as interpersonal skills are crucial to being an effective leader, so too are the intrapersonal skills required to manage yourself—in your career and in your life. When these skills are developed, not only will your work and your life be balanced, but each will be a resource for the other, and the stress you experience in general can be moderated. This chapter will help you keep your career and yourself healthy.

◆ ◆ ◆

Throwing the Right Switches:
How to Keep Your Executive Career on Track

Craig Chappelow and Jean Brittain Leslie

Even the shiniest, highest-performing locomotives can run off the rails if the right measures aren't taken to prevent it. The same is true of executives. High-level managers with impressive track records, who are seen by themselves and others in their organizations as being on their way to the top, may have no concerns about their careers derailing. That type of complacency, however, can set them up for a wreck.

Many high-performing executives have one or more blind spots that they ignore as long as they continue to meet their business goals. Others rely heavily on a specific strength, then find themselves lacking the necessary skills when their work environment changes. These factors and others can play a role in derailing the careers of once-promising managers.

Since 1983 the Center for Creative Leadership has studied the career derailments of male and female executives in North America and Europe. By comparing successful executives with those who derail, CCL has identified specific characteristics that lead to success and other characteristics that force formerly successful careers off track. Executives who are aware of these characteristics and who combine that awareness with an honest self-assessment of their leadership behavior can do a lot to keep their careers headed in the right direction.

This article examines two of the factors that are key to determining whether executives will successfully further their careers or derail—the ability to establish strong interpersonal relationships and the ability to adapt and develop during periods of change. Other factors may be involved, but these two are among the most critical. In addition to looking at how deficiencies in these characteristics can cause executives to derail, we will look at related strategies that successful executives use to realize their full potential and stay on track.

What Is Derailment?

It's important to first understand what we mean by derailment and success. CCL's research has defined successful executives as those who have reached at least the general manager level and who, in the eyes of senior executives in the organization, remain likely candidates for promotion. Derailed executives are those who, after reaching the general manager level, are fired, demoted, or held on a career plateau. Right up to the point of derailment, the superiors of the derailed executives saw them as having high potential for advancement, impressive track records, and solidly established leadership positions. (For the purposes of this study, executives who have simply advanced as far as the company hierarchy allows or who voluntarily decide to stay at a particular level are not considered derailed.)

Interpersonal Skills

The ability to work well with others is a key factor for long-term career success. This characteristic clearly separates executives who succeed from those who derail. Executives who are perceived as adept at building and managing effective interpersonal relationships are described by their bosses, peers, and direct reports as

- Good listeners
- Available to others
- Collaborative
- Sharing responsibility
- Nonauthoritarian
- Teamwork oriented
- Supportive of others' ideas
- Honest
- Trustworthy
- Straightforward
- Ethical

Consider the following story about an executive who took part in CCL's research. He displayed a strong sense of connection with the people in his department and was seen as adept at building strong relationships:

A woman in the office had recently become engaged, and the department had taken up a collection to purchase a wedding gift for her. The executive suggested giving her an engraved cake knife. He had received one on his wedding day, and on every "cake occasion" he and his wife use the knife. It always reminds him of his wedding day and how much he loved his wife on that day and continues to love her to this day. The woman who was engaged was very touched by this sense of emotion and openness, and the gift took on a meaning for her beyond just something to cut a cake with. She felt more loyal to the executive as a result.

The most common reason for career derailment is an inability to relate to people in meaningful ways. Executives who are unable to establish strong interpersonal relationships are described by their bosses, peers, and direct reports as

- Insensitive
- Competitive with others
- Self-isolating
- Dictatorial
- Overly critical
- Overdemanding
- Easily angered
- Arrogant
- Emotionally explosive
- Manipulative
- Aloof

Many managers are hired originally for their contributions as individuals, and at first their value to the organization is measured in terms of bottom-line results. As they move up in the organization, however, they find themselves judged not only on results but also on how well they manage relationships with people inside the organization and outside the organization, such as customers. If they grow resentful because they feel that fostering relationships was not part of the original bargain, they will resist developing the skills needed to establish strong interpersonal relationships.

Let's look at the case of an executive who ignored the importance of interpersonal relationships and suffered the consequences:

> A company lacked strategic direction. The CEO set up a five-day meeting to explore strategic alternatives. All the key senior officers participated, and everyone worked hard for five days. After the meeting, however, nothing more on the matter was heard from the CEO, who had virtually no contact with the meeting participants. Five months later he put everyone through a fire drill to put together one-year and five-year plans. Because of the earlier lack of follow-up and relationship building, the whole process lacked credibility—and so did the CEO.

One reason that a lack of interpersonal skills plays such a large role in executive derailment is that the behaviors associated with those skills are difficult to change. A turnaround is not impossible, however. It doesn't require a personality transplant. What it does require is an honest assessment of the executive's behavior and an action plan to improve interpersonal competence.

Executives can begin by asking themselves a series of questions:

- How would I describe my interpersonal skills?
- Have my boss, peers, direct reports, or customers given me feedback about my approach to relationships?
- What did they say?
- How do I feel about what they said?

Answering these questions will help executives assess their relationship-building skills, then set goals and take action to improve their interpersonal competence. Here are some strategies executives can follow to take the next steps in developing interpersonal skills.

Identify the People with Whom You Want to Improve Your Relationships

Select specific places, times, and situations for practicing new behavior aimed at improving the identified relationships. For example, you might tell yourself: "I will not interrupt Mary in our Tuesday morning staff meetings during the question-and-answer period." Such a small action might seem insufficient for addressing such a large problem. The power of this strategy, however, is in developing individual plans for interacting with each person with whom you want to improve your relationship.

It's important to set plans that are specific. Setting a goal to "improve my working relationship with Mary," for instance, would be ineffective because it wouldn't address changing a specific behavior. Also be careful to avoid tunnel vision. Executives are often tempted to focus on their toughest cases, but they should set specific interaction plans for all the people with whom they have contact.

Build on Your Existing Relationships

Scheduling a weekly lunch meeting with each of your direct reports to get to know them better may seem like a good idea, but is it really what they want? Spending their lunch breaks with you may be the last thing they want to do.

A better idea is to take advantage of the regular interactions you already have. Changing your behavior during short face-to-face interactions with others can make a big difference in how they view your interpersonal skills. Be attentive, genuine, and open. Ask for their opinions, ask how you can help them get their work done, and listen to what they say.

Avoid coming across as insincere. For instance, don't use a tired icebreaker such as "How's the family?" unless you're familiar with the family members' names and interests. Also don't assume that people want to chat with you about their personal lives. It may be better simply to act more pleasantly when discussing work issues.

Display Empathy Toward Others

Whether you're dealing with your boss, your peers, or your direct reports, take the feelings and perspectives of others into account. Listen without judging. Don't cut off people in the middle of a sentence. If you're talking with a direct report, be aware of and diplomatic about the power relationship between managers and subordinates.

Be careful not to use humor inappropriately. Your closest friends may appreciate your dry wit and sarcastic asides, but those you work with may not. Also, if something is said to you in confidence, keep it private. If you make private information public, you will lose credibility and trust, both of which are essential to effective leadership.

Learn to Listen

Hearing and listening are not the same thing. If you're holding a conversation with someone in your office, turn away from your e-mail and the papers on your desk. Separate your opinions about the person from what he or she is saying. Ask questions to make sure you understand what has been said, and take notes to help you remember.

Don't be a passive listener, and don't let information go in one ear and out the other. Participate in the conversation, but don't monopolize it. Translate what you hear into concepts, but don't get stuck on one idea. If the person with whom you're talking makes a particularly intriguing point, take a note on it and get back to listening.

Collaborate

Be willing to share information with others to achieve mutually beneficial goals. Involve others in making decisions but don't lock yourself into collaborating on every decision or action. Effective leadership is partly about making decisions and partly about reaching consensus—and knowing when to do which.

Don't, however, keep others in the dark about your decision-making process. If you gather new facts that prompt you to reach a new decision or to change direction, share those facts with others so they can understand why you acted as you did.

Change and Development

Successful executives make mistakes; it is the ability to learn from mistakes that distinguishes successful executives from those who derail. The ability to adapt is an important component of executive success, and successful executives tend to take responsibility for their own development and improvement. Executives who are flexible in the face of change are described by their bosses, peers, and direct reports in the following terms:

- Handles mistakes with poise and learns from them
- Is open to feedback and learns from it
- Is self-assured and stays composed under pressure

Many executives who derail do so because they are unable or unwilling to adapt. They may be unable or unwilling to change their management style. Or they may resist making changes because their past success indicates to them that they don't need to change and they fear that any changes might lead to failure. Executives who are unable or unwilling to adapt are described by their bosses, peers, and direct reports as

- Avoiding risk
- Disliking authority figures
- Defensive
- Not open to diversity
- Resistant to learning from mistakes
- Closed to feedback
- Not handling pressure well
- Having narrow interests

Like interpersonal skills, the skills of flexibility and adaptability to change can be developed with effort. Again, such development begins with an objective assessment of the executive's behavior and a plan to adopt behaviors that lend themselves to an openness to change.

Executives can begin by asking themselves a series of questions:

- Am I resistant to change?
- Do I look for opportunities to learn new skills and take new perspectives?
- Do I admit and accept my mistakes and learn from them?
- What kind of feedback have I received about my adaptability and openness to change?

The answers to these questions will help executives assess their adaptability and openness to change, then set goals and take action to improve those skills. Here are two strategies that executives can follow to develop adaptability.

Become More Self-Aware

Self-awareness is important to remaining flexible and being comfortable with change. Recognize your emotional reactions to change. Maintain standards of honesty and integrity. Know your values and be comfortable with them; they can be an anchor during times of transition. Don't let success go to your head and interfere with your willingness to learn from mistakes.

Work on understanding which leadership style best fits a given situation and putting that style into use. Leadership styles range from command and control (making decisions unilaterally and passing them down to direct reports) to collaboration (defining and solving problems in concert with direct reports).

Seek and Make Use of Feedback

Feedback given to you should focus on a specific situation, describe your behavior in that situation, and communicate the impact of your behavior. Effective feedback is based on fact, not opinion. It's important to act on the feedback you receive and not dismiss it. Your sources of feedback—both at and outside the workplace—should be people whose opinions you trust and respect and who will support you in making changes based on the feedback.

Staying on Track

Career derailment is often highly predictable by co-workers, but the executives themselves are usually unaware of or unwilling to fix the flaws that lead to derailment. Executives need to commit to their own professional development before reaching the critical point beyond which there is no salvaging their careers. Executives who have potentially derailing flaws but who also have an ability to assess themselves and to learn and develop can avert career failure and progress smoothly up the management ladder.

Suggested Reading

Browning, H., and Van Velsor, E. *Three Keys to Development: Defining and Meeting Your Leadership Challenges.* Greensboro, N.C.: Center for Creative Leadership, 1999.

Leslie, J. B., and Van Velsor, E. *A Look at Derailment Today: North America and Europe.* Greensboro, N.C.: Center for Creative Leadership, 1996.

Morrison, A. M., White, R. P., and Van Velsor, E. *Breaking the Glass Ceiling: Can Women Reach the Top of America's Largest Corporations?* Reading, Mass.: Addison-Wesley, 1987.

Van Velsor, E., and Leslie, J. B. "Why Executives Derail: Perspectives Across Time and Cultures." *Academy of Management Executive,* 1995, 4(4), 62–72.

◆ ◆ ◆

Putting Some Life into Your Leadership

Marian N. Ruderman and Patricia J. Ohlott

If you were to ask executives and managers where they get the most influential and effective developmental training, the likely answer would be "on the job." It's widely accepted in organizations that experience gained from job assignments and formal training helps managers develop their skills in areas such as implementing agendas, working through relationships, creating change, and increasing personal awareness.

Often, however, managers discount what can be learned from experiences outside of work. The popular media often portray the intersection of work life and family life as fraught with career peril. Phrases like *mommy track* define how some women's careers are handicapped when they take on the role of mother. The label *daddy stress* is placed on the conflict men can feel when the expectations to excel at work and the desire to spend more time with family clash.

Although nonwork roles and responsibilities can limit and interfere with performance at work, there is another side to the story that is richer in possibilities and rewards. Interests, roles, and responsibilities outside of work can also serve as creative and supportive sources for learning how to be a more effective manager.

It's important to see that ordinary nonwork activities such as organizing a fundraising event, coaching a youth sports team, and even advocating for a community cause are not irrelevant to or disconnected from your work activities. Such activities provide both the practical skills and the psychological support that can enhance your leadership effectiveness on the job. You don't have to try to be superman or superwoman, having and doing it all. You merely need to recognize that off-the-job experiences can hold powerful managerial lessons. Be careful not to misunderstand the relationship between outside activities and work. Contrary to popular belief, activities that take place outside of the regular workday contribute to a leader's effectiveness as a manager.

Note

This article draws from work conducted at CCL over the past fifteen years that focuses on the relationship between multiple life roles and effective performance at work. One study was conducted with alumnae of CCL's Women's Leadership Program. The study shed light on the ways in which personal life roles enhance professional ones.

The practical advice in this article also draws from information in the book *The Lessons of Experience: How Successful Executives Develop on the Job,* in which McCall, Lombardo, and Morrison examined the developmental experiences of male executives. They concluded that events in people's personal lives, and not just job experiences, teach managerial skills.

What You Can Learn

The lessons taught by off-the-job experiences can affect your on-the-job leadership competency in many ways. If you know how to harvest those lessons, you can bring them to bear on leadership challenges. You can also get valuable leadership practice. The first step in making the most of your life lessons is to be aware of the leadership opportunities provided by off-the-job experiences. Consider the following examples of what you can learn from nonwork experiences. As you read, think about similar experiences in your own life.

Interpersonal Relationship Skills

Community work, friendships, parenting, and spousal relationships are some of the sources from which you can draw to develop the interpersonal skills needed for managerial success.

Susan and Lawrence were co-chairs of a benefit event supporting a local mental health organization. The two possessed very different leadership styles. Susan was a good strategic thinker and excelled at motivating volunteers. Lawrence had a degree of determination and persistence that Susan lacked. Initially, Lawrence felt impatient with Susan's careful consideration of all the "what ifs" and her insistence that volunteers should have input into the plans. At the same time, Susan regarded Lawrence as a control freak, incapable of listening to or valuing other people's ideas. During the six months they worked together, they discussed budget, logistics, and publicity. Their conflicts surfaced in these meetings. They both had a strong commitment to success, however, and that gave them the courage to openly discuss their differences. Those conversations revealed a combination of strengths suited to designing and managing a complex project.

A community volunteer experience in which you do not choose your working partner can provide you with a deeper appreciation of having to work with people whose approach to life is different from yours. That appreciation can in turn make you more effective on the job when working with people whose personalities or working styles are different from yours. It can help you with a staff member you inherit or someone new to your organization.

Margot employed an au pair, Ingrid, to take care of her two children. Ingrid had studied English in school in her native country, but she still had difficulty understanding Margot's instructions and expectations. Margot soon realized that she had to change her communication style to make sure her messages were understood. She spoke to Ingrid more slowly and eliminated slang and colloquial expressions. Sometimes she demonstrated tasks and procedures instead of describing them. Margot found that explaining things more than one way helped Ingrid understand more clearly.

By paying attention to your communication style and focusing on how to communicate more effectively, you can learn how to make your messages to subordinates, peers, and your boss more effective. Communication differences don't happen just between cultures or nationalities—you can use your off-the-job experiences with people of other ages, the opposite gender, a different race, and so on to learn how to communicate effectively.

> George had been a star tennis player in his teens. It so happened that he got the opportunity to coach a young tennis player, Michelle, who was preparing for her first tournament. In this role he was a natural coach, providing feedback, setting goals, and offering support when she doubted herself. As a result, Michelle entered the tournament with confidence and skill, and George knew he had played a significant role in her development.

Serving in a coaching role outside of work can be valuable in learning how to play the same kind of role on the job. You can learn to see subordinates as budding stars and—using a mix of feedback, support, and challenge—help them bring out their best efforts.

Broad, Practical Knowledge

Sometimes a job calls for more than what's in the job description. There are occasions when having a personal knowledge of a product, an industry, or a customer's needs can prove invaluable.

> Tina's father had worked for the State Department, and the family had lived in several different countries during her childhood. As a girl she endured changing schools, leaving friends, and learning new customs and languages. But as an adult Tina discovered that she was better prepared than most of her co-workers when the company she worked for developed a global strategy. She was sensitized to cultural differences, had a working knowledge of several languages, and had learned from her childhood experiences to be flexible and adaptable. She became extremely valuable to her company and was sent as part of the advance team when new offices were opened overseas.

As you move forward in your career and in your development as a manager, remember to consider the wealth of experiential learning you've accumulated at the different stages of your life. Rather than tucking those experiences away and moving on, bring relevant pieces of your background experiences into the foreground as an aid to developing leadership skills.

Your Leadership Potential

Leadership opportunities can be hard to find. In some organizations it's difficult to get the leadership practice you need because all the players are already at the table.

> Carl, a systems analyst, eagerly wanted a promotion to a management position in his company. His earlier career advances had been based on his technical proficiency. He hadn't had much opportunity to test his leadership potential and was unsure about his ability to lead people.
>
> Unexpectedly, Carl was asked if he would serve as president of a local child advocacy organization. Carl had served on the organization's board for several years but had never aspired to be an officer. In light of his career goals, he decided to accept the nomination. As board president, he got opportunities to run effective meetings, to involve other people in decision making, and to motivate others to achieve financial, educational, and service goals. When a management position in his company opened up, Carl felt confident that he would be able to handle the job. He knew he could be effective as a leader.

Away from the job, you can often find ideal situations for exploring your leadership potential and practicing your leadership skills. In volunteer activities, for example, you can often lead without being hampered by how things have been done in the past. Accountability for results makes such an experience real and useful without the pressure of, for example, a career performance review.

Family roles such as organizing a family history project, planning a reunion, or recognizing significant family milestones can help you practice such management skills as budgeting, delegating, leading teams, managing projects, and maintaining interpersonal relationships.

Promoting Leadership Development

There are three important ways in which private life encourages and enhances leadership development.

The first is by providing you with opportunities to develop psychological strength. No doubt you have noticed that events in your personal life can from day to day have different effects on your outlook and concentration. Your personal responsibilities and relationships contribute to your general sense of how strong, secure, confident, and capable you feel.

A second way is by supplying you with the support of family relationships and friendships, which can encourage and advise you.

A final way is by providing you with learning opportunities. The roles you play off the job can be your laboratory for mastering management skills.

To enable nonwork experiences to enhance your managerial effectiveness, you must first become aware of their developmental potential. Instead of focusing on how your personal commitments and activities detract from your career objectives, examine how such activities strengthen your professional ability by providing psychological strength and supportive individuals and by motivating skill development.

Increase Your Psychological Strength

A busy work life in a demanding career is often associated with stress and pressure. You might be angry with yourself over how you handled a situation, be frustrated with your subordinates, be discouraged at the results of your initiatives, or be anxious about decisions you have made. During those times it's enormously helpful to have experiences away from work that serve as a source of gratification and pleasure.

When you've had a week of nonstop crises and chaos, for example, a weekend spent doing what you like with people you like has enormous power to calm and cure. Opportunities to be playful, follow an interest, or experience joy can provide great benefits to the busy manager.

Think about the activities you have outside of work, the ones that really recharge your batteries. They don't all have to be high-action pursuits. You may enjoy gardening or reading; others may enjoy a sports activity or attending a concert. Everybody has a place of refuge that can be used to gain perspective. That place of refuge may be a literal place, like a favorite room or a house of worship. Or it may be more abstract, like a favorite book or movie. Whichever you choose, such an activity can act as a buffer to the stress of work.

Make a list of those sources of refuge as a way of discovering buffers for those times when the challenge of work is very high. Can you give any more time to any of those activities to build an even stronger buffer? Are there activities or relationships or other resources you want to add to as a balance to the challenges of work?

Gather Support for Challenging Times

To successfully meet challenges at work, it helps to have a support network from which you can get feedback and learn new skills and with which you can try out ideas. But you can also build a support network among the people you know outside of work. Family, close friends, neighbors, and community partners can all be drawn on for support, and you can transfer the benefits of that support to your work. Knowing that there are supportive resources available can give you the confidence you need to take risks and to move out of your comfort zone. A solid support network outside of work is a foundation for facing new challenges, addressing personal weaknesses, and leveraging personal strengths.

Think about the individuals in your private life who will support your taking on the leadership challenges at work. Make a list of family members, friends, and others you can count on to encourage your risk taking and growth.

Friends, family members, former colleagues, and all of the other components of your personal support network can be a valuable resource to you. You can often use your support network to help you handle the hard parts of leadership. If you're working through a knotty organizational problem with political overtones, for example, it may be safer to do your processing with someone outside your organization who has no stake in the outcome and who can give you an objective opinion. Your spouse might make the perfect sounding board.

Perhaps you have a work initiative that is meeting resistance. Friends outside the company can give you a broader perspective and help you to see the other side so that you can understand that resistance and negotiate a solution. You can also use someone from outside the organization for help with more routine tasks such as practicing a presentation.

Seek Opportunities That Motivate You to Learn

Experiences outside of work are rich in opportunities for learning practical management and leadership skills. Sometimes these opportunities come without warning—as hardships, for example. More often we can choose experiences that build specific leadership skills.

Learning is most likely to occur when you are faced with a challenge, because such a situation offers the opportunity and the motivation to learn. These learning opportunities arise in many ways. For example, a particular situation might provide a stage for you to try a new behavior. If you have wanted to try your hand at public speaking, consider delivering a sermon at your place of worship. Another opportunity for learning lies in a demand to take action. A family crisis would fit the bill here. You can also learn when you are faced with incompatible demands or when you can be assured of getting feedback (which is sometimes difficult to get at work).

Nonwork situations can also motivate you to learn because the outcomes of off-the-job experiences can have significant power in your life. Playing fast and loose with interpersonal relationships is one thing at work, but it's another thing when your spouse files for divorce. You may avoid office politics at all costs, but when the local airport plans a new runway adjacent to your property, you may suddenly find yourself learning all about local politics.

On-the-job learning occurs when the opportunity and motivation for learning interact, creating the need for development. This interaction can happen away from work, too.

Fitting It All Together

Your whole life is filled with opportunities for developing your leadership skills. Developmental experiences don't happen only at work. Learning opportunities don't happen only at home or in your community. Information, skill, and practice can come from a variety of sources. The key is to identify your own development needs and then find sources both at and away from work that can support your achieving those goals. Those sources can be people or they can be tasks.

Once you have a developmental plan in place, you can use nonwork activities to fill developmental gaps. Off-the-job experiences can provide skill training, leadership practice, and emotional support. Integrating your experiences—on the job and away from work—is fundamental.

Serving as a Role Model

As you begin to experiment with integrating your work life with the rest of your life, you may find opportunities to act as a role model for others. Communicate your actions so that others can identify you as a potential role model for their own development. Let people know what you're doing:

Suggested Reading

Bateson, M. C. *Composing a Life*. New York: Plume, 1990.

Crosby, F. J. *Juggling: The Unexpected Advantages of Balancing Career and Home for Women and Their Families*. New York: Free Press, 1991.

Hansen, L. S. *Integrative Life Planning: Critical Tasks for Career Development and Changing Life Patterns*. San Francisco: Jossey-Bass, 1997.

Kaplan, R. E., Drath, W. H., and Kofodimos, J. R. *Beyond Ambition: How Driven Managers Can Lead Better and Live Better*. San Francisco: Jossey-Bass, 1991.

Kofodimos, J. R. *Balancing Act: How Managers Can Integrate Successful Careers and Fulfilling Personal Lives*. San Francisco: Jossey-Bass, 1993.

Lombardo, M. M., and Eichinger, R. W. *Eighty-Eight Assignments for Development in Place*. Greensboro, N.C.: Center for Creative Leadership, 1989.

McCall, M. W., Jr., Lombardo, M. M., and Morrison, A. M. *The Lessons of Experience: How Successful Executives Develop on the Job*. San Francisco: New Lexington Press, 1988.

"I'm taking Wednesday morning off to watch my daughter perform in her third-grade play."

"Come with me and shoot some hoops at lunchtime. I always work better after releasing some physical energy."

"The time I spend in my garden is what gives me a larger perspective on this organization."

In some work settings it may feel risky to bring in personal experience and insights. But if you have the courage to take this risk, you will bring more honesty and humanity into your organization.

You'll help free other people from the burden of hiding their sources of psychological strength and practical learning. You'll help others to escape the fragmentation that drains their energy. And you'll demonstrate how drawing on all life experiences enhances and enlivens people and work.

◆ ◆ ◆

Stress Takes a Toll on Leaders

Sharon McDowell-Larsen

For leaders, stress comes with the territory. The increasingly competitive nature of global business, the pressures to succeed quickly and the fear of failing, the physical demands of late nights and constant traveling, and the increasing difficulty of balancing work with personal and family needs are just some of the things that fill executives' lives with stress. Consider that the average participant in CCL's Leadership at the Peak program, for top-level executives, works more than sixty hours a week and that many of these leaders are on the road for up to a third of the year. In fact, according to *Jobs Rated Almanac, 2001*, the position of senior corporate executive is the third most stressful job, behind president of the United States and firefighter.

Over time, the stresses that executives must inevitably endure can exact a considerable toll on their psychological and physiological health. It's common to hear recently promoted senior executives say that since their advancement they have stopped exercising regularly, have gained weight, and have seen their cholesterol and blood pressure levels rise. But how harmful to health are the stresses that accompany the executive role, what are the implications for leadership performance, and what can executives do to cope with stress?

All stress is not created equal, and stress is not always negative. There is a spectrum of stress, and some stress is normal, even desirable and healthy. The terms *eustress* and *distress* are used to distinguish between "good" and "bad" stress. When stress is controlled, it can provide a competitive edge in performance-related activities such as athletics, public speaking, acting—and leadership. However, what may be eustress for one person may be distress for another.

Essentially, stress is the interplay between an individual's resources and the demands placed on that individual, and responses to stress are influenced by genetic factors and social support systems. When perceived demands exceed perceived resources over an extended period of time, distress results, and physiological systems can no longer bear the load. This can lead to health problems, including heart disease, obesity, asthma, ulcers, and allergies.

Hidden Response

The psychological aspects of distress, in the form of negative thoughts and uncomfortable feelings, are often immediately recognizable. Physiological responses, although just as intense, are not always as easily recognized. A cascade of hormones, primarily cortisol and the catecholamines epinephrine and norepinephrine, is released—the same hormones that are released when someone faces physical danger or a challenge that requires effort. This highly adaptive hormonal response has proved effective for survival in times past, inciting a fight-or-flight reaction to danger. In today's world, however, this response can be a disadvantage because in many cases it is no longer socially appropriate.

Research suggests that excessive secretion of these hormones over long periods of time can be a major contributor to stress-related health disorders, particularly cardiovascular problems. Damage to the myocardium of the heart, for instance, may require the simultaneous presence of the catecholamines and cortisol, whereas prolonged elevations of cortisol are associated with increased risk of infection, bone and muscle loss, premature aging, and memory loss.

The factor of *personal control* appears to play a large role in determining the intensity and quality of responses to stress, and this is where executives and other top managers seem to have an advantage over people in lower-ranked jobs when it comes to stress. Research has shown, for instance, that people in jobs that allow them to use creativity and initiative to perform demanding tasks—people such as artists, scientists, entrepreneurs, and top executives—experience an increase in epinephrine but have low levels of cortisol. This type of response tends to be less harmful to health than a response in which levels of both hormones are elevated. Epinephrine is a general indicator of mental arousal or effort and increases whether the effect is positive or negative, whereas cortisol tends to increase in times of distress.

Both hormones have been found to increase in those whose jobs impose unpredictable demands, leave little room for individual discretion, fail to use personal skills and abilities to full potential, and provide little opportunity for personal control and growth—a situation typical of lower-ranking jobs. This may predispose such individuals to increased risk of heart disease and premature death.

The different responses to stress not only affect individual health but also appear to be reflected in organizational and societal health. Studies of British civil servants have shown that age-adjusted ten-year mortality rates are highest among those in the lowest ranks and decrease significantly with each step up the positional ladder—through clerical, professional, and top administrative jobs.

Other studies in Great Britain have shown that although the causes of death have changed over the years, death is delayed in those with higher socioeconomic status.

The reasons for these phenomena are unlikely to be purely genetic, and it has been suggested that the different death rates can be explained partially by different patterns of response to stress. Those in upper management or the upper classes are more likely to have a response to stress that is typical of people who have a high degree of personal control and who are able to use creative problem solving and initiative. Those in the lower ranks of organizations or society are more likely to lack personal control, autonomy, and involvement in decision making and therefore are more likely to show more negative responses to stress. This raises an important point for leaders: participative management not only may be good leadership but may also make for healthier employees.

No Cure-All

Although having personal control in a job or situation appears to have an advantageous influence on response to stress, it is by no means a universal antidote for stress. For instance, one study showed that people with borderline hypertension do not benefit as much from personal control as do people with normal blood pressure.

There are also gender differences in stress-response patterns and use of control. In one study, women managers reported having less control than men at work but appeared to benefit more than men from the control they did have. Men tend to use control to work harder, whereas women tend to use it to work in a more relaxed way.

Gender differences have also shown up in managers' responses to stress at home. A study of male and female managers with similar job roles found that their norepinephrine levels were similar during the workday. After work, however, norepinephrine levels increased in the females but decreased in the males. As the males were winding down, the females were winding up. One possible explanation for this is that traditional female after-work tasks such as grocery shopping and cooking dinner are performed with more regularity and urgency—meaning with little control over their scheduling—than are traditional male after-work tasks such as home improvement projects or washing the car.

Staying Healthy

Health can be maintained during periods of stress either by reducing the extent and degree of the strain or by becoming more resistant to its effects. Two ways that have been shown to increase resiliency to stress are securing a strong social support system and improving physical fitness.

Just as well-built foundations and sturdy construction materials make buildings strong, the support of others and physiological strength allow people to bear heavier loads of stress. Studies have found correlations between mortality and having a social support network—in other words, there is strong evidence that friends and family help individuals live longer.

Regular exercise has also been cited as an important strategy for coping with stress. The catch is that stress itself may keep people from exercising regularly and that people who experience little stress may be more likely to exercise. Exercise is itself a stressor, but it also helps to dissipate the hormones released in response to stress. Aerobic exercise in particular, because it is rhythmic, induces relaxation and calmness and decreases depression. Exercise can also replace negative behaviors that are typical responses to stress, such as smoking, poor eating habits, and drinking.

A Wider View

Now that you have a better idea of what stress is, how executives and others tend to respond to it, and some possible ways of coping with it, you can look beyond what stress means for you as an individual leader to its implications for your organization. Stress-related health costs can be significantly reduced by ensuring a supportive work environment, giving people at all levels of the organization more personal control and opportunities to use the full range and depth of their abilities, providing opportunities for development, and making it easier for employees to engage in regular exercise. Creating a workplace that keeps the lid on stress in these ways is one of the biggest challenges of leadership.

Part II

Creating Healthy Organizations

Chapter Six

What Is Leadership Development?

Your primary goal as a leader is to ensure the viability and improvement of your organization. Beginning with a consideration of how the understanding of leadership is changing, this chapter will help you distinguish between two important organization-improvement efforts that are often confused: the systematic development of individual leaders and the development of effective and systemwide collective leadership.

◆ ◆ ◆

The Third Way: A New Source of Leadership

Wilfred H. Drath

Do you feel confused about leadership? I often ask groups of managers and executives that question, and when I do, heads nod affirmatively all over the room.

Those managers and executives are not alone. Most of us, despite being awash in advice about how to practice leadership, are confused about leadership itself.

Why? Because what used to be a widely shared understanding of leadership is showing the cracks and strains of a rapidly changing world. Many things that once were agreed upon about leadership are now open to doubt and questioning. When people no longer have a shared understanding of leadership, its practice becomes confusing.

The confusion starts with a basic question: Where do we expect leadership to come from? The answer would seem to be a no-brainer: leaders, of course, are the source of leadership. Although this answer makes sense in many ways, it is also the cause of a lot of the confusion about leadership. It is the basis for the widely held understanding of leadership that has prevailed for so long. But it is also an idea that does not work as well in the world we are moving into.

In a world that is globally interconnected; that is networked electronically, economically, often culturally, and even spiritually; and in which differing views of life are held in a dynamic tension, the concept of *leadership from a leader* is much less workable than it was in a world where people stuck more or less in like-minded groups. Leadership from a leader still seems to make sense on the surface, but it often doesn't work as expected. And that's confusing.

What people are looking for is a new source of leadership. It's a little like running out of a precious natural resource. Leadership is needed just as much and maybe more than ever before, but the traditional source—the individual leader—is drying up. A new source is needed, and I believe it's right under our noses: leadership can come from the activity of people making sense and meaning of their work together.

In this article I will show how this source of leadership is just as powerful as leadership from a leader—and is even more workable in today's changing world. I will also look at some of the practical implications of thinking about the source of leadership in this way.

Leadership as Personal Dominance

To understand this new source of leadership, it will help to review the logic of thinking about leaders as the source of leadership. Let's start with the idea of personal dominance.

When leadership literally involves going first, dominance is critical. Imagine a group of humans thousands of years ago setting out on a journey into unknown territory. Everyone except the leader has someone to follow. The leader, who goes first, must face danger before anyone else and make decisions about which obstacles to confront and which to avoid. The leader must also overcome the fears and doubts of followers to retain their loyalty. The leader has to be strong, cunning, inventive, and resourceful. The capacities for personal dominance and for leadership are thus logically and closely linked.

It is a short step to viewing leadership as an aspect of the leader's individual being—physical presence, personality, character, and psychology. The nature of leadership is tied to the nature of the leader. If the leader is harsh and demanding, leadership will have the same qualities. If the leader is kind and caring, leadership will be the same.

Because leadership comes from the leader, there is only one way to make leadership happen: the leader must provide it. Leadership occurs as the leader acts on followers. Directing, inspiring, motivating, evaluating, rewarding, and punishing are logically seen as leadership behaviors.

Whatever needs are seen as leadership tasks—for example, the need for direction and commitment or to face major challenges— are what the leader is expected to accomplish for the community. If the leader is effective at completing these tasks, the community or organization moves in accordance with the leader's vision, aligns with the leader's plans, responds to the leader's call, and adapts as the leader adapts. If the leader fails at these tasks, the community or organization drifts aimlessly, loses its sense of purpose, and falls apart. Followers thus depend on the leader not just for direction, commitment, and adaptation but also for their sense of meaning and belonging.

The Limitations of Personal Dominance

Because leadership as personal dominance is so logical and compelling, people have learned to understand and accept personal dominance as leadership. In many circumstances it has been and remains a workable notion of leadership. But there are circum-stances in which leadership as personal dominance is limited.

For one thing it requires the continuing presence of the domi-nant person. If the leader is taken away, leadership is lost. The only remedy is to find another dominant person. And this can fail be-cause the original leader's leadership cannot be duplicated. When leadership is directly linked to the leader's individual being, the new leader may not be seen as providing the type of leadership that is needed.

Another major limitation is that the dominant person must have an almost perfect understanding of all the factors involved in the leadership tasks. This becomes more difficult as these factors become increasingly complex. Even when the factors are beyond the comprehension of any one person, however, if both the leader and the followers believe that the leader grasps them, it can be enough to keep leadership working fairly smoothly. But the leader may come to recognize that the factors are too complex for one per-son to handle. And if glaring failures occur often enough, the fol-lowers' faith in the leader may waver.

Thus personal dominance is also limited by the need for conti-nuity among followers. If there is a loss of followers who believe in and are committed to the leader and who are willing to face the challenges identified by the leader, leadership can falter. The fol-lowers may physically depart, or they may begin to question their reliance on the leader and demand that they be included in lead-ership tasks.

We have seen some of the ways by which the power of personal dominance to make sense of leadership can be lost. When this hap-pens, a new source of leadership is needed. Interpersonal influence has been this new source.

Leadership as Interpersonal Influence

At first glance, interpersonal influence may seem to be little more than a softening of personal dominance. But it differs radically: it is a way of understanding leadership that overcomes the limitations of personal dominance. Unlike personal dominance, interpersonal influence opens up leadership to the participation of followers. The leader's voice is no longer solo and dominant. The source of leadership becomes the negotiation of values and perspectives between the leader and followers. The leader's voice becomes a *compound* voice that includes the voices of followers.

In this view, truth, which the dominant leader spoke without question, is open to a process of reasoning and argument. It is also open to doubt. The leader's mode is persuading rather than telling. Persuasion in turn is accomplished by connecting and shaping the diverse values and perspectives of the leader and the followers. Interpersonal influence emphasizes the relationships among the hearts and minds of people in a community.

So how is the leader distinguished from the followers? If the leader is not dominant and everyone in the group or community is open to influence, the person who emerges as having the most influence is understood to be the leader. This is a big step forward in the understanding of leadership: new leaders can emerge as conditions change. Someone who was a follower can become a leader if he or she has gained the most relative influence in the context of a changed environment.

Interpersonal influence as a source of leadership is not a total departure from the personal dominance principle because personal attributes such as knowledge, persuasiveness, intelligence, authority, power, and creativity count as influence. But these attributes do not themselves constitute leadership; they only allow a person to become relatively more influential. Leadership thus comes from a relationship in which influence is negotiated, and a person becomes a leader by participating in this process.

The Limitations of Interpersonal Influence

Leadership as interpersonal influence is an advancement on leadership as personal dominance: it provides a new source of leadership to replace one that is less and less workable, and it overcomes the limitations of the latter.

But does interpersonal influence also have limitations? Although they are just beginning to become evident, the limitations of interpersonal influence will become increasingly important.

Global transportation and communication and the interdependence of economies have created a growing need for leadership that can deal with significant differences in values and worldviews. Interpersonal influence allows people to make sense of situations in which there are some differences in values and perspectives, but its effectiveness in contexts in which worldviews are dramatically different is less certain.

For example, when EgyptAir Flight 990 crashed in 1999, U.S. and Egyptian crash investigators agreed on one thing: they had to determine what caused the Boeing 767 to plunge into the ocean off Nantucket Island, Massachusetts. Yet in considering a critical piece of evidence—the meaning of words uttered by the copilot when the plane began its rapid descent—the two groups of investigators arrived at disparate interpretations. Did the copilot's prayer indicate that he was committing suicide by crashing the plane deliberately, or was it just a normal reaction in the face of imminent disaster? The U.S. and Egyptian interpretations of the copilot's words were based on widely divergent ways of understanding the world. People who don't share a general view of the world can find themselves in disagreement about so-called facts. Leadership as interpersonal influence involves negotiating values and perspectives, but that is difficult to do without some basic agreements about reality.

Challenges to interpersonal influence are encountered in other contexts as well. In nations throughout the world, for instance, there has been a slow but inexorable movement toward recognizing the legitimacy of diverse voices in community life that once were stifled. The views of people outside the mainstream, of immigrants and other newcomers, and of disenfranchised communities are now being heard. These once-marginalized groups are now in a position to voice concerns and to exert influence on traditionally entrenched sources of power.

There are fundamental challenges that can prevent these once-marginalized groups from gaining the legitimacy needed for influence in the leadership process, however. Mutual influence can be viewed as a loss of power by the traditionally enfranchised and as acquiescence and assimilation by the disenfranchised. This can lead to resistance and frustrating stalemates.

So, like personal dominance, interpersonal influence has limitations that decrease its viability as a source of leadership. This creates a need for a third source of leadership: the activity of people making meaning and sense of their work together.

Leadership as Relational Dialogue

Personal dominance and interpersonal influence are recognizable as leadership in everyday interactions in communities and organizations. They seem obvious, perhaps because we have seen them so much. The accepted notion is that leadership is either a leader taking charge, being commanding and forceful (dominance), or a leader being participative, open to input, and a facilitator (influence). People tend to think of these as differences in the style of the leader, but they may be better viewed as differences in ways of knowing and recognizing leadership.

Underlying our traditional ways of knowing and recognizing leadership is the assumption that leadership is about something a leader does. Personal dominance and interpersonal influence both depend on a leader to make leadership happen. But what if situations and contexts arise in which it is unlikely or impossible that a single person can make leadership happen? The U.S.-Egyptian investigation into the crash of Flight 990 is one example, but in the business world the context could be a labor-management task force on worker safety or a customer-supplier partnership. Such examples are becoming more common every day.

These contexts require a kind of conversation that is not just respectful of different perspectives but also opens every perspective to the possibility of transformation. Also called dialogue, such conversation is sometimes used as a tool in interpersonal influence, but in contexts in which no single individual can make leadership happen it must become more than a tool—it must become the source of leadership itself. In short, the activity of people making sense and meaning of their work together becomes the source of leadership.

Relational dialogue creates the rules about what is true and what is real. It is not just agreement about goals, not just shared knowledge, but is more pervasively the creation of a world in which it makes sense to have shared goals or shared knowledge in the first place. Thus relational dialogue is the source of leadership needed for Americans and Egyptians to step away from a strictly Judeo-Christian or Islamic worldview and create a world in which a joint understanding of the facts about Flight 990 can be articulated. In a business context, relational dialogue is the source of leadership needed for management and labor to disengage themselves from the home base of their identities and create a ground upon which they can work together.

This new source of leadership will be needed in the world we are making. However, people will have to be able to recognize relational dialogue as a source of leadership just as they recognize dominance and interpersonal influence.

People will recognize relational dialogue as a source of leadership when there is a mutual acknowledgment of shared work but no common ground on which to do the work. Many of the examples already cited fit this paradigm: differences across cultures, attempts at cooperation between labor and management, and efforts to bridge the gaps between the traditionally powerful and the traditionally marginalized. Whenever people share work across enduring barriers and conflicts, this new source of leadership will become more likely to be recognized.

In such contexts, there will sooner or later come a time when differing and even opposing worldviews will need to be judged as equally worthy. The commercial developer will acknowledge that the environmentalist's view of reality is equally worthy, and vice versa. Once differing worldviews are acknowledged as being equally worthy, relational dialogue will be the only workable source of leadership. No individual will be able to make leadership happen; it will require joint action across worldviews to make a new sense and meaning of shared work.

This view of where leadership is headed might sound hopeful, impossible, misguided, or even dangerous. These are all likely reactions because relational dialogue as a source of leadership is only beginning to emerge. The process by which it will come to make enough sense to enough people that leadership can be created has only begun. Yet even now there are some ideas that will constitute the *logic* of relational dialogue as a source of leadership.

A New Source in the Making

The first idea is that people become individuals through relational processes. Each person is individual and unique only through interrelations with others. The terms *leader, follower, parent, child, introvert, entrepreneur,* and *artist* all describe relationships more than they do individuality.

The second idea is that people construct the realities of life in participation with others. People rarely know what is real or possess meaning alone; it is usually a shared achievement. People get their sense of what is true and real from participation in communities, families, work, church, clubs, and so forth.

The third idea is that just as individuals and reality are relationally constructed, so truth and meaning cannot be discovered or found but must also be constructed. The claims that truth and reality have been discovered, revealed, or found are supportable only within a given worldview. The moment we acknowledge shared work across worldviews, the moment we try to create a new context for new truths and meanings, we must step away from a commitment to our truth as *the* truth and work across worldviews to construct truth and meaning.

But isn't this more like the end of leadership than a new source of leadership? What about the undeniable power of individual leaders to change minds, shape events, and inspire followers? The construction of this new source of leadership will also require an understanding that all leadership is shared leadership. This will allow for the recovery and reconstruction of personal dominance and interpersonal influence as sources of leadership, reenergized by a relational turn. From this viewpoint it's evident that even the most heroic brand of personal dominance is achieved through the leader's participation in a community that does not just bow to that dominance but creates it as well.

Moving Toward Action

To begin clearing up the confusion about leadership in order to practice it more effectively, we need to start asking new questions about leadership. For instance: How do people working together in teams, groups, organizations, and communities bring leadership into being? How can their capacity for leadership be increased? What role do individuals play in creating, sustaining, and developing leadership? What contexts are being created in your organization or community for which personal dominance and interpersonal influence cannot

Suggested Reading

Cooperrider, D. L., and Srivastva, S. "Appreciative Inquiry in Organizational Life." In R. Woodman and W. Pasmore (eds.), *Research on Organizational Change and Development*. Greenwich, Conn.: JAI Press, 1987.

Drath, W. H. *The Deep Blue Sea: Rethinking the Source of Leadership*. San Francisco: Jossey-Bass, 2001.

Drath, W. H., and Palus, C. J. *Making Common Sense: Leadership as Meaning-Making in a Community of Practice*. Greensboro, N.C.: Center for Creative Leadership, 1994.

Gergen, K. J. *Realities and Relationships: Soundings in Social Construction*. Boston: Harvard University Press, 1994.

Kegan, R., and Lahey, L. L. *How the Way We Talk Can Change the Way We Work: Seven Languages for Transformation*. San Francisco: Jossey-Bass, 2000.

be the source of leadership? What practices are already under way in your organization or community that might be considered leadership as relational dialogue? Is it worthwhile for you to support the development of these practices? If you are responsible for leadership development in your organization or community, what changes would you need to make to recognize and support the emergence of a new source of leadership? What implications would such a source have for current practices in your organization or community with respect to authority, accountability, decision making, and human resource planning?

These questions and hundreds more like them will drive us as we struggle to construct a new source of leadership that is workable and fit for the world we are making.

◆ ◆ ◆

The Missing Link: Organizational Culture and Leadership Development

Vidula Bal and Laura Quinn

Nearly everyone has had the experience of feeling like an outsider in a different culture. When people find themselves in a place where what they see and hear is unfamiliar, they often feel awkward and nervous. And if their new surroundings are completely different from what they're used to, they might think they've landed on another planet.

> Imagine that you're a sales manager making your first visit to the offices of a new client in the high-technology industry. You're excited about the visit because you have heard positive things about the company's creativity and innovation. As soon as you walk in the door, however, you start to feel uncomfortable. You're wearing a business

suit, but the employees at the high-tech company are dressed casually, to put it mildly—some are wearing shorts and sandals. You fidget as you wait in the reception area. When someone comes to take you to the meeting with the company's executives, you notice as you walk through the corridors that some employees have brought their pets to work. There are a few dogs, some cats—even a ferret. When you reach the meeting room, you're astounded to see a tent set up nearby. You ask what the tent is for. "It's there for anyone who wants to take a nap," an employee explains nonchalantly.

If you had stepped into an office where the employees wore suits and where the atmosphere was closer to a traditional business environment, you probably wouldn't have given it a second thought. But you have encountered an organizational culture that is new and different to you. And although that culture is consistent with the high-tech company's focus on and support of creativity and innovation, it feels strange to you. This points up a common dualism in perceptions of organizational cultures: although people are quick to recognize cultures that are different from their own, they are usually so ensconced in their own cultures that they take them for granted and have a hard time even acknowledging their existence.

Shaping the Culture

Organizational culture is an organization's values, beliefs, practices, rites, rituals, and stories—all of which combine to make an organization unique. These cultural features often derive from the strategic business drivers of the organization—elements such as quality, innovation, results, speed, and agility. These business drivers affect policies and procedures throughout the organization, thus creating its culture.

In the example of the high-tech company, its business drivers have created an organizational culture that emphasizes casualness and physical comfort as a way to encourage and support creativity and innovation. Although you might feel as though you're in a *Twilight Zone* episode, your experience during your visit is really not so unusual. You've just been turned upside-down because the company's culture has been shaped by business drivers that are different from those of your organization.

Practicing managers and academics alike have long recognized the existence of organizational cultures. Most managers, however, do not take culture into account as they devise plans and strategies for developing leaders in their organizations. One reason for this neglect is the difficulty that most people have in recognizing their own organizational cultures. But failing to acknowledge the crucial role that organizational culture plays in developing leaders can be costly. Although the culture that results from the policies and procedures affected by a company's business drivers typically reinforces those drivers, sometimes this culture ultimately works against the drivers, the company's interests, and its development goals.

CCL's Sustainable Leadership Capacity team is focusing directly on how organizations can best provide *systemic* support for leader development. The team has found that many executives make the mistake of believing that merely sending employees through leadership development programs will automatically produce the quantity and types of leaders needed to handle the challenges ahead. But there is more to it than that: to build sustainable leadership capacity, organizations must pay attention not only to development but also to the *context* in which development takes place. Organizational culture is a major part of this context, so managing the *fit* between an organization's culture and its efforts to develop leaders is vital to building sustainable leadership capacity.

A good way to begin your organization's leader development efforts is to review the organization's business drivers and assess its culture. Then you can determine which kinds of developmental strategies best support those business strategies, and learn how to leverage your culture's strengths while minimizing its weaknesses.

Cases in Point

In the following illustrations, leaders can find both some green lights and some caution flags to consider as they establish and evaluate their organizations' efforts to develop leaders.

Going Overboard

Vanessa is the director of leadership development for a successful manufacturer and retailer of personal care products. She has been with the company from its inception, and the organization's strategy has always been driven by a spirit of innovation and creativity. The company devotes a great deal of its resources to research and development, for instance, and it gives members of the marketing staff the time and freedom to come up with creative approaches to their jobs.

Vanessa's job responsibilities include devising structures for training the retail staff members and outsourcing development programs for the company's managers and executives. In doing so she has always taken into account the company's emphasis on innovation and creativity. She tries to incorporate every new spin on training and leadership development, she is constantly on the lookout for new and better providers of leadership development programs, and she has even instituted an in-house award given to employees who come up with the most innovative sales techniques.

Vanessa has embraced the company's business drivers in her efforts to develop leaders, and that's commendable. But her approach might have some downsides.

Vanessa's strategy mirrors the value that the company places on new ideas. In this organization, people who want to change old habits are encouraged to practice new behaviors, for which they are then recognized. An organizational culture that encourages and recognizes new behaviors goes a long way toward building sustainable leadership capacity.

Such a culture also presents pitfalls for leader development, however. In an organization that places a high value on anything that is *new*, things can get old pretty quickly. Vanessa emphasizes the adoption of cutting-edge leader development practices, but if she constantly changes the company's approach to leader development to fit whatever is trendy, the developmental efforts could gain a reputation for being flavor-of-the-month. This approach runs the risk of undercutting sustainable leadership capacity.

Driven by Diversity

Wanda is the vice president of human resources for a mineral mining company. The Western state in which the company is based has an increasingly diverse population, but the company's workforce is fairly homogeneous. Before Wanda was hired, the company's executive team, wary of lawsuits, decided to include an appreciation of diversity among the company's core values. Wanda, who has a background in working with diversity issues, has made progress in implementing this value, but one challenge is that the company has a stable workforce without much turnover—some employees have been with the company for more than twenty-five years.

Wanda is working not only to increase the diversity of the company's workforce but also to incorporate the driver of diversity into the company's efforts to develop leaders. She believes that diversity means not only recognizing the contributions of diverse groups of employees but also ensuring egalitarian treatment of those contributions. One philosophy she has embraced, therefore, is that everyone in the organization, from mine workers to the chief executive officer, is entitled to some type of leadership development. Wanda realizes that not everyone needs the same type of development, so she has created different outlets for different groups of employees. One step she has taken is to ask the older, more experienced employees to attend classes on how to become mentors. Then the highest-potential younger employees are assigned mentors from this group. Wanda has also established specialized training opportunities for minority employees.

The mining company's decision to make diversity one of its business drivers will have an impact on the organization's ability to build sustainable leadership capacity. But there could be negative as well as positive effects.

The notion that everyone deserves some type of leader development will strengthen the organization by making all employees feel included and valued. The danger in providing different types of leader development for different groups is that it could prevent the organization from having a common leadership development language and make it difficult for people to relate to one another. Wanda will need to ensure that the different developmental efforts have enough elements in common that they all produce the desired impact at the organizational level.

Profit and Risk

Larry is the director of corporate training and development for a high-tech company that is facing increasing pressure from shareholders to increase profit margins and stock value. In the past the company had always been able to ride out the ups and downs of Wall Street, but the recent downturn in the economy has made it difficult for the organization to maintain its historical profit margins. The company's long-standing reputation for consistently producing above-target results is now in danger. Concerned about the company's vulnerability in the marketplace, the senior management team has dictated that all operational activities be focused on results and directly linked to organizational strategy.

With results now the principal business driver, Larry has had to justify any expenditures on training and leadership development. But Larry believes that the challenge of doing more with less has actually been advantageous because it forced him to take a hard look at the company's training and development programs and link them directly to the business outcomes sought by the organization. This led to a revelation: he realized that the company had not been applying the same strategic intent in its training efforts that it was applying in all other operational areas. This finding prompted him to create a training program that is focused not only on developing employees but also on furthering the company's results-oriented strategy.

The business driver of improving profit margins and results is helping the company stay competitive in the marketplace. But Larry's decision to incorporate the emphasis on the bottom line into the company's efforts to develop leaders introduces another level of competition that could be detrimental to the building of sustainable leadership capacity. If the imperative of achieving the best results as quickly as possible continues unchecked, it could foster a climate of internal competition. Although a certain amount of such rivalry is desirable, it can have negative consequences if carried too far.

For example, employees who participate in these leader development experiences may not share what they have learned with their co-workers. They may feel they can gain an advantage over their colleagues by keeping their new insights to themselves. Discouraging the sharing of learning could have a negative impact on the company's profit margins and results. So despite Larry's best intentions, his strategy for developing leaders could end up working against the company's principal aims.

No Mistakes

Tim is a manager at a long-established retail company that decided three years ago to pursue quality as one of its principal business drivers. The executive board, knowing that the initiative would have to permeate the entire organization to be successful, insisted that all the company's departments had to commit to the effort before the board would support the investments necessary for the undertaking.

Tim is in charge of the quality program, which includes a monthly meeting of all employees at which any instances of compromised quality—and the person or people responsible—are highlighted for everyone to see. During the three years of the initiative, fewer and fewer instances of substandard quality have been reported. So on the surface the program appears to have been a resounding success. But Tim has just now begun to notice a phenomenon that is causing him concern: people aren't reporting mistakes because they are afraid to.

Many organizations have had success with quality initiatives. But such initiatives can have insidious effects on organizational culture and the building of sustainable leadership capacity.

Although the retail company appears to have made great strides in improving quality, Tim now realizes that people have become fearful of making mistakes on the job—and especially of admitting such mistakes. They are afraid they will face humiliation at the monthly meetings. In addition, no one wants to tarnish what appears to be a three-year track record of steady quality improvement by admitting that there is any need for learning.

Improvement cannot come without learning, and one of the foundations of learning is being able to make mistakes—up to a point at least—and to concede them. Mistakes, whether they are your own or others', provide learning opportunities. When employees are discouraged too vigorously from admitting mistakes, learning opportunities are lost and the organization suffers.

A Key Ingredient

Executives who make investments in their organizations' leadership development are sometimes puzzled when they don't get the expected returns on those investments. They could improve their returns by acknowledging that organizational culture plays a vital role in the development of leaders and then factoring organizational culture into their developmental efforts.

First, however, they must be able to recognize their organizational cultures—no easy task because they are so embedded in those cultures. But there are clues to be found.

Ask yourself some questions: What does it *feel* like in your organization? What stories are told over and over in your organization, and what values do those stories promote? What are the drivers of your organization's business strategy, and how have they shaped the organizational culture? Once you have a clearer understanding of your organizational culture, you can pinpoint how it may be hindering or enhancing leadership development efforts in your organization.

◆ ◆ ◆

Leading Together: Complex Challenges Require a New Approach

Wilfred H. Drath

People in organizations want and need to work together effectively and productively. Individuals long to be part of a bigger picture that connects them to a larger purpose. This is what they expect leadership to accomplish. They expect leadership to create the direction, alignment, and commitment that will enable them, working together, to achieve organizational success.

The trouble is, it's getting harder and harder to make this happen. Creating direction, alignment, and commitment—the work of leadership—is becoming more difficult than ever.

There are a number of reasons for this. As organizations break down functional silos and develop greater global reach, people more often work with others who are not like them. It's harder to get people who don't share a common set of values and perspectives to get behind a common direction, to align, and to commit to one another.

Adding to this difficulty, people don't work side by side as much anymore. People working together might be scattered over several regions and time zones, even over different countries.

Subtle and not-so-subtle barriers to communication and trust are created by the lack of simply being in the same room together. It's harder to shape a common purpose and get people aligned, and it's more difficult for people who don't see each other face-to-face to commit effectively to one another.

It's also getting harder to make leadership work because of changes in the attitude toward traditional ways of practicing leadership. Increasingly people without formal authority want to be involved in setting their own direction and in designing their own work and how they will coordinate with others. They are less willing to commit themselves to work in which they have had no say. Yet people may not be prepared to participate effectively in leadership this way. They may knock on the door demanding to be let in on leadership without actually knowing how to enter into it. It's harder to create direction, alignment, and commitment when there are different and sometimes competing ideas of how to best accomplish this leadership work and when people have differing levels of readiness for participating in leadership.

Facing the Unknown

In general, leadership is more difficult today because of what Ronald A. Heifetz, in his book *Leadership Without Easy Answers*, calls *adaptive challenges*, which can also be thought of as complex challenges. A complex challenge is more than just a very complicated problem. Complexity implies a lack of predictability. Complex challenges confront people with the unknown and often result in unintended consequences.

This unpredictability also means that a complex challenge is quite different from a technical problem. Technical problems are predictable and solvable. Using assumptions, methods, and tools that already exist, people can readily define the nature of a technical problem and prepare a solution with some confidence in the results. So, for example, if a key supplier changes the pricing on critical components, and such changes are expected to happen from time to time (the problem is already understood), and there are established ways of responding (tools for solving the problem already exist), then this is a technical problem. A technical problem arises and is solved *without any fundamental change* in assumptions, methods, or tools. Also, the people who solve a technical problem don't themselves have to change.

A complex challenge cannot be dealt with like this. Existing assumptions, methods, or tools are no good in the face of a complex challenge and may even get in the way. To be faced successfully, complex challenges require altered assumptions, different methods, and new tools not yet invented. Complex challenges require people and organizations to change, often in profound and fundamental ways. This is where things get unpredictable. Some examples of current complex challenges are the need for companies that have merged to bring about culture change, for the health care industry to address the nursing shortage, for many companies to make the transformation from product push to customer pull, and for social agencies to get diverse constituents with differing perspectives to work together on such deep-rooted issues as reducing the number of youthful offenders.

Complex challenges are made even more difficult by the fact that no one can say with any authority or accuracy just how things need to change. This is where leadership starts to get a lot harder. Because the complex challenge lies beyond the scope of existing assumptions, the frameworks that people use to try to understand the nature of the challenge itself are not adequate. So, for example, it's not just that people in an organization that needs to undergo a culture change don't know how to make the change happen. It's worse than that. They have no way of being sure what sort of new culture is needed. No one who is part of the existing organization has any kind of especially gifted insight into the needs of the new, changed, still-unknown organization of the future. Everyone has ideas, of course, and everyone has a point of view and may be quite attached to it. Only by virtue of position and authority are anyone's ideas given special status. Unfortunately, although having a lot of authority may make it possible for a person to make sure his or her views hold sway, that doesn't guarantee the effectiveness of those views.

If all of this makes it sound as though a complex challenge requires a lot of talk and reflection among a lot of people in an organization, it does. And all of that talk and reflection takes a lot of time. Because the complex challenge is not only complex but also a challenge, however, it demands a response now, not someday. So facing a complex challenge puts people in a bind and ensures that they will experience some stress as they try to think and reflect together without letting analysis lead to paralysis.

No Going It Alone

In the face of complex challenges, a leader, no matter how skilled and otherwise effective, cannot simply step into the breach, articulate a new vision, make some clarifying decisions, and proclaim success. Because a complex challenge requires a whole system and all the people in it to change, it lies beyond the scope of any individual person to confront.

Complex challenges make it virtually impossible for an individual leader to accomplish the work of leadership, and individual leadership therefore reaches a distinct limit in the face of complex challenges.

Since about the 1920s (in the writings of Mary Parker Follett) there has been talk of the possibility of distributing or sharing leadership and making leadership more inclusive and collective. If leadership is still needed (and who can deny that it is) and if no individual alone can provide leadership in the face of a complex challenge, then perhaps what is needed is the collective action of many people. It's conceivable, even compelling, that everyone in an organization could contribute in some way to facing a complex challenge. The possibility that a more inclusive and collective way of leadership could help organizations meet complex challenges and be more effective is promising.

The problem has always been—and remains today—*how* to get more people involved in leadership and *how* to make leadership more inclusive and collective.

Two critical problems continuously block the way. The first could be called the *too-many-chefs* problem: the effort to make more people into leaders seems doomed to collapse in a cacophony of differing visions and values as too many individuals exhibit leadership. The second could be called the *diffused accountability* problem: when people share leadership, it seems inevitable that accountability will also get shared until, as everyone becomes accountable, no one is really accountable at all.

Both of these problems are real. Attempts to make leadership more inclusive and collective have often—if not always—foundered on just these obstacles. Such failures have made many people realistically pessimistic about the utility of a more inclusive and collective approach to leadership. Yet the promise of such leadership grows brighter as complex challenges surpass the ability of the individual leader to respond.

The problem is how to develop more inclusive and collective ways of making leadership happen without running afoul of the twin problems of too many chefs and diffused accountability. Somehow we need to develop the whole process by which direction, alignment, and commitment are created—not just develop individual leaders. We at CCL call the development of individual leaders *leader development*; the development of the whole process for creating direction, alignment, and commitment we call *leadership development*. Both leader development and leadership development are needed. But even though leadership development is becoming more critically important every day, it lags far behind leader development in most organizations.

Defining the Tasks

A good place to start developing a more inclusive and collective leadership is to think of leadership (both individual and collective) as a process that is used to accomplish a set of *leadership tasks*. This makes it possible to focus not on the way leadership is practiced but rather on what people hope to *accomplish* with leadership. A useful question is, What work is leadership expected to get done? As already suggested, leadership is expected to set direction, create alignment, and generate commitment—or some similar list of desired outcomes.

The too-many-chefs problem that often comes up in trying to share leadership is created when organizations try to get more people to act as leaders and exhibit leadership. This is subtly but importantly different from getting more people involved in the process of accomplishing the leadership tasks.

Getting more people to act like leaders does little more than multiply the individual leader approach. In the face of a complex challenge, simply having more people trying to say what should be done is unlikely to be effective.

In the same way, the diffused accountability problem is created when organizations make more people accountable by designating more people as leaders. This is also little more than a way to multiply individual leaders. Many ways of trying to share leadership in order to make it more inclusive and collective are actually still firmly rooted in the tradition of the individual leader—designating more leaders can just add to the difficulty of accomplishing the leadership tasks in the face of complex challenges.

So having more leaders is not the answer. Instead the answer is to create richer and more complex processes of accomplishing the leadership tasks. Focus on how to create direction, alignment, and commitment in the face of complex challenges, and forget about how many people are, or are not, leaders.

Putting the accomplishment of the leadership tasks at the heart of leadership frames different and more useful questions: What are the obstacles to clear direction, effective alignment, and solid commitment? What resources exist in the organization for creating direction, alignment, and commitment as a complex challenge is being confronted? What different approaches to accomplishing the leadership tasks are possible for the organization? How might people act in new and different ways to accomplish the leadership tasks?

Answering questions like these can help organizations avoid the traditional problems of shared leadership by getting them past the idea that more inclusive and collective approaches require making more people individual leaders.

Three Capabilities

Complex challenges require richer and more complex ways of creating direction, alignment, and commitment. The ways people talk, think, and act together—the culture of the organization along with its systems and structures—are what need to become richer and more complex.

At first this may seem to be a bad idea. When facing a complex challenge, surely the last thing needed is more complexity. Yet the very complexity of the challenge calls for an equally complex capacity to respond. A complex capacity to respond means something different from just a more complicated process. It means a more varied, less predictable, more layered process capable of greater subtlety. At CCL we believe that making the leadership process more collective, pushing the process beyond one that depends primarily on individuals, enriches the process of leadership to the level of sensitivity and responsiveness required by a complex challenge. Continuing to depend on individual leaders (no matter how many) to lead people through basic and profound changes is risky. This is because any individual leader, no matter how capable, may be unable to make such changes personally. Getting more people working together in more ways increases the likelihood that people who are able to make the needed changes themselves will become influential in the leadership process. We call this *connected leadership*.

Three collective capabilities can be useful for organizations needing to achieve connected leadership: shared sense-making, connection, and navigation.

Shared sense-making. Complex challenges do not come wrapped with an explanation. By their nature they cause confusion, ambiguity, conflict, and stress. They are immediate, so they press for a solution now. But they also force people to change toward the unknown, so they also require reflection. Moving too fast can make things worse. What seems to be required is the capability to engage in shared sense-making.

This is not problem solving; it's not even problem defining. It's a process that must come before a challenge can even be thought of as a problem with solutions. The outcome of this sense-making is shared understanding. It involves people in paying attention to both the parts and the whole of the challenge. It requires people to experience multiple perspectives and to hold conflicting views in productive tension. It answers the persistent question about difficult change: Why change? Without an understanding of why change is required, people are rightly suspicious of it.

Connection. The process of leadership is realized in the connections between people, groups, teams, functions, and whole organizations. Complex challenges threaten existing connections. Think of what happens in an organization seeking to become more customer focused. The existing structures and boundaries that differentiate and coordinate such entities as production, marketing, sales, and finance begin to be more like impediments than workable ways of organizing. Facing complex challenges requires people and organizations to develop and enrich their forms of connection.

The outcome is relationships made to work in new ways both within and between groups and communities. Getting relationships to work in new ways requires people to see patterns of connection (and disconnection) in order to explore the root causes of the complex challenge and clarify differing and sometimes conflicting values. Often, new language emerges.

Navigation. Because a complex challenge is not a familiar problem to be solved but a reality to be faced through change and development, the process is one of learning from shared experiments, small wins, innovations, and emergent strategies.

No one can set a goal whose achievement will resolve the complex challenge. It is a journey whose destination is unpredictable and unknown. A key to success is the ability to be keenly sensitive to the forces of change as they happen, like mariners who sail a ship by making minute, mutual adjustments in response to one another and to the elements of wind and current.

These capabilities cannot be taken on by individuals. They can be developed only between individuals and between groups, functions, and whole organizations. Too often the move to more inclusive and collective approaches to leadership is attempted without making this move into the space in between. More inclusive approaches to leadership have often been expected to flow from a change in the competencies of individual leaders, such as when leaders are called on to be more empowering and inclusive and to share leadership. The persistence of the obstacles to more inclusive and collective leadership comes from the failure to let go of long-held and long-valued assumptions about the individual nature of leadership.

Making Gains

In facing complex challenges, people, organizations, and communities can develop ways of accomplishing the leadership tasks that give more people a sense of being responsible for setting direction, creating alignment, and generating commitment. Successfully facing complex challenges will support a sense of shared power and collective competence.

It will also create the possibility for leadership strategy. Because strategy means making choices among alternatives, no strategy is possible without alternatives to consider. So if the development of connected leadership, of a more inclusive and collective leadership process, adds to the alternative ways that leadership can be carried out, it also creates the possibility that choices can be made about leadership. Leadership then would no longer be a matter of making a single kind of practice work for every context. Instead of seeing leadership as simply a natural force to which humans are subject and that comes in only one naturally determined version (such as the forceful leader taking charge), people would come to see leadership as a process that humans control and that can be shaped to human needs through intentional choices.

Note

The ideas in this article are drawn from an ongoing research and development project at CCL called Connected Leadership. The purpose of this project is to identify and test ways of enriching organizational processes, culture, and systems to support more inclusive and collective approaches to leadership by and among groups, teams, departments, and the whole organization. Its goal is to contribute to making leadership more effective in the face of complex challenges.

We invite readers of this book to join us in exploring and developing the potential of connected leadership by contacting us through our Web site at www.ccl.org. We are seeking collaborators in two broad categories. The first is people, organizations, and communities who believe they are developing and practicing some form of what is described in this article. We wish to learn more about the real-world experience of developing leadership as the property of whole systems. The second category is groups, teams, agencies, governmental entities, organizations, and communities that wish to collaborate with us in developing connected leadership. We believe the best way to develop the practice of leadership is through collaborative action.

Chapter Seven

Creating the Leadership Pipeline

Your organization's success depends on maintaining the quality and continuity of its leadership. Consequently, the decisions that are made about the systems and processes for choosing leaders are essential. This chapter offers specific advice to guide decision making in this area.

◆ ◆ ◆

Ending the Board Game:
New Leadership Solutions for Companies

Jay A. Conger

The accounting and fraud scandals at Enron, WorldCom, Global Crossing, Tyco, and other companies raise a critical question: why did their boards of directors fail to take a strong leadership role and preempt these disastrous outcomes? After all, a board has a legal responsibility for the management of its company. There are numerous reasons why the boards of these particular companies failed to take a proactive role, but one crucial contributor was the nature of leadership on corporate boards today.

Many current corporate governance policies and practices are intended to ensure a balance of power between the CEO and the directors, but reality usually gets in the way. Among the vast majority of U.S. companies, leadership is vested largely in the hands of a single individual—the CEO. But it's becoming increasingly clear that relying on one person to lead both a company and its board can be a serious mistake. To halt the procession of corporate scandals, leadership needs to be shared.

Inside Knowledge

If you look closely at today's boards, you'll see that in most cases the CEO is the unquestioned leader. This is largely because of the natural advantages of the CEO's position.

For one thing, the CEO has far greater access than other directors to current, comprehensive information about the state of the company. The other directors usually have extremely limited knowledge of company affairs. Their enlightenment is restricted by the fact that they usually are company and even industry outsiders with a part-time role. Although their external perspective has some important advantages, it is a liability when it comes to cultivating knowledge and information about the company and its industry. Most directors are well aware of this gap in their understanding and, as a result, willingly concede authority to the CEO.

Directors also tend to see their primary role as serving the CEO; to them, providing oversight is a secondary role. Most directors are CEOs themselves, so they share an unwritten but binding etiquette that frowns on aggressively challenging a fellow CEO and on probing too deeply into the details of someone else's business. Many fear that they will end up micromanaging CEO responsibilities. All these factors encourage directors to defer to the leadership of the CEO.

As a result the CEO usually determines the agenda for meetings and controls the type and amount of information that directors receive. The CEO often is the one who selects board members and appoints the members of the board's various committees. These and other powers and prerogatives generally make the CEO the de facto leader of the board. The only exceptions—the only times when a board feels *it* must take the lead—typically come during the selection of a new CEO or during a change of company ownership.

Dual Titles

The CEO's effective leadership of the board is magnified and solidified in most companies by the fact that the CEO is the leader not only in essence but also in name—he or she is the board chairman. From a CEO's vantage point, there are clear positives to this dual leadership role.

- It centralizes board leadership and accountability in a single individual, so there is no question about who leads the board.
- It eliminates the possibility of a dysfunctional conflict or rivalry between the CEO and the board chairman, which might result in ineffectual compromises and drawn-out decision making.
- It avoids the potential problem of having two public spokespeople addressing the organization's stakeholders and possibly delivering conflicting messages.
- It achieves efficiency in that the board chairman is also the person who is most informed and knowledgeable about company affairs. The CEO doesn't have to spend a lot of time and energy on updating a board chairman on company and industry issues before each meeting.

For companies there may be another advantage—at least in the current environment—to combining the roles of CEO and board chairman. Research has shown that CEOs, almost without exception, strongly believe that they should also hold the chairmanship of the board. When it comes to recruiting the best CEO talent, companies whose policy is to hand the reins of the board to the CEO are therefore likely to have an advantage over companies that don't have this policy.

Superficially, at least, it appears that there are a number of advantages to having the CEO and the board chairman be one and the same. But there is a critical drawback to relying on this CEO model of board leadership—a drawback that has become painfully evident during the recent corporate scandals. Under the CEO model, too much leadership authority is concentrated in the hands of the CEO, and the company often has no effective system of checks and balances when it comes to leadership.

One way to balance power is to create another source of leadership, and organizations have at least three options available to achieve this: an independent, nonexecutive chairman (someone from outside the organization who has never held the CEO or other executive position in the company); a lead director; or strong, autonomous board committees.

Split Decision

The idea of a separate, nonexecutive chairmanship has been circulating for at least a decade. Few companies, however, have adopted this option—only about 10 percent of the largest firms in the United States have a chairman who is not also the CEO. This suggests fairly strong resistance to the concept among the top echelons of corporate America.

What are the arguments for having a separate, nonexecutive chairman? Perhaps the principal one is that it increases the ability of the board to monitor the CEO's performance. A board led by a fellow director will likely feel it has greater latitude to challenge the CEO and his or her actions when necessary. In addition, having a separate board chairman may enhance a company's standing among investment fund managers, who often assume that CEOs seek to serve themselves first and shareholders only secondarily. In the eyes of these fund managers, a separate, nonexecutive chairman with a mandate to elevate shareholder value is less likely to be compromised than a CEO-chairman.

There are a number of qualities and characteristics that a separate chairman should possess to be effective and successful. First, the chairman should not be a former CEO of the company. (A former CEO would likely have been involved in the selection and often the mentoring of the current CEO, so his or her objectivity could be compromised.) Second, the chairman should have the confidence and admiration of the directors, along with self-confidence and sufficient knowledge of the company and the industry to fit naturally into the leadership role. To gain this knowledge, the chairman must be dedicated to putting in the time and effort to closely follow the company and its industry.

This requirement means it's not a good idea for the outside chairman to be a board member or CEO of another company (although a recently retired CEO might fit into the role perfectly). Being a separate, nonexecutive chairman can be highly demanding—in large, diversified companies the chairman may need to spend seventy-five to a hundred days a year keeping abreast of the company if everything is going well, and even more if the company encounters a crisis.

Because the separate chairman will work closely with the CEO, it's important that the CEO be involved in the selection process. For this model of board leadership to function effectively, the chairman must feel that his or her allegiance is not solely to the CEO and must feel free and unafraid to challenge the CEO. At the same time, there should be strong positive chemistry between the two individuals—again because they will be working together so closely. However, the chemistry must not be so powerful that it could override the chairman's objective viewpoint. During the selection process, it's best if the chairman candidate and CEO decide for themselves whether chemistry exists between them. However, the scope of the potential chairman's ability to challenge the CEO is best determined by the sitting directors. In light of this, the best selection method is for the CEO to provide his or her input on each candidate on the roster submitted by the board nominating committee and then for the board to make the final choice.

Establishing from the start clear and negotiated expectations of the roles the separate chairman will assume is also critical to the success of this model of board leadership. Tasks and responsibilities to be placed under the purview of the chairman might include setting meeting agendas in consultation with the CEO, assigning tasks to board committees, facilitating full and candid deliberations of matters that come before the board, and annually reviewing the board's governance practices.

Despite the potential that this board leadership model holds for breaking up the concentration of authority and reducing the chances of scandal, it's unlikely to be widely adopted by U.S. companies. The primary stumbling block is CEOs themselves. As noted earlier, most CEOs are strongly biased toward having a single leader—themselves. They believe that sharing leadership of the company and the board is cumbersome and inefficient. In addition, candidates for the role of separate, nonexecutive board chairman face greater legal risks than other directors do—risks for which they might not be willing or able to get liability coverage. Moreover, they must be willing to make a much greater time investment than that required of a typical board member. For most people who would be considered qualified outside candidates, such an investment would be impractical.

There are strikes against the nonexecutive chairman form of board leadership, but companies looking to break away from the status quo have two other alternatives to consider.

Process Pilot

A form of board leadership likely to be more palatable to many CEOs is having a lead director—an individual who does not assume the formal role of chairman but acts as the directors' representative to the CEO. Through this intermediary function the lead director can bring to the CEO sensitive issues or concerns that individual directors might not raise on their own or want discussed in a public forum. In this alternative the lead director *leads* not so much in the sense of influencing the board's stands on various issues as in the sense of piloting the boardroom process.

The lead director is both an ombudsman and a facilitator of the governance process. His or her role can include overseeing and preparing the agenda for board meetings, discussing controversial business issues one-on-one with the CEO, and conducting exit interviews with executives who are leaving the company to determine whether their resignations reflect problems in the organization or with the CEO's style and approach. In addition, lead directors might meet on occasion with major shareholders to determine their expectations and concerns. Such smaller meetings, without the presence of company management, could encourage more open, revealing, and helpful discussion than occurs at annual, public shareholder meetings.

What characteristics should be sought in a lead director? In addition to being from outside the organization, the ideal lead director should have significant executive experience, should be highly respected by other members of the board, should serve in another board leadership capacity (as chairman of a board committee, for example), and should possess the strength of personality and background to effectively challenge the CEO when warranted. The lead director should not be selected on the basis of seniority on the board; although boards are prone to honor an elder member with the lead directorship, this criterion is often unlikely to be a good indicator of an individual's ability to lead effectively in a changing business environment.

The lead director model of board leadership looks like an attractive alternative to leaving power solely in the hands of a CEO-chairman, yet less than one-third of the Fortune 1000 companies have opted for it. Many CEOs—and indeed, many board members—continue to believe that having a lead director merely gums up the works and is appropriate only in times of emergency. However, CEOs tend to be more amenable to the idea of the third option—giving board leadership to the board committees.

Making Headway

Board leadership that is shared by the board committees has emerged as the most prevalent alternative to the CEO-chairman model. There are a number of reasons for this shift in power, but one of the most obvious is that CEOs, caught up in setting corporate strategy and overseeing day-to-day operations, realize that they have their hands full and don't have the time to be active members of each board committee. As a result, they often feel comfortable in assuming a consultative or advisory role and allowing the committees to lead themselves—and by extension to lead the board as a whole.

The growing use of board committee leadership has also been driven by the increased reliance on outside directors, who of course become committee members and chairmen. With the proliferation of outside directors, the practice of CEOs' handpicking committee chairmen has largely been replaced by a system in which committees select their own chairmen.

In companies that have elected to turn to board leadership by committees—at least on a trial or experimental basis—committee members should take a number of steps to ensure that their panels not only retain their leadership but also enhance it. For outside directors to take full advantage of their relatively newfound majority status on boards and committees, they often need to develop action plans and positions that are independently produced rather than dictated or guided by the CEO and senior management. Board and committee meetings and other activities are generally the only opportunities the directors have to accomplish this. So it's important that some committee meetings be held without company executives present so the directors can discuss sensitive issues—such as those surrounding corporate performance and executive succession. These committee meetings also may be the only chance panel members have to arrive at strong positions that they believe are in the best interests of the company but may be contrary to the stated preferences of senior management.

It is critical that committees be able to meet on short notice when the members believe this is called for by an event such as a corporate crisis or rapidly developing change. It's also important for committees to ensure that they have the ability to seek and retain outside specialists who can make objective assessments of the company's operations—and that they can do so without the permission of senior management.

What's Ahead

To date, strong leadership from board committees is the area in which the most progress has been made in achieving governance practices that provide more balance in corporate leadership. Considering the resistance to board leadership by a separate, nonexecutive chairman or a lead director, it's probably also the area in which the most progress will continue to be made for the foreseeable future.

But certain trade-offs involved in relying solely on board committee leadership may make it fall short of being the best option of the three. When leadership is splintered across a number of individuals, there is no single director who takes comprehensive responsibility for the board and for ensuring that its activities are well coordinated and meet high standards of governance. There may be no central ombudsman to give the full board a collective voice. In addition, because committees have a narrow focus, they can at best shape only portions of the overall agenda.

All these drawbacks suggest that committee leadership is only a partial approach to building a method of board governance that is truly effective and optimal for the well-being of companies. In the final analysis the practice of using empowered outside chairmen or lead directors should be the means of countervailing the corporate leadership practice of putting too much power in the hands of one person. In companies, as in governments, an effective system of checks and balances is critical to ensuring both successful performance and integrity.

◆ ◆ ◆

The Ins and Outs of Selecting Successful Executives

Valerie I. Sessa and Jodi J. Taylor

As goes an organization's top leadership, so to a large extent goes the organization. With so much riding on the success or failure of senior managers ranging from CEOs to two levels below, the selection of these executives is paramount and demands a painstaking, well-thought-out process. Despite these apparent truisms, evidence shows that many organizations have been shooting from the hip—or worse, shooting themselves in the foot—when it comes to executive selection.

Many newly selected executives are judged to be unsuccessful once in the position; estimates of the failure rate of these leaders range from 27 percent to as high as 75 percent. The reasons for these failures are myriad, and there are no simple explanations or remedies. But it is clear that top executives in many organizations do not approach the selection of leaders with the same enthusiasm

Note

In our research project, we worked with 494 top-level executives who were participants in CCL's Leadership at the Peak executive development program. The executives filled out questionnaires and were interviewed about selection processes they had been involved in at the very top of their organizations (CEO and two levels down). This information is the foundation of our book *Executive Selection: Strategies for Success*.

In that book we discuss a selection system that goes to the heart of what we have learned from our research. The book offers a sequence of activities to pursue when considering top-level selections:

Choose the selection committee. The importance of this part of the process is often underrated, but it can be one of the most crucial ingredients of selection. Teams make better selection decisions than individuals, and teams that are diverse in terms of the members' jobs in the organization and their demographic characteristics make better selection decisions than do teams with less diversity.

Prepare for the search. Decision makers should begin preparing for the search by taking a holistic, context-rich look at the corporation and the job and connecting their findings with the candidate or skill with which they approach other challenges facing the organization. All too often, selection decisions are made in an illogical and haphazard manner, even though these choices are often crucial to organizational survival in the current competitive business environment.

CCL, in an effort to put executive selection on a firmer footing and determine how it should be done, has for the past several years conducted large-scale research on the subject. In one major study, hundreds of executives told their stories of selection, good and bad. In a second study, a multimedia simulation developed at CCL revealed a great deal about the decision-making styles of those who

requirements. Three important steps need to be taken: perform an organizational assessment, assess the position requirements, and develop the candidate requirements.

Recruit the right candidates. A selection decision is only as good as the executives in the candidate pool. When evaluating whom to consider, decision makers should keep in mind that a diverse group of applicants is better.

Make the match. There is no simple formula for selecting executives. What seems to be important in this step is the type of information gathered and used. We found that it is important to gather information on factual and measurable attributes (such as track record, experience, and past performance), on soft-side skills (such as personality and values), and on fit with the organization.

Follow up. Most decision makers never consider what to do after the selection is made. Processes need to be integrated into the overall system of selection to guarantee that the person selected receives support during and after the transition. Also, the outcomes of the selection—including hard-side skills, soft-side skills, and fit issues—should be monitored so the new leader can be given feedback on performance.

choose top-level executives. We supplemented that research with our own knowledge derived from dealing with top executives, all with the goal of helping such executives develop processes for selecting leaders who will be successful.

One finding that emerged is the growing practice of hiring high-level executives from outside the organization. Nearly one-third of today's CEOs are outsiders, compared with 9 percent three decades ago. The same phenomenon is occurring one and two levels down, with estimates that around 41 percent of those selected are external. Our interviews with executives involved in the selection process uncovered a definite bias: they said that when they were open to considering both internal and external candidates, they chose an external candidate 75 percent of the time.

Yet those same selectors estimated that the failure rate for external hires was substantially higher than for internal hires—35 percent compared with 24 percent. And if those selected performed poorly on the job, the external executives were more than twice as likely to be fired as internal executives, who tended to be demoted or otherwise shunted aside.

This predilection for external candidates by otherwise astute and experienced leaders, who know exactly what is at stake for their organizations, seems to fly in the face of logic. But we believe there are three related explanations for this paradox:

- Organizations hire outsiders for different reasons than they hire insiders.
- The selection processes for internal and external candidates differ, with the result that the external candidates appear more favorable to those making the ultimate decision.
- Once on the job, those brought in from the outside are treated no differently than internal hires are. They are, however, evaluated differently.

So there appear to be a *selection gap* and an *evaluation gap* in the process and aftermath of hiring top leaders. A closer look at the three explanations might help those who make the hiring decisions close those gaps and increase their success rate.

Separate Sets of Reasons

Organizations approach the hiring of top leaders with certain broad goals. Not surprisingly, when a company defines a job as a developmental challenge for whomever it selects, it generally settles on an executive from within the organization. Perhaps more unexpectedly, when a company is looking for a leader who can create a new or different vision, it also tends to select an internal candidate. This runs counter to today's conventional wisdom that insiders lack the perspective needed to change an organization. But selectors apparently believe that only a candidate with an extensive background in the company and insight into its history, culture, and products can create a realistic and attainable vision for it.

However, when an organization wants to introduce new technology, start a new business, or develop its workforce in general, it more often turns to an outside candidate. These situations represent fundamental changes for organizations, changes that present demands different from those the organizations would face if they remained the same or embarked on incremental change. So selectors lean toward outside candidates, believing that only they can bring the fresh perspective, new skills and knowledge, and objectivity needed to achieve these goals.

But making fundamental changes in an organization is a tough challenge, particularly for outsiders, who are not familiar with the established way of doing things and do not have a support network of relationships in place. This could largely account for the fact that outside hires are far less likely to succeed than are internal hires.

Unequal Selection Processes

In addition to considering differing organizational needs in hiring internal and external executives, selectors receive information from different sources when evaluating the two kinds of candidates, resulting in divergent selection processes. Although some of the same tools—interviews, résumés, and references—are used for both types of candidates, selection committees rely more heavily on these tools in evaluating outside candidates. They are also more likely to use search firms to cull information on external candidates, whereas in considering internal candidates they tend to lean more heavily on performance appraisals, succession plans, and feedback from subordinates.

Because external candidates can more easily control the information provided on résumés and in interviews—and even, to a large extent, that obtained through search firms and references—this information is not only less extensive than that gathered on internal candidates but is also biased toward the positive. The information collected on inside candidates is more balanced in depicting strengths and development needs.

Additionally, we found that selectors rely on three main categories of information in looking at candidates, and that the reasons for selecting internal or external candidates differ within each category. We divided the types of information into hard-side characteristics, soft-side characteristics, and fit.

- *Hard-side characteristics.* Companies more often choose external candidates on the basis of business or technical expertise that they believe will match their particular needs. Internal executives are more often selected because they have successful track records in the organization or for their own development.

- *Soft-side characteristics.* When a selection committee puts a premium on interpersonal skills, it is more likely to go with an external candidate, often because the internal candidates have demonstrated a lack of such skills. Again, internal candidates tend to be chosen because they are known quantities who have shown enough merit to qualify for further development.

- *Fit.* External candidates are more often selected because they are perceived to be a good fit with the organization's culture or because other candidates in the pool are not considered a good fit. Internal candidates are chosen because, even though they might not be seen as a perfect fit with the organization's culture, they are known to the selectors and deemed worthy of development.

Relying on separate sources and types of information can result in flawed decisions and unsuccessful hires. Because of the tendency to make direct comparisons of information obtained on external candidates with that obtained on internal candidates, selectors often conclude that the external candidates look more positive. One selector we interviewed told us: "The internal candidate was excluded on the basis of weak leadership skills. But externals were not assessed on leadership skills." Another executive said: "I am aware that people tend to rate external candidates less candidly than internal ones. With internal candidates, you can talk with people who have worked with the candidate and you will receive an honest evaluation."

Different Grading Systems

Our research found that once a hiring decision has been made, the divergent paths of internal and external executives coalesce on at least one front: the way they are managed. In general, neither type of executive is supported in any special way once in the new position, and executives hired from outside the organization do not receive any more support from their superiors than do internal hires. Interestingly, even though internal candidates are often selected to give them an opportunity to develop, once hired they are just as unlikely as external executives to be purposely given on- or off-the-job assistance in development.

The similar ways in which internal and external hires are treated does not carry over to how they are judged. During the first five months in a position, external hires are less likely than internal hires to be measured on organizational results. They are, however, likely to be evaluated more harshly on their individual performance, and these judgments often are made almost immediately after they take their position.

Even though interpersonal skills are frequently one of the criteria on which external executives are selected, once on the job they often are seen as having problems with their peers. This is hardly surprising. External executives are expected to enter the organization with the expertise and skills to immediately solve problems and effect the changes they were hired to make, and yet also to get along with peers who might have been passed over for the position. So by fulfilling their performance mandate, external executives may at the same time harm their relationships with other executives.

In sum, external executives are initially seen as assets with few weaknesses and little need for development. They are expected to be perfect and are punished for not being so. Internal hires are treated as potential assets to be nurtured. They are seen as being in need of development, so their performance is not expected to be perfect.

What Can Be Done?

We believe that selectors use two different paradigms when selecting internal versus external candidates. Internal executives are selected when the organization perceives that it is in a steady state. The candidates are seen through a developmental paradigm as an asset to be nurtured and developed. In contrast, external candidates are hired when the organization is changing or believes it is missing something. They are seen through a selection paradigm as assets acquired fully equipped and ready to solve the organization's problems. These paradigms largely account for the growing preference for outside candidates and their disappointing success rate. The opposing paradigms are thus a liability, but there are a number of steps that organizations can take to close the selection and evaluation gaps and improve the chances of executive success— regardless of the type of hire.

Combine the developmental and selection paradigms. Assess what the candidates can do for the organization and what the organization must do to support and develop the selected candidate. Do both whether the candidate is internal or external.

Don't overestimate the capabilities of external candidates. By the same token, don't underestimate the capabilities of internal candidates. Keep in mind that you may see only the "beauty marks" of the external candidates while you see both the "beauty marks" and the "warts" of the internal candidates. Realize that the information available to assess internal candidates is probably more extensive and paints a more realistic picture than that available for external candidates. Acknowledge that external executives, not just internal executives, have development needs.

Use the same sources of information for all candidates. For example, if you use a search firm to find external candidates, also use it to evaluate potential internal candidates. At Maytag Corp., selectors treat internal and external candidates for leadership positions equally. Both types of candidates are put through the same external assessment process, and selectors even wait to interview internal candidates until the external candidates arrive for their interviews.

Clarify what constitutes a good fit. Develop a precise understanding of what an executive, whether internal or external, needs to be a good fit—with an organization's culture and its values and with his or her boss.

Give new executives a breaking-in period. They need time to learn the new job, get acquainted with a new role, meet their new associates, and generally get comfortable. This is especially true of outside hires, who are often brought in to make changes and must also learn a new organizational culture and develop relationships with new people.

Don't develop a hiring strategy that favors either internal or external candidates. Hiring mainly from the inside may limit the fresh ideas and perspectives an organization needs to adapt and thrive. Giving preference to outside candidates reduces opportunities for internal executives and saps their commitment to the organization.

Conclusion

Factors such as economic globalization and the information technology explosion have placed many organizations today in a constant state of change. So it's only natural that executive selectors are more likely to look to the outside for candidates with the experience, skills, knowledge, and other credentials that may be missing from the organization and are needed to keep the organization evolving and on the cutting edge. But the expectations for external executives once on the job often turn out to be a fatal onus. Internal candidates, in contrast, are more often chosen when the organization believes it will do just fine under the status quo and with an executive who can be given the time and room to develop.

We suggest that combining selection and development into one paradigm in the selection process would substantially improve the success rate of newly hired leaders. The bottom line is that executives should not be selected unless they bring the necessary strengths to the position. Yet all executives, internal or external, need to be developed in some areas to be successful.

Suggested Reading

Sessa, V. I., Kaiser, R., Taylor, J. K., and Campbell, R. J. *Executive Selection: A Research Report on What Works and What Doesn't.* Greensboro, N.C.: Center for Creative Leadership, 1998.

Sessa, V. I., and Taylor, J. J. "Choosing Leaders: A Team Approach for Executive Selection." *Leadership in Action,* 1999, 19(2), 1–6.

Sessa, V. I., and Taylor, J. J. *Executive Selection: Strategies for Success.* San Francisco: Jossey-Bass, 2000.

◆   ◆   ◆

Finding Success at Succession

David Berke

In recent years, succession planning—which aims to ensure continuity in key leadership and management functions—has become increasingly important for organizations. There are many reasons for this, but perhaps the most obvious is demographics. The oldest of the baby boomers are getting close to retirement, and the group following the boomers, Generation X, is not large enough to replace them.

Demographics, however, is not the only reason why organizations and their leaders should pay attention to succession.

Turnover at the CEO level has grown substantially. According to *strategy+business* magazine, CEO turnover at major corporations increased by 53 percent between 1995 and 2001. And when a CEO leaves, it is not unusual to see change occur at the next levels of the organization.

Mergers and downsizing in the 1990s stripped out middle-manager positions—traditionally the place where future executives were identified and developed skills, company knowledge, and contacts. And finally, the emphasis on growth in the 1990s may have led companies to focus on hiring from the outside rather than on developing people they already employed to ensure a sufficient pool of candidates.

There is no one best succession planning approach; too much depends on the specifics of a company, its culture, and its business situation. Let's examine two common approaches to succession planning and the lessons that can be drawn from each.

Follow the Leader

A common response to the need for succession planning is to find a successful program and copy it. The system that Jack Welch used at General Electric is very popular—and with good reason. But

copying it is a poor idea unless your company has a corporate culture, resources, and support systems that are very similar to GE's,
not to mention a CEO who is willing to dedicate the time and attention to succession planning that Welch apparently did.

A succession planning system must be built to fit the organization in which it will operate. It should reflect corporate elements
that are highly specific to the organization, such as strategy and
culture.

Different strategies require managers and executives to have
different skill sets. One thing is clear, however: to devise an effective succession planning system, leaders must know where the company is going—or at the very least its likely direction as described
in the strategic plan—and what types of resources it has. The greater
the uncertainty in the environment, the greater the argument for
developing a diverse talent pool, one that can meet both antici-
pated and unanticipated needs.

As for culture, although it has many elements, there are three
that are the most important for succession planning:

- The extent to which the CEO is willing to own the outcomes
  of the succession planning process.
- The organizational philosophy of development and the extent to which development is supported with resources, both
  of money and people.
- The viability of the performance management system, which
  can provide useful data for managing development and
  movement.

Other questions that must be answered within the context of
the organization concern the goals of the desired system and the
status of systems to support implementation. In the end it is better
to identify a few key goals and successfully implement them than
to attempt to adopt some other company's approach in toto.

Stick with Tradition

Many companies already have succession planning systems. It is likely that the core of most of these systems is a process of identifying potential or probable replacements for specific positions. This is called *replacement planning*.

It's certainly important to have an idea of who may be ready and able to move into a position if it becomes vacant—particularly at senior levels or in functions that have strategic significance. However, building a succession plan around the identification of potential replacements has critical limitations—especially if this is the sole or primary activity a company engages in while preparing for succession.

A replacement planning approach typically has the following steps:

- The top executive assigns the human resource department to ask executives and line managers to identify high-potential people who could replace them in perhaps three to five years.
- HR meets with line managers and executives to discuss their selections and to gather data so that appropriate documentation, such as succession charts, can be completed.
- HR prepares one or more books of information on possible replacements.
- HR subsequently meets annually or at some other regular interval with managers from various levels of the organization to update succession charts and discuss the replacement candidates who have been identified, how they are doing, how close to being ready they are, and so on. Performance appraisal data may be referenced. All this information is kept up to date in a database.
- Material is prepared for a review meeting with top management. Talking points related to potential candidates are identified.

This may seem like a solid approach, and it is in fact a solid *administrative* approach to producing reports for a high-visibility meeting. Whether it serves the goal of ensuring continuity is another question, however.

Here's why: this system is built around preparing for an event rather than focusing on an ongoing process. This means that unless extreme care is taken, the system is more likely to drive preparation of reports than preparation of people for succession. And if the process is to be ongoing, review meetings need to be held more often.

Because this approach focuses on replacement of an incumbent in a current position, it assumes, first, that those naming replacements will be able to predict who can best meet the organization's future business needs. It also assumes that the organization's current structure and strategy will continue indefinitely.

Taking the second point first, this may have been a safe assumption in more stable times, but it certainly isn't now. As for the first assumption, it is entirely possible to name likely replacements at the lower levels of specific organizational functions, but this approach falters at higher organizational levels, particularly the corporate level. Additionally, this approach can raise questions about the role of diversity—in skills and abilities as well as race and gender—in the company's succession planning process.

The manager of the possible successor simply has a responsibility to report on how or whether someone is developing. If the manager knows what to pay attention to and does so, the discussions between HR and the manager can be helpful and informative for the HR person who is gathering the information. The discussions can be even more useful for the CEO to hear if he or she is taking an active role in the succession planning process.

Finally, in what is essentially an administrative process, HR can become the process owner—and it often does by default. Administrative processes are often perceived as busywork; facilitating development is not something that most executives or line managers want to do or know how to do. It takes them away from what they and their organizations see as their primary job.

Nevertheless, both research and experience suggest that a succession planning process will not produce the desired results unless the CEO and executive team visibly and actively engage in the process and take responsibility for its outcomes. If a company's top team follows the steps described earlier, the CEO is likely to become aware of only a small subset of the people who should rightfully be considered as having high potential for key executive positions, even if the CEO is actively engaged in the annual review meeting.

Take It from Here

What should a company do about succession planning? Here are some general recommendations:

- Make sure the succession planning process fits the organization. There's nothing wrong with studying successful efforts and identifying specific elements that could be adapted and implemented. The danger comes when an entire approach is mandated without weighing what will and will not work in a particular company culture.

- Ensure that roles are clear. HR should act as the facilitator of the succession planning process; the CEO and executive team should own the outcomes. In part this means that the CEO must accept that he or she cannot delegate this role without jeopardizing the success of the process.

- Make development a key element of the process. Focus on developing talent pools instead of just identifying and reporting on possible replacements. Talent pools should contain the diversity necessary to meet unexpected business challenges. If resources are available, broaden the development process.

- Continue to gather and maintain relevant data, but consciously examine and decide what data are relevant and develop systems to provide that data.

- Finally, realize that implementing a succession planning process with development at its core can be a significant change for the entire organization, including HR. It will require time, good planning, regular follow-up, and ongoing support from the top.

Chapter Eight

The Leadership Context Is Diversity

The ranks of management are changing. They are getting younger; more varied in terms of gender, race, and ethnicity; and harder to get a fix on with respect to attitudes about what organizations and leaders should be. Whether you are a member of one of the new groups coming into management or a member of the traditional white-male group, the challenges you face in dealing with increased diversity are significant. This chapter will help you gain a better understanding of how to act in this dynamic situation for the benefit of yourself and your organization.

◆ ◆ ◆

Telling the Untold Story:
A Conversation with Stella M. Nkomo

Stephen Rush

Stella M. Nkomo is a professor at the University of South Africa Graduate School of Business Leadership and a member of CCL's Board of Governors. Her book, from the Harvard Business School Press and cowritten with Ella L. J. Edmonson Bell, an associate professor at the Dartmouth College Tuck School of Business, is *Our Separate Ways: Black and White Women and the Struggle for Professional Identity*. Based on years of research, the book looks at how the combined effects of race and gender create for black and white women not only far different organizational identities and career experiences but also very disparate paths to the corporate world.

I recently talked with Nkomo about her latest work and what it means for leaders. Here are some excerpts from the interview.

SR: I thought we could start by talking about the research on which the book is based, and what led you and Ella Bell to engage in the research.

SN: As professors in business schools, Ella and I had an interest in women in management. As we looked at the literature on that subject, it was obvious that the books and research did not speak to the experiences of African American women. We wondered what it is like for black women in corporate America—how race and gender affect their experiences. There was some literature on black managers, but most of it looked at men. So we felt that black women managers as a group were falling between the cracks. Their stories were not being picked up.

We wanted to find out what was happening to those women—how they got into corporate America, where they were, and what their experiences were. Ella and I had never met each other, but people who knew both of us knew of our common interest and put us in touch with each other. After we finally met, we wrote a research proposal and won a research grant competition sponsored by the Rockefeller Foundation.

We wanted to look particularly at the first big cohort of women—both black and white—who entered corporate America, in the 1970s. The Civil Rights Act of 1964 helped bring a lot of women into management, but it didn't really have a big impact until the seventies. So we wanted to track these pioneering women, and we decided that to make apparent what was different for black women, we needed to compare their experiences to those of white women. When you put two things side by side, you get a better sense of how they are similar and different.

SR: Tell me a little about the details of the research, which was very extensive and was conducted over a period of eight years.

SN: We wanted it to be the definitive telling of the story, so we did a two-part process.

One part was what we called *life history interviews*, because we had found that previous management literature about women always talked only about their careers, never about their early childhood. We wanted to know the whole story of every woman in our study, so we did 120 interviews—averaging about eight hours apiece—in which we got each woman's entire life story. The interviews also were done in two parts, with the first half dealing with early life up until about college, and the second half going from that point until current career history.

The second part of the process was a survey. We sent out surveys to about 1,200 women who had graduated from business schools in the seventies and early eighties, and we ended up with 825 completed surveys. So we had both qualitative and quantitative data.

The interview data were very rich. The first question we asked was, "Tell me about where you grew up." So we took the women way back—we were looking for formative experiences, significant life events that would offer clues about why these women ended up in what at the time was a very nontraditional career for women. It sounds strange today because women now make up 48 percent of management, but in the seventies and eighties it was a new thing to have women as managers.

We wanted to know who these women were, what shaped them, where they grew up, their educations, and the influence of their parents. Essentially what we ended up with is 120 biographies. It took about two years to do the interviews—some of the interviews are a hundred pages—and then a lot of time to get everything transcribed and to interpret all the data.

SR: Once you had all these data, I imagine your big challenge was to distill them and present them in a way that wouldn't be overwhelming because of their sheer magnitude and that people could really connect with.

SN: After we had all the data and started making sense of our findings, the problem we faced was how to tell the story to other people. We knew we could have done a very typical kind of analytical, numbers-based research report. But we decided that once we understood the themes, we would look for the women who best epitomized the themes and who had poignant stories that would illustrate the major themes. So we focused on seven black women and seven white women, and we juxtaposed their stories throughout the book.

In that way the women became our main characters. When you read about somebody else's life story, you can't help but think about your own story—so this approach draws people in and adds richness to what we found. Quantitative data are good, but when you see a figure of 60 percent it doesn't give you a sense of the emotion. The women were generous and very candid, and we feel we heard authentic things from them.

SR: Was there anything that emerged from the research that really surprised you?

SN: I think the thing that surprised me most was how deeply the women's early life experiences and the early messages they got about being female or being female and black stayed with them. A lot of the significant events in their early childhoods had a profound effect on the way they made sense of the world later on.

For one of the women, her father telling her early on that she could be anything she wanted became her anthem for the rest of her life and got her through a lot of tough times. Another woman learned from her parents that as a black woman she would face discrimination but that she shouldn't let it paralyze her. That stayed with her.

I was struck by the extent to which the things that happen to us early in our lives echo in our heads and stay with us. Those early experiences are a major determinant of our basic self-concept and self-esteem.

Another thing that struck me was that all of these women, regardless of their background, were incredibly smart and talented. They had all been excellent students and shown leadership abilities in school. Often I would get angry when I was talking to a woman and thinking that with her intelligence and all she had accomplished, she should be CEO by now—but she wasn't.

The amount of resolve was a common denominator among the black and white women. One of the things that made these women successful was their perseverance. They showed a great deal of fortitude and professional will in always getting up and tackling the next obstacle and dealing with the challenges of breaking into a field where they were an anomaly at the time.

SR: You looked at both the differences and the similarities in the paths that black and white women follow to managerial success and in their experiences along the way. What differences did you find?

SN: One thing that was interesting was that as young girls, the majority of the white women were not prepared by their families or by their social lives for the fact that they would run into sex discrimination. For the most part they were given a gender-neutral message. In their interviews, many of the white women said they were upset that no one had prepared them for gender discrimination. Many of them didn't encounter discrimination until they got to college or the corporate world. But the black women were clearly armored against *racial* discrimination. Their parents prepared them to face such discrimination but told them not to let it stop them.

Another difference was the way that black and white women behaved once they got into the corporate world. The white women, because of this gender-neutral message and also basically because of white privilege, took the attitude that *I will be accepted; eventually I will be accepted. Because I have to belong here. I don't think it's a problem. So let me do what they tell me to do, let me work really hard, and I'll be OK.* The black women were much more skeptical about ever being truly accepted for who they were and about racism and sexism going away. Black women are much more guarded in their interactions with corporate America because they have never been fully accepted.

We also found that the black women were much more likely to speak out against injustice and push for change. The white women were more like, *Look, I know bad things are going on here, but I need to do my job and work hard and I'll be OK.* So there was a different reading of the environment and how they would behave in that environment. The black women talked about a *concrete wall* as opposed to a *glass ceiling*, because they were dealing with not only sexism but also racism. And the racism was almost a daily occurrence.

Another thing we found was that for the black women, their identity and pride as black women and the way they thought about their culture were sources of strength for them. They wanted to be recognized and accepted for who they were because it was a source of pride for them.

The big difference was the intersection of race with gender, which created disparate experiences that have a lot to do with the relative position of each woman to white men. The black women were different from white men in terms of not only gender but race. It wasn't easy for either group to be successful in the corporate world; they just took different approaches and had different experiences.

SR: What did you find about the role that race plays in professional relationships between black and white women managers?

SN: This is the part that caused us a lot of pain; we were asking ourselves, *Should we write about this?* At the time these women were growing up, especially in the South, there was still segregation. Most of these women did not have any interaction with women of a different race. For many of them, the first time they encountered one another on a close basis was in the corporate world. And we found that each group stereotyped the other with some of the oldest, most damaging stereotypes of women.

For example, some black women referred to white women as sellouts who were putting their lot in with white men or were always flirting with white men to get ahead. Some of the white women saw the black women as militants with chips on their shoulders, who wanted to advance but didn't want to work hard to do so, relying instead on affirmative action. So in our research, at least, the idea that women unite and bond and are empathetic with one another was not the case. And I understand why. The fact is that the corporate world would allow only a few women to be successful, and the women understood they were in competition for the few jobs available.

So the black and white women had a lot of mistrust of each other, in equal amounts—call it a mutual inability to comprehend each other. In the last chapter of the book we talk about how black and white women need to be authentic with one another and really listen to one another's stories. Both groups are dealing with difficult situations, and it shouldn't be about who is worse off or better off—women just need to come together.

The uneasy relationship between black and white women has been going on for a long time. It's a delicate, sensitive issue, but Ella and I decided to include it in the book in the hope that it would help women begin a dialogue. And we also hope that white men who read the book will realize the kinds of things they do that end up pitting women against each other.

SR: As leaders strive to improve diversity in the workplace and the situation for women managers, what lessons can they draw from your research and book?

SN: The first thing is that leaders need to recognize that there is diversity among women, that not all women managers have the same issues. If leaders are setting up programs for women managers, they need to pay attention to how the issues might be slightly different for women of color. And the way to find that out is to ask. Ask the women: "If we do this program, will it address your needs? How will it impact you?"

The second thing is that although mentoring is great, women—especially black women—want and need sponsorship. They need someone who is willing to champion them and to resolutely say, "This black woman has the skills and is ready for the next position." Black women feel that when leaders are thinking and talking with one another about promotions, especially to the higher levels such as senior vice president, the black woman is the last person on their minds. What many leaders and companies do with affirmative action is that when they think of a woman, they usually think of a white woman, and when they think of a man, it's probably a black man. And the black woman remains invisible.

The last thing is that leaders should encourage black and white women to network. Looking at the large numbers of white women currently in middle management, I have no doubt that ten years from now there will be many women in senior management positions. White women are going to be the next group that will have to know how to manage diversity. And given that white women now tend to have poor relationships with women of color, companies need to start taking action to ensure that women have the ability to network with one another and to learn to work together.

◆ ◆ ◆

X Marks the Spot:
Developing and Retaining Emerging Leaders

David Baldwin and Stephanie Trovas

In an increasingly competitive, global, and technology-driven marketplace, leaders must keep a constant vigil over the management ranks in their organizations. The ability to recruit, train, develop, and retain people for top leadership positions is essential if organizations are to succeed—or even survive—in such an environment. A big part of this challenge involves people who are members of the group commonly known as Generation X—defined here as people born between 1964 and 1978. A segment of this generation—rising managers and professionals who are under thirty-five years old, that is, emerging leaders—is being studied through a CCL research project.

There are, of course, members of Generation X who have already emerged as leaders. Some are moving into middle management and others are up-and-coming vice presidents of major multinational corporations, already in crucial positions and playing a major role in deciding strategic direction. A number of Gen-Xers have started high-tech companies. In fact, according to the *Los Angeles Times*, approximately 70 percent of current start-up businesses in the United States were founded by people under thirty-six. And in some corporations, Gen-Xers are being promoted above older colleagues.

The focus of this article, however, is on people who are just beginning to take on significant leadership and management roles. Researchers, management experts, and leaders of organizations have all been devoting a lot of effort to understanding how to prepare these emerging leaders, how to work most effectively with them, and how to make the best use of their distinctive skills and talents. Three considerations are important when trying to gain insight into emerging leaders:

- There are fewer managers to choose from and develop in this age group than there were in the preceding generation.
- Evolving employment patterns have affected this generation's attitudes toward employers.
- The newest generation of managers views authority differently than previous generations did, and this has a notable impact on emerging leaders' attitudes toward leadership.

A Smaller Pool

One of the unique challenges of working with emerging leaders is demographic. To put it simply, there are too few of them. In the past, organizations usually had a sizable pool of adequately trained people to draw on for managerial and leadership positions, but now the number of workers with the skills needed to take on the critical leadership challenges companies face is smaller. This is partly a result of the robust U.S. economy during the latter half of the 1990s, which provided more work and pulled more people into the workplace but didn't necessarily make workers more competent or better trained. Basic demography also plays a part: there are simply fewer people in Generation X than there are in the Baby Boom generation—those born between 1946 and 1963. The meteoric rise of the technology industry during the 1990s is another factor. That industry has created new places for younger workers, spreading the workers who are qualified or have potential for leadership positions across old-economy and new-economy companies and so reducing the number available to either.

The consequence is that established leaders must take even more care to make sure that emerging leaders are developed—even though changing work patterns and worker attitudes make this task more challenging than in the past.

Changing the Contract

Since the 1970s, employment patterns have been undergoing fundamental changes. For instance, the implicit understanding that employers and employees have about their relationship—sometimes referred to as the *psychological work contract*—has changed. Employees no longer expect to stay with one company for their entire careers; in fact, emerging leaders have little expectation of remaining with the same company for even ten years. Estimates of the number of organizations that members of Generation X will work for by the time they reach age sixty-five vary from six to ten. Hanging onto emerging leaders for the long term has thus become a serious concern for many organizations.

This change in the psychological work contract has been cited by some people who look askance at Gen-Xers. However, this change has come about not just because of Generation X but because of other generations as well. So even though it's been suggested that Gen-Xers are not willing to pay their dues as previous generations did, the reality is that many emerging leaders, a good number of whom saw their parents suffer through downsizings, simply don't trust an organization to be there for them in the long term. And emerging leaders tend to believe that people should be promoted, compensated, and given responsibility based on how competent they are rather than on how long they have been in the workforce or with a single company.

Another change in employment patterns has been a shift away from the traditional hierarchy. In the past it was generally accepted that younger people would report to older people, but now it is becoming more common for younger people to be promoted over their elders. In some industries and competitive environments—the Internet marketplace, for example—the general perception is that younger employees have some skills and abilities that older workers don't. This not only creates generational conflict but also raises the possibility that some emerging leaders are being thrust into positions before they have had the opportunity to develop the necessary management and leadership skills.

Earned Esteem

Past generations tended to at least acknowledge if not always acquiesce to positional authority, but many if not most emerging leaders do not accord people respect just for their rank. Gen-Xers frequently don't acknowledge authority or assume that it arises from position. Their prevailing view of authority can be summed up as, "Don't listen to leaders until they prove they can actually do the work themselves." If managers can't demonstrate that they can accomplish work themselves in addition to getting others to do it, Gen-Xers are unlikely to grant them the same degree of authority as previous generations did. Gen-Xers expect managers to earn their stripes and don't give much weight to superior position or long experience.

That attitude about authority is frequently taken as an indication of disrespect for elders in general and bosses in particular. However, Gen-Xers' viewpoint may be more aptly described as skepticism—bosses need to prove that they are still capable. This skepticism may arise from the fact that emerging leaders came of age with few heroes or leaders they could claim as their own—scandals, for example, removed a number of potential political heroes. It may also be a result of Gen-Xers' being raised in a period of heightened consumer marketing, which may have succeeded primarily in making them suspicious of anything that smacks of hype—perhaps including overblown war stories about being "self-made" told by leaders of the organizations in which they work.

This skeptical view may also be rooted in the limited experience that emerging leaders have in the workplace. In their organizations, managers from a previous generation may have proved their technical expertise years before the emerging leaders came on board. As the older workers shifted from technical to managerial positions, they developed leadership skills that complemented but were different from the technical skills that carried them through the earlier stages of their careers. Newer workers don't see those technical skills and may assume they don't exist, which reinforces their doubts about managerial authority. Alternatively, technological changes may have, at least in the view of emerging leaders, outpaced the older managers' technical skills.

What They Want

Examining emerging leaders' core values and preferences about leadership reveals how they may prefer to behave as leaders and how they want their bosses to act. Emerging leaders prefer a hands-off approach in leading others and in being led, with an emphasis on delegation. Additionally, they prefer honest and direct communication and feedback, an openness to changing directions quickly, pragmatism, a career path or development plan, and a relaxed, casual work environment.

Emerging leaders do respect authenticity and the ability to get things done, so a good approach when working with them—an approach that will lend itself to achieving good results—is to focus on tactics that communicate authenticity and sincerity. Managers of emerging leaders may also find it effective to act as mentors and develop personal relationships with them to understand what motivates them as individuals. Although more research needs to be done, it appears that this relationship approach to developing emerging leaders may be critical to helping them.

Emerging leaders' attitudes toward leadership and authority are influenced by the times in which they came of age. The members of each generation are to some degree similarly affected by important events that occur during critical times in their lives and development. To understand today's emerging leaders, it is useful to take note of the important events that occurred as they grew up (see sidebar, "The Main Events").

These events seem to have influenced emerging leaders to behave in ways consistent with self-protection. The consequences of corporate downsizings and government scandals appear to be significant drivers of their behavior. Moreover, emerging leaders tend to want to establish themselves in their careers and to build their résumés before committing to having a family. One piece of evidence is that this generation is marrying later than previous generations. According to *The New York Times Almanac* for 2001, in 1998, the median age at which men first married was twenty-seven, and for women, twenty-five. In 1960, men married at a median age of twenty-three and women at a median of twenty.

It's also useful to consider the social trends during the years in which Gen-Xers grew up. Divorce rates skyrocketed, and children's quality time with their parents diminished. Gen-Xers were immersed in technology, which advanced by leaps and bounds and whose influence burgeoned.

All of these factors influenced perceptions, values, and beliefs about the world in general and leadership specifically. They predisposed emerging leaders to have less certainty, trust, and loyalty than previous generations did.

To understand emerging leaders—and to develop and retain them—it's also helpful to know their defining characteristics and what they expect from the workplace. Research by CCL and others has identified some of these characteristics and expectations, and although they can exist for individuals from any generation, they are more pronounced in emerging leaders.

Characteristics. Emerging leaders tend to be technologically savvy, independent, and skeptical of institutions and hierarchy. They are entrepreneurial risk takers who think globally, learn experientially, and embrace change. They are efficient and focused on outcomes, open to and appreciative of differences, and socially responsible.

The Main Events

A number of historical events over the past three and a half decades—some of general social importance and some arising from the technological revolution—have had significant impacts on the lives and worldviews of today's emerging leaders.

General

1968	Martin Luther King Jr. assassinated
1969	Men land on the moon
1973	Watergate scandal begins
1973	Roe versus Wade abortion decision
1975	Vietnam War ends
1976	Energy crisis
1979	Iran hostage crisis
1981	Centers for Disease Control's first published report on AIDS
1981	Reagan assassination attempt
1984	Ozone depletion detected

Workplace expectations. Emerging leaders tend to prefer direct communication and informality. They value freedom, flexibility, and a sense of community. Work-life balance is important to them—quality of life takes precedence over money. They want continuous and immediate feedback, an individually customized development plan, and a genuine relationship with a mentor or coach. They want their work to be meaningful and challenging, and they expect their rewards to be immediate.

Free Agents

Some if not most emerging leaders have agendas to build their skills and résumés, with the aim of giving themselves a sense of job secu-

1984	Extensive corporate downsizing begins
1986	Space shuttle disaster
1986	Chernobyl disaster
1989	Berlin Wall falls
1990	Persian Gulf War
1991	USSR dissolves

Technological

1971	Intel's first chip developed
1972	First e-mail management program
1974	Videocassette recorder introduced to the consumer market
1975	Microsoft founded
1975	Personal computer introduced on the consumer market
1979	First commercial cellular telephone system
1980	CNN begins 24-hour broadcasting
1981	MTV launched
1983	Compact discs mass-marketed
1991	World Wide Web launched

rity beyond their current organizations. They appear to be more committed to the vocation than to the organization. The free-agency concept popularized in professional sports is an apt metaphor for the attitude emerging leaders carry into the workplace: they will stay with an organization as long as it's the best offer on the table. Savvy companies that are aware of this agenda, such as Intel and Nike, are providing opportunities for their emerging leaders to leave the organization, acquire skills elsewhere, then be rehired in a new capacity.

Why should organizations invest in the development of emerging leaders who are liable to job-hop to the next opportunity available?

First, organizations need to accept that they will not be able to keep all of their emerging leaders. Second, organizations that are aware of the needs of emerging leaders and are willing to take the time to build a trusting relationship, which includes providing challenging opportunities for growth, may well be able to reap the benefits of extended employment and commitment. For example, at Bank of America, newly hired emerging leaders are offered a one-year investment program similar to an extended graduate school program. They are provided a mentor, they work on projects involving real-world problems and present their solutions to upper management, and they receive feedback on their work from their peers and their boss. The program is aimed at fostering the emerging leaders' trust in the company by making them feel they are part of a community of peers and the organization is investing in their future. The long-term success of this development and retention strategy remains to be confirmed by experience. But one thing is certain: when investment and challenge end, emerging leaders begin to look elsewhere.

Understanding how emerging leaders view trust in an organizational system can be complicated. Some emerging leaders have suggested that they give and receive trust in exchange for the freedom to accomplish work on their terms. As one emerging leader said:

> More freedom gets people to do things. Organizations must be grounded in choice. I want to feel empowered. I want my organization to assume that people do want to work hard. I don't want to be micromanaged. They need to realize that if they give you freedom, they'll keep you. Tapping into the people—empowering and motivating versus power, authority, control, and position—[is what is important].

Although emerging leaders want independence in accomplishing their work, they appear to also want a sense of community, of belonging to a group of people who are as committed as they are. At times the need for independence and the need for community can collide and result in personal tension for emerging leaders, and this is a phenomenon that merits further attention in devising effective leadership development for emerging leaders.

Emerging leaders want authentic relationships with their mentors and other co-workers. They want to be appreciated for what they do rather than be told they are too young or don't have enough experience. Consider these two comments:

> I want to be mentored by and to mentor the older generation, too. We learn together. I would like the older generation to be open to being taught. I can learn from them; I want to know why they think they don't have anything to learn from us.

> I need an organization that is patient and understanding as I ask lots of questions. I feel inexperienced and know that I'll make some mistakes. It helps if people are open to listening and sharing experiences.

Emerging leaders also have a thirst for feedback—both receiving it and giving it. They want to know when they are doing well and when they're not—and they prefer to know immediately rather than through a yearly performance review.

The current economic climate and vying for top talent have made retention an increasingly critical human resource issue. Organizations can adopt a number of tactics to retain Generation X employees in general and emerging leaders in particular. Most of these tactics involve nonmonetary reward systems such as vacation time, employee control over schedules, developmental opportunities, positive reinforcement and acknowledgment from people whom younger workers respect, coaching, and mentoring. As one emerging leader put it:

> Organizations need to know how to reward without using money; money isn't the reward desired. We need to keep variety in our jobs. We need help in figuring out where we're going. We want job-pathing and development. We want expectations that we can understand.

Suggested Reading

Deal, J., Peterson, K., and Gailor-Loflin, H. *Emerging Leaders: An Annotated Bibliography.* Greensboro, N.C.: Center for Creative Leadership, 2001.

Holtz, G. T. *Welcome to the Jungle: The Why Behind Generation X.* New York: St. Martin's Press, 1995.

Howe, N., and Strauss, B. *13th Gen: Abort, Retry, Ignore, Fail?* New York: Random House, 1993.

Raines, C. *Beyond Generation X: A Practical Guide for Managers.* Menlo Park, Calif.: Crisp Learning, 1997.

Tulgan, B. *Managing Generation X.* New York: Norton, 2000.

Zemke, R., Raines, C., and Filipczak, B. *Generations at Work: Managing the Clash of Veterans, Boomers, Xers, and Nexters in Your Workplace.* New York: American Management Association, 2000.

Taking Action

It's not overstating things to say that the current and future effectiveness and success of organizations is in the hands of emerging leaders. Established leaders can take a number of specific steps to develop and retain emerging leaders:

- Listen to and follow their input on how they would like to be developed.
- Offer them control over their time and space.
- Provide short-term, performance-based rewards.
- Be available as a mentor.
- Provide the resources they need.
- Give timely and consistent feedback.
- Encourage a fun, relaxed environment.

- Offer choices of on-the-job training.
- Assess their motivation, and find out what kind of perks and benefits they want.
- Introduce entrepreneurial opportunities.
- Give them ownership of their work and responsibility for bottom-line results.

◆ ◆ ◆

Across the Divide: Grasping the Black Experience in Corporate America

Ancella B. Livers and Keith A. Caver

Blacks and whites work closely together every day in corporate America, successfully handling a range of difficult organizational tasks. Despite the high level of accomplishment, these interactions are often very frustrating for blacks in ways that their white colleagues are largely unaware of.

Whites too can be frustrated, sometimes confounded, by the way a seemingly innocuous interaction takes a wrong turn.

The result is that performance, both individual and organizational, is not as good as it could be. And given the serious problems faced by organizations today, anything less than a best effort can severely diminish an organization's chances of not only thriving but also surviving.

What can be done to achieve a best effort? First, it is crucial that whites understand how their black colleagues experience the corporate environment. To accomplish this, the parts of blacks' experience that are invisible to whites need to be made visible. Second, both whites and blacks must take action to improve communication and thereby understanding.

A Second Job

Over the years we have worked with more than one thousand African American professionals. They have told us time and again of their frustration with misunderstandings—often serious misinterpretations—of their behavior. This situation is like having a second job. Like other managers, these blacks have the job of setting direction, creating alignment, gaining commitment, and promoting adaptability. But they also have the job of dealing with the misunderstandings and the feelings that those misunderstandings cause.

This second job, which makes blacks' experience in the workplace distinct, has many parts. However, there are four that are fundamental.

Notes

The ideas in this article have been shaped by our personal and professional experience. As faculty members at CCL who regularly train corporate leaders, both black and white, we have had the opportunity to hear what hundreds of executives have to say about their work experiences.

To follow up on the ideas we heard in those conversations, we drew upon thirty-nine in-depth interviews conducted with African American executives by CCL researchers (in 1996 and 1997), surveyed approximately 270 African American professionals (in 1999 and 2000), and personally interviewed another 20 black professionals in depth.

In the course of this work we were struck by three things. First, we noted how similar the stories from black professionals were, regardless of the individuals' education, organization, job level, or geographic region. Second, we realized how closely their stories mirrored our own work experiences. And third, we were fascinated by the ways in which the experiences of black professionals differed from those of their nonblack—mostly white—colleagues.

Responsibility

"You don't forget where you came from. You have a moral obligation to bring somebody else along." When we heard this from a senior African American manager, we nodded in acknowledgment. Many African Americans feel that their professional responsibility is a mixture of work, personal duty, and racial obligation. In fact, more than 90 percent of the managers we surveyed said they felt obligated to help other African Americans in their organization. This arises from their respect for and feeling of accountability to those who came before them and struggled to get them and other blacks into corporate America. It includes a tacit agreement that they will, in turn, help those blacks who strive alongside them and those who follow them.

Furthermore, most leaders surveyed believe there is a link in the minds of their white colleagues between their job performance and that of other African Americans. Nearly 90 percent said that if they are successful in their jobs, other African Americans will be seen in a better light. About half also believe that their nonblack colleagues generalize the mistakes of one African American to others in the organization. A vice president of a major polling firm stated it this way: "If I fall and stumble, other African Americans are adversely affected. Senior managers are risk averse, and African Americans are still seen as being a risk."

In the workplace, what does taking responsibility mean for black managers? In addition to their normal responsibilities, black managers may be assigned by the organization or may pursue on their own such tasks as taking care of blacks and black issues. This may include mentoring other blacks and networking with or speaking up for newer or less well-known blacks in the company.

Many blacks take on these responsibilities because they believe it is the right thing to do and they feel the organization expects them to do it. As a result they may feel a constant, stress-inducing struggle between what they feel they owe one another and what they think is due the organization.

The concept of responsibility can be a burden in other ways as well. For instance, spending time helping other blacks can lead to concerns about the amount of time that a manager devotes to this activity. It also might be seen as covering for someone who is performing poorly. At the same time, not hewing to the organization's expectations that blacks will give extra time and attention to racial issues can be perceived by other managers as being uncooperative. For the black manager such expectations deny him or her a choice about the kinds of responsibilities that are seen as discretionary for others.

Gender

The issues of race and gender can be challenging when regarded separately; taken together they become even more complex. Women are not just women, for example, they are white women, black women, and Asian women. Each combination tends to evoke different connotations in the corporate setting and elicit a different reaction from others. And the same holds true for men.

This creates unique nuances for black managers. For instance, it adds to the stereotypes they must manage. In addition to the general stereotypes that men are independent and in control of their emotions, black male managers may also be seen as angry, intimidating, athletic, or sexually predatory. One self-described "big-framed" manager at a chemical company lamented that he has to pay special attention to his actions, behaviors, and mannerisms to avoid being viewed as intimidating.

For women the general stereotype is that they are supportive, cooperative, nurturing, less competent than men, and treated as sexual objects. Black women are also forced to deal with a set of perceptions beyond those. They are often considered aggressive and too direct, assertive, and flashy for corporate America. One woman told us that there are about fifteen other black professional women in her organization, all of whom have very different personalities and work styles, and yet at some point in their careers all of them have been told that they are too direct.

How do these factors play out for black managers? Gender, race, and the combination thereof can affect the degree to which an individual is given responsibilities and opportunities in the workplace. Areas in which inequalities appear include salary, access to important projects and people, promotions, and job responsibilities. What's particularly important to remember about the combination of race and gender, though, is that individuals have no control over these two characteristics, and each holds its own position in the hierarchy of status and influence.

There is also the issue of the gap between black men and black women. Census figures from 2000 suggest that there are about 800,000 more managerial and professional black women in the workforce than black men. The argument in the black community is over who is doing better or worse at work—black men or black women. One human resource director we spoke with said that black women in her organization have a more difficult time moving up, being visible, and getting opportunities than do black men. However, a senior manager in a large corporation told us, "I think the person that's on the bottom of the totem pole, as far as getting promoted, is the black male. I think the white female is next and then the black female is above that." Black men and women often interpret this tension as competition between them.

The stress arising from the combination of race and gender is just one more factor contributing to the overall pressure of existing in the business environment. A vice president of a manufacturing conglomerate said, "I would like to think that my performance plays a larger role than my race and gender. But I don't know that for a fact, and I don't think I will ever know."

Networking

Networking is often extolled as beneficial to an executive's career. Yet it can be difficult for blacks to network with whites because of a lack of trust. Black managers are not sure which whites they can trust in the workplace and therefore don't know whom to access.

Because of this lack of trust and the apparent inability of others to see or understand the black work experience, many black managers find it hard to develop anything more than perfunctory relationships with their white colleagues. Consequently these managers may feel the need to keep up their game face, rarely letting their true personas show through. (Because of this many whites think their relationships with blacks are stronger than they are.) Keeping up with this convoluted set of relationships can be enormously taxing for black managers who want to use corporate resources to advance their careers.

At the same time, networking with other blacks, although beneficial, can be problematical. A recent CCL study revealed that blacks who network with other blacks at high levels are seen as more effective leaders than those who don't. This is despite the fact that many blacks are directly and indirectly advised to avoid being regularly seen with other blacks.

Another factor is that despite the generally accepted value of networking, many blacks avoid it because they don't believe it is important for them. A vice president of a major bank told us that at first: "I just didn't get into it. Networking is not my culture." However, as her career progressed she came to acknowledge the importance of networking. The many difficulties African Americans face in the workplace are precisely what makes networking critically important for them. It can be a major aid to maneuvering around these obstacles while learning about opportunities, becoming aware of pitfalls, increasing visibility, and forging alliances.

To network or not to network, and the reasons why, are just two more pieces of the extra workload for black managers. And many African Americans don't want to network because they don't want to maintain their bicultural facade any longer than they have to. For many, being around whites is not relaxing—it's work.

Mentoring

"Should my mentor be black or white?" Black managers often ask themselves this question, and many African Americans who responded to our survey said they preferred a white mentor because he or she could open more doors in the organization. Others said they preferred a black mentor because he or she would know where they were coming from.

One operations director said he had had the opportunity to work with a black mentor but passed it up. He wanted somebody white, who had influence and power. The way the operations director saw it, he had black friends for support if he needed it. Conversely, a logistics manager told us that he sought out a black mentor so he could be shown the ropes by someone just like him.

The problem is that there are few African Americans available at the appropriate level in corporate America to be mentors. And because mentors tend to choose people with whom they can easily relate and most mentors are white, the question shifts to, "Can I get a mentor at all?" This is a question that most white leaders do not have to ask. The mentor pool is broad and available for them.

Despite this, once the mentoring relationship has been established, African Americans find it to be quite valuable. In an article in the April 2000 issue of *Harvard Business Review*, David Thomas, a professor of organizational behavior at the Harvard Business School, writes that minority executives in particular benefit from mentoring. He says that mentors give critical advice and counseling, open doors to challenging assignments, and appropriately confront those who unfairly criticize their protégés—particularly when such behavior seems racially motivated. However, Thomas also reports that cross-race relationships can have difficulty forming, developing, and maturing.

From the mentor's perspective, some blacks whose organizations ask them to be mentors just because they are black find themselves feeling vulnerable and, again, without a choice in the matter. Or they may struggle with multiple loyalties—to themselves, to other African Americans, or to their organizations. One black executive told us that he struggles with whether to tell younger African Americans some hard truths about racial issues in the company or to hide them so the employees will not look elsewhere for work.

Whether one is a mentor or being mentored, the "Should I or shouldn't I?" questions are one more extra burden for blacks in the workplace. The mental calculations alone are tiring and can use up time that these executives wish could be devoted to the work itself.

What Whites Can Do

Everyone, of course, has a stake in improving interactions across races. There are a number of communication-related activities that whites can do to help them see what they have been missing:

Keep issues in perspective. When talking to African Americans, it's important to appreciate the difference between individual concerns and matters of race. Be careful not to hold individual blacks responsible for national racial issues or assume that their personal perspective represents the perspective of their group. At some point almost every African American has been questioned by someone demanding an explanation for the behavior of Louis Farrakhan or Jesse Jackson. In a similar vein, it is important to understand that when a black person champions an issue it is not necessarily a black issue. Be careful not to arbitrarily introduce race as an element in issues where it does not belong.

Learn about the experience of being black. Make an effort to read about, listen to, attend events with, and generally get to know African Americans. Take an inquiry approach, without necessarily peppering your black colleagues with incessant questions. Be aware of your assumptions going in so they don't impede the process. One black technical specialist we spoke with said that whites "don't really know what it's like to be black, to grow up as a colored person, become Negro, and then evolve to be black. If they understood that better, we would have more harmony at work." With time and effort, honest outreach between blacks and whites in the workplace can occur.

Speak openly and provide feedback. Most important, listen to and seriously consider all perspectives, and share your insights with black managers in a way that is engaging, not condescending. Be as honest with them as you are with your other colleagues. If praise and encouragement are due, don't be stingy. If developmental feedback is called for, back it up with data and don't worry about accusations of racism.

If you are being accused of racist behavior, you should examine your motivation for giving this person feedback and assess the manner in which you do so. Would you give the same feedback if the person looked more like you, and would you give it in the same way? If the answer is yes, do you then have the data to support the feedback? Finally, are you willing to help this person improve? If you can answer all these points satisfactorily, you should proceed with feedback despite claims of racism.

Keep mutual respect paramount. The experience of many black managers is that respect is hard to come by. Only about half of the survey respondents felt that they were respected in their organizations.

You might want to examine the degree to which you mete out respect to others. You can do this by paying attention to how you communicate. Consider your language and others' verbal and nonverbal responses, and ask for feedback as appropriate. You might also take an honest interest in others' lives. Another way to show respect is simply to listen to blacks' ideas as well as their concerns.

What Blacks Can Do

Blacks can also take actions that contribute to effective communication and understanding. Here are some suggestions:

Know yourself. Self-definition is important, particularly for African Americans, because so many others are inclined to define them and, potentially, to define them negatively. If you are not sure of yourself, you can unconsciously fall into believing others' perceptions of you. Knowing yourself is perhaps the best defense you can develop against the many complications of the workplace; it allows you to lead from a position of strength. Know who you are, what you believe in, where you are starting from, what resources you can draw on, and where you want to go. Be clear about your strengths and weaknesses and ask yourself such questions as what you value about your work and what you are willing to put up with in the organization. You can gain knowledge about yourself through assessment tools, formal development programs, and self-reflection.

Determine and expand your areas of influence. You may not be sure that you are qualified to exert influence in areas in which you want to be a player. So it's best to develop an accurate understanding of the areas in which you are not influential so you can realistically determine whether they are appropriate and whether you should try to expand your influence into new areas. Note the areas in which people seek out your expertise and those in which they don't. Keep track of the subject area discussions in which you are included and those from which you are excluded. Observe when your suggestions are incorporated into a final decision and when they are not considered.

If you find that you're not as influential as you should be, there are some strategies that can help you add to your influence. First, make sure you have the requisite experience and expertise. Second, ask yourself and others if interpersonal behaviors are limiting your sphere of influence. Third, consult with colleagues to try to determine why you have been overlooked in certain situations.

Balance assertiveness with approachability. For African Americans, being assertive and confident may be interpreted as being pushy or threatening. The solution is not to try to be less assertive but to adopt behaviors that help to manage others' perceptions of you. Use behaviors that make you approachable, such as maintaining a pleasant countenance, cultivating ways to make small talk, and having a firm but not crushing handshake. Being sociable is a way of carrying yourself so that others in the organization want to get to know you.

Build trust. Trust is the cornerstone for forming and strengthening relationships and maintaining professional interactions, yet because of personal experience and historical precedent trust between blacks and their white colleagues is often tenuous. Building trust involves giving up some control and making yourself vulnerable. That might be a frightening prospect, but the consequences of not making the effort to build trust are dire.

To expand your sphere of trust, consider the following steps. Determine what information, tasks, or confidences you are willing to trust others with. Identify individuals who you believe are trustworthy. Then begin to place your trust in these individuals in small ways, gradually trusting them with more significant things as they prove and solidify their trustworthiness. Give people the benefit of the doubt before you assume they have intentionally broken your trust.

Seeing the Light

Of course, not all whites are completely unaware of what their African American colleagues must deal with in corporate America. But whites often rationalize that they face the same things, so blacks don't really shoulder an extra burden. A lack of appreciation for the second job that blacks must do, explaining it away or underrating its long-term effects, is as much a threat to productivity as being oblivious is. Fortunately, both whites and blacks can use the actions described here to begin to increase communication and improve understanding about the experience of blacks in today's corporate America.

Chapter Nine

Creating Teams That Work

Despite their recent popularity in organizations, teams are not generally well understood and often don't accomplish what is hoped. This chapter defines issues that are crucial as you lead the launch of a team, and as you work to enhance team effectiveness.

◆ ◆ ◆

Making Sure That a Team Is the Right Way to Go

Michael E. Kossler and Kim Kanaga

Many organizations take pride in describing themselves as *team based*. Scores of business books and magazine articles have exalted the formation and operation of teams over just about every other kind of organizational initiative. It's easy to see why. Information technology and the heightened competition in global markets have created flatter organizations, which have turned to teams to replace a top-down approach to addressing business challenges and to supplant individual effort with group strength. Teams have enabled some companies to take giant leaps forward in such areas as timeliness, innovation, customer service, and quality of goods and services.

But teams are not always the best way to accomplish a job. Organizations often ignore the difficulties and costs of launching teams. Teams typically need more time and more training to achieve results than do other kinds of work units. Teams may fly in the face of a company's established culture and reward system. These challenges can block a team from operating at peak performance.

When teams are assigned to the right task, composed of the right people, and supported in the right environment, they can achieve breakthrough performance. Determining whether these three criteria have been met is a critical step that many managers pass by in their zeal to build a team. This article will help you determine whether a team is the right way to accomplish a specific job.

How Teams Work

Teams are often temporary, yet they can help an organization gain strength by discovering new products and services, developing new ways to serve customers, and creating new systems that enhance efficiency.

Let's say your organization has put you in charge of an important business initiative. Forming a team could be the best way to tackle that challenge—but before you start recruiting, determine whether this is in fact the case. For certain kinds of work, it's more efficient and less expensive to have individuals or work groups handle the job.

Teams are often the best choice for addressing complex problems and issues that affect many parts of the organization—enterprise resource planning, for example, or developing an Internet business model. Team members can represent the thinking of a broad spectrum of stakeholders and act accordingly.

Teams can also help address controversial organizational change. When an organization expects resistance to a new business initiative, for example, team members can promote acceptance of and commitment to the initiative by communicating with employees in their respective functional areas and breaking down the us-versus-them mentality.

Simple, straightforward tasks generally don't require a team. Teams seldom perform well right off the bat because it takes time for people who don't know each other and who don't normally work together to merge their different interests and viewpoints. So setting up a team to accomplish a simple task with a short time frame usually isn't a good idea.

Innovation Engines

If your organization has assigned you a challenging task but has given little guidance on how to accomplish that task, forming a team may be your best strategy. Teams are excellent vehicles for driving toward innovative answers to thorny business problems.

Teams spark innovation because they create a climate in which various opinions and viewpoints rub against one another. This friction can lead to perspectives with more creative potential than the perspective of any individual team member. In other words, teams can be greater than the sum of their parts; they often produce results that go beyond what might be expected from the qualities and strengths of their individual members.

A team can be an effective engine for imagining and designing new systems, structures, and processes. But once a system is in place, managing it doesn't require a team—in fact, it's a waste of time and energy to create a team to manage a familiar system.

The Five Work Units

Look around your organization and you will find various types of work units. Broadly speaking, an organization can bring five categories of units—individual, work group, collaborative work group, team, and high-performance team—to bear on business challenges. Once you understand how each of these work units gets results, you can determine which of them has the degree of collaboration needed to achieve the organization's goal. If the task doesn't require a great deal of interdependent collaboration, a team isn't needed.

Individual. Some kinds of work can and should be handled by a single person. That individual has all the expertise, knowledge, and skills needed to do the job and is solely accountable for getting the job done. If the workload increases so that one person can no longer handle it, the company might create additional positions, each requiring a subset of the skills needed to do the whole job.

Work group. This unit consists of a number of people who may work together and who all do essentially the same kind of work but who are not dependent on one another for the information and skills needed to accomplish the job. In the human resource department of a large organization, for instance, all the staff members responsible for administering benefits constitute a work group. They all perform similar or related tasks, because the amount of work is too large for one person.

Collaborative work group. Individuals in these groups need information from one another to achieve results. The work might be handed off from one individual to another, as in a manufacturing system. Each individual completes one step in a complex process that leads to a finished product. In collaborative work groups, one person's errors in execution affect the ability of others in the group to do their work. Effective collaborative work groups may look like teams, but they differ in that each individual is accountable for his or her work and is rewarded for individual performance. Another difference is that collaborative work groups are often permanent parts of an organization (a department, division, or branch office, for example), whereas teams are usually created to perform a specific task and are dissolved when it is completed.

Team. A team is a small group of interdependent individuals who collectively have the expertise, knowledge, and skills needed to complete an assigned task or ongoing work. Team members have clear roles and responsibilities, share a vision and sense of purpose, and are collectively accountable for completing tasks and reaching the team's goal. It's harder to create a team than a work group or a collaborative work group. In organizations that prize individual achievement, building and leading an effective team can be difficult.

High-performance team. High-performance teams are characterized by an unusual degree of synergy among their members. They commonly exceed the performance that might be expected from an aggregation of individual contributors, and each team member

When Is a Team Not a Team?

Sports provide our most common model for what teams are and how they operate. But not all athletic units fit the definition of a team given here. Wrestling teams, golf teams, and swim teams, for example, are groups of people who perform the same or similar tasks. Each person in the group may train individually. During training and competition, the group members don't need to cooperate or even communicate with one another. They perform separately, one at a time. Such teams are more akin to work groups.

Soccer, basketball, and baseball teams bring together people with different yet complementary skills. No individual player can win a game. All team members need to know what the game strategy is so they can play their individual roles accordingly. The actions that each player takes depend to some extent on the actions of other team members, as does the timing of each player's actions. The team members are interdependent. Interdependency and shared purpose are part of what defines a team. These same qualities are reflected in teams that work in the business world.

often displays an extraordinary commitment to the other members' personal growth and success. It's not unusual for members to sacrifice individual rewards to secure success and rewards for the team. High-performance teams are so internally well coordinated and interdependent that team members are able to anticipate what other team members will need and provide it in advance.

Support Is Imperative

You may now have decided that achieving the results your organization expects of you clearly warrants forming a team. But no team works in a vacuum. Teams have to function in the context of the organization and its culture. Recruiting team members doesn't guarantee that they will work as a team. Even if you choose the members with great care and consideration of their skills and expertise, the group may never jell into a team. If your organization can't or won't support the team you plan to form or if it won't reward team achievements as well as it does individual achievements, then you don't need a team. You and your organization will be better off addressing critical business challenges through some other kind of work unit.

For example, if your organization won't give teams authority outside the chain of command, it can't make the most of a team designed to explore solutions that cross functional boundaries. If your organization doesn't support the idea that a team should be composed of skilled people with diverse viewpoints, then it can't take advantage of a team built to reach consensus or to make a strategic decision—and it won't get innovative perspectives on business challenges. Teams take longer to get results than do other kinds of work units, so if your organization doesn't have the time to allow a team to develop, it shouldn't form a team.

To determine whether your organization really needs and can support a team, examine the organization's support systems. Consider traditional types of resources such as budgets, appropriate staff, and necessary space and technology for team members as well as development programs, team-oriented financial systems, and systems that provide companywide support.

Assessing Support

To understand the support your organization is likely to give a team, identify the team-oriented resources and processes it has in place. Use the following questions to assess your organization's support of teams in the areas of development programs, financial systems, and mechanisms that show companywide support.

Development Programs

For a team to be effective, organizations need to provide development programs that teach team members basic interpersonal competency skills and team processes.

- Does the organization offer any training for teams in such areas as conflict management and collaboration? Do teams conduct 360-degree surveys on team performance?
- If the organization does not have any formal training for teams, is it acceptable to go outside the organization for that training?
- Where does the training budget reside? Is it part of the team's budget? Is it part of the individual development budget? Is the money in a centralized organization budget?
- If there are no dollars for training, is there a process through which the organization's teams could visit teams in other organizations to learn from them?

Financial Systems

Teams often cross two or more functional areas, but many organizations tie financial systems to single functional areas. Organizations need to provide financial systems that support teams and policies that protect team budgets.

- What is the organization's budget process for teams?
- What are the budgetary implications when a team is made up of individuals from two or more functional areas with independent budgets?
- What needs to be done to make sure that the team will have its own budget with no strings attached?
- If the team needs additional money, what is the process for getting that money?

Companywide Support

It takes more than a sponsor and an e-mail announcement to support a team. Organizations should provide effective and consistent communication tools and channels that support the team and appropriate political support to gain companywide endorsement of the team's work.

- Are there successful teams in your organization? What processes were put in place to make those teams successful? How was support for those teams communicated, not only at the top of the organization but also throughout the organization?
- Which people in your organization have successfully led a team? What could you learn from them?
- What teams in your organization have been ineffective from the organization's perspective? What contributed to their lack of success?

Group Rewards

Beyond these three support areas, organizations also support teams through reward systems that recognize group achievement alongside or even in place of individual achievement. If your organization doesn't have such reward systems, then it's not likely to get the results it wants from its teams. To assess your organization's team reward system, consider the following questions:

- How does your organization reward team performance?
- What special efforts have you seen in the organization to show appreciation for especially effective team performance?
- How does the organization balance the rewards for individual efforts and for team accomplishments?
- What tangible, nonmonetary rewards are typically provided to teams in your organization?

If the Shoe Fits . . .

Given the necessary support and resources, and the right mandate, teams provide exceptional value to organizations. In a complex world and in complex organizations, very little can be accomplished by a single individual. Business challenges often need the diversity of ideas and the close collaboration that characterize teams.

When employees work and experience success as team members, they often find the work to be particularly satisfying. The larger perspective that teams can give individual members often allows them to find greater meaning in their work. Teams are often a key ingredient of organizations that are perceived as good places to work; they foster the employee commitment and loyalty that all organizations want.

Your organization may need teams for its own good. Teams are often the best means by which organizations can learn. They are innovation engines and are often the organization's best chance for building new ideas, products, services, and solutions. But teams are not the best answer for every business challenge, and sometimes they aren't even a good answer. To get the powerful benefits that teams promise, managers need to be sure that a team is what is needed for any specific business goal and that the organization will support a team in its work.

◆ ◆ ◆

The Right Start: A Team's First Meeting Is Key

Kim Kanaga and Sonya Prestridge

The use of teams has become an increasingly important approach to conducting business. Teams can produce innovative solutions to complex problems, enabling organizations to be faster, more responsive, more competitive, and more successful in meeting their missions.

But it's difficult for a team to be successful if it hasn't had a well-planned and well-executed first meeting. The essential business of this meeting is to get the members well on the road to being a team—that is, to bring this group of disparate and formerly disconnected people with varied skills, experiences, and styles to bear on a challenge.

Team members will learn why they have come together as a team and will get to know each other, begin to trust each other, and learn to work together outside of and across their usual channels and boundaries. They will set up the terms on which they will interact with one another to achieve their shared purpose.

The best format for a first team meeting is face-to-face. The meeting can be as short as two hours or as long as three days. But it's essential that the meeting include the team leader as well as all the other team members, plus the upper-management sponsor of the initiative. Sometimes it's helpful to also have a meeting facilitator.

In today's business environment, one significant challenge that often faces nascent teams is getting all the members together in one place. Teams are likely to be geographically dispersed, separated by time and distance. Videoconferencing and other communication technologies may seem like the best route to take, but the benefits of at least one initial face-to-face meeting are so significant that every effort should be made to make it happen.

Getting Ready

The first meeting should define and begin work on the four elements that are critical to team success: purpose and direction, roles and responsibilities, procedures and practices, and cooperation and relationships.

It's up to the team leader to prepare team members to address these four issues during the first meeting. One effective way to do this is through one-on-one meetings with the members. The team leader may also use e-mail bulletins or broadcast voice mails.

In any case, the communication must contain information that is useful. New team members will want to know the date and location of the first meeting; travel and lodging information, if applicable; and all the team members' names and contact information, along with the members' responsibilities.

Sharing this kind of practical information not only helps people connect to their new roles as team members but also introduces members to one another and begins to define their roles. The team leader can also use premeeting communication to explain to team members why they are being brought together and what they are expected to accomplish. By contacting the team members early, the team leader lays a groundwork that will encourage them to feel responsible for accomplishing a common goal.

Setting the Compass

A lack of clarity about purpose is a major cause of team problems and failure. The first team meeting should be used to establish the purpose of the team. The team leader should present relevant background information such as the forces and conditions that led to the decision to launch the team, the business challenges the team will address, and the ways the team and the organization will measure progress toward the team's goals. The team also needs to know the deadlines for accomplishing its work, what resources are available, and any challenges or constraints it faces.

Successfully setting purpose and direction for the team at the first meeting and beyond hinges on several factors:

Understanding the team's mission. Members should have a common conception of why the team exists and what it has been chartered to do. A good way to establish the big picture is to develop a mission statement that can serve as the basis for setting priorities, making decisions, and allocating resources. It's best if the group creates its mission statement early on, perhaps during the first meeting.

Identifying critical success factors. The team has to translate its mission into action. The team leader should ask the team to think about what it will take for the team to be successful, directing the discussion away from statements of hope, fear, or other intangibles that are difficult to pin down or manage. Each critical success factor should be necessary to the team's mission. Taken together, the critical success factors should be sufficient to accomplish the mission. Aim for a mix of strategic and tactical statements.

Creating and owning the team's goals. The amount of energy team members will expend on reaching goals is significantly affected by the level of participation they have in creating those goals

Crafting a Mission Statement

At a team's first meeting or shortly thereafter, the leader or sponsor, a facilitator from outside the team, or a team member experienced in facilitating should lead the group through the process of creating a mission statement. One effective way to get the process going is brainstorming. Try the following process.

To begin, consider these questions:

What purpose does the team serve?

Who are the organization's customers?

What do they have to gain from the team's work?

What are the team's unique capabilities?

What does the team want to change?

What gives energy and urgency to the team?

What are the team's core values, and how do they relate to the organization's values?

What do the team members want the team's legacy to be?

For each question, use at least one sheet on a flip chart, and have team members call out ideas that relate to the question.

and determining how they will be achieved. Goals should be closely aligned with the team's mission. If the goals are mandated by outside sources, the team members should be given an opportunity to determine how to accomplish them.

Goals that are challenging yet attainable can motivate team members. The goals should also be well defined and specific; this helps everyone on the team work efficiently toward the goals and know when the goals have been achieved. For example, setting dead-

Record all suggestions, no matter how wild, until the energy level in the room begins to drop.

Then post the sheets of paper around the room and have everyone go around and look at them. Have the group identify patterns and themes that emerged from the brainstorming exercise, looking for common words and repetition. Discuss how these themes might fit together to form a mission statement.

Have the group draft a mission statement, using this strategy: First, ask individual members to write a statement for the team. Then bring team members together in groups of three or four and ask them to share their individual statements and create a mission statement from them within their group. Finally, bring the entire team together to share the small-group statements and to build from those a single statement for the entire team.

If time allows, the team can continue the discussion to arrive at a final, polished version. It is equally effective to assign a subgroup to make revisions and bring the statement back later for approval by the whole team.

Whichever method is chosen, make sure that the completed statement is understandable, particularly to people who are not members of the team. It also should refer to specific customer needs; indicate how the team will conduct its work; reflect challenging but achievable goals; and be expressed in a way that will focus effort, guide decisions, solve problems, and provide inspiration.

lines for and applying measurements to goals—such as sales numbers or client contacts to be achieved in a specific period of time—can help the team better organize and use its resources and certify when goals have been met. Establishing milestones also provides the team with a way to assess its progress toward its goals.

If time is short and the team is facing a long agenda for its first team meeting, it may be tempting for the team leader to simply tell the team what its purpose is and how results will be measured. However, the process of creating a mission statement inspires and motivates team members, helps them take ownership of strategies, and encourages them to take responsibility for their individual contributions.

Central Casting

When a team performs below expectations or fails altogether, confusion about individual roles and responsibilities is often a prime reason. For a team to be successful, each member needs to agree to his or her own role and responsibilities and to have a clear understanding of what is expected of the other members.

It's typical for team members to assume they know what is expected of other members, but these assumptions are often wrong. Differing perceptions about roles and responsibilities can lead to misunderstandings and conflict among team members. So the things that are expected of each member should be discussed and agreed on before the team members begin working on the task at hand, because these expectations largely determine what members will do and how they'll do it.

There is at least one potential pitfall teams should be aware of as they determine roles and responsibilities at the first meeting. If two or more members have overlapping roles but they don't see it that way, conflict can result. So it's important that everyone is clear about which responsibilities are individual and which are shared, and that each team member understands who will work with and depend on whom to get a task accomplished.

Standard Procedures

An effective team consistently uses the processes and guidelines its members have agreed on for managing the flow of work, making decisions, solving problems, and managing meetings. For members to function well in their efforts to accomplish their goals, they must be aware of, agree to, and manage several factors:

Decision making. It's critical that team members understand and concur on who is empowered to make decisions in specific areas— the team leader, the team as a group, individual members, or some combination of these. Yet most teams don't discuss or reach agreement on the most effective method for making decisions.

It's not unusual for a conflict to erupt over who is responsible for a specific decision. In other instances no one feels responsible for a decision, so no decision is made. It's especially important that the team leader's role in decision making be clearly stated and understood by the entire team.

Communicating. Team communication is typically handled in one of two ways: either team members don't communicate with each other as much as they should or every bit of information is communicated to every team member, even if it's irrelevant. Neither method helps a team's productivity. Effective team communication requires that the team not only manage the quality, quantity, and timing of communication within the team but also have a specific strategy for communicating with outside individuals and groups.

Understanding and agreeing to team norms. During the team's first meeting, it should establish guidelines for acceptable and desirable behavior for individuals on the team. These norms are essential because team members often come from different functional areas of the organization and sometimes from different geographic areas. Each team member arrives with different ideas, assumptions, and expectations.

In some organizations, for example, it may be normal for people in certain departments, business units, or localities to interrupt, tease, and engage in friendly put-downs. In other parts of the organization these behaviors may be seen as totally out of line. In some organizations it's customary to start meetings late, but in others promptness is the rule. In some workplaces disagreement is welcomed, but in others it's considered rude and hostile. Therefore, having an agreed set of team norms for behavior will help unify team members.

Building Trust

The last area that should be covered at the team's first meeting depends heavily on the other three. Cooperation and relationships emerge when team members know what is expected of them and follow guidelines they have agreed on that help them work together. With a common purpose and direction, clarity about roles and responsibilities, and agreement about processes and practices, the chances of effective collaboration are high. To start building cooperation among team members and between the team and the rest of the organization, attention should be paid to these factors:

Establishing a sense of camaraderie. Team members work effectively together when they support, trust, and respect one another. During the first meeting, ask people to describe their previous experiences as team members—what went well, what needed improvement, and the lessons learned. They might talk about experiences with other projects of a similar nature and their expectations for the current team's work. Team members should state why they think they were asked to be on the current team and what they can bring to the team.

Reviewing and monitoring external relationships. It can be helpful to identify the key relationships between the team and its stakeholders inside and outside the organization and to work out processes for developing and maintaining those relationships. This is also the time to think about the specific people and groups from whom the team will need help and support, how the team might extend into the territory of other groups, and whom the team needs to keep apprised of its work.

Discussing the relationship between the team and its leader. Leadership style affects a team's communication, cooperation, decision making, and work processes. Some effective team leaders are authoritarian; others are more participative. The team leader should be aware of the style he or she tends to use and the impact that style may have on the team's effectiveness. Team leaders aren't locked into any one style; in fact, some of the most effective team leaders are able to adapt their style of leadership to fit different situations.

The team's leader is in a powerful position to influence the team's realization of its potential. Team members need to feel inspired by the opportunity before them and confident that they will have the resources and support needed for success. They need to have positive feelings about the people they will depend on to accomplish the team's mission. A strong first meeting sets a clear direction, delivers an inspiring challenge, and instills a cooperative spirit that will enable the team to achieve its highest potential.

◆ ◆ ◆

Cultivating Teams

Robert C. Ginnett

"You know what the problem is with teams?" a senior executive once asked me. "You just can't make them work right. You can't order teams around. You can't make them develop and you can't make them perform."

His statement suggested two things to me. First, he definitely liked to control things around him and he probably didn't like to be controlled much by others. This was not a great flash of psychological insight on my part. He fit the pattern of many senior executives in that regard. I'm not exactly sure why this occurs. One hypothesis is that they have to be controlling because the position they are in requires them to be that way. But I don't think much of that supposition because there are too many outliers: excellent senior leaders who are not control freaks. I believe the data reflect a pattern found among a generation for whom the principal organizational unit is the individual performer. In that kind of system you can order some, if not all, individuals around.

And that realization tied directly to the second thing his statement suggested—that he had had a lot of experience with teams that had problems.

My observations of him aside, he was absolutely correct. You can't order teams to develop—but you can grow them.

Prepare the Ground

Think about it this way. Suppose you wanted to grow a beautiful, award-winning flower garden. First, you would need to select a spot with appropriate amounts of sun and shade. Then you would need to prepare the soil. This takes a lot of work, especially near the Rocky Mountains, where I live. The soil must be tilled and augmented to the proper particle size. Organic material such as humus or compost must be added. The soil must contain the proper chemicals to nurture the plants you want to grow. The pH must be measured and adjusted. Next come the living things such as bacteria and fungi—and don't forget the earthworms. After all that, you plant the seeds and ensure they are kept moist until they germinate. Then comes daily watering, adding appropriate amounts of fertilizer on a regular basis, and pruning. This is, indeed, a lot of work.

And do you know what's wrong with flowerbeds like this? You can't *make* them grow! You can't order them into beauty. All you can do is create the best possible conditions so they can do the work of growing and producing beauty.

Teams function pretty much the same way. You can't order teams to grow or develop or be high performing any more than you can order flowers to do these things. But if you are a creative and forward-thinking leader and have decided that you need high-performance teamwork to achieve your vision and mission, then you can create the best possible conditions for teams, giving them a fair chance of growing, developing, and achieving high performance. And as with the flowerbed, most of the work of leadership is done up front—not in controlling but in creating.

If you accept this analogy, you probably won't be surprised by the next part. Creating the right conditions for teamwork takes a lot of hard work at three distinct levels. At the individual level you want to select people who have the interests, skills, abilities, values, attitudes, and interpersonal orientation not only to do the task work but also to do the teamwork. Moving up to the team or group level, you want to ensure that the task is designed appropriately for teamwork; that the composition of the team is appropriate in skill, scope, and size; that there are appropriate norms in place to foster team behaviors; and most important, that the team leader exercises appropriate authority behaviors. Finally, and perhaps most difficult, the leader needs to examine and create or develop appropriate structures and systems to support teamwork. These include team-oriented reward, education, information, and control systems throughout the organization. Although changes in systems are the most difficult to make, they are also the most powerful in creating the appropriate conditions for teamwork to occur.

Let's return once more to our flower garden. Assuming that you've done all the hard work and that nature has cooperated, your garden is just about to reach its peak of beauty. You may think everything will be fine—but not so fast. You could make a serious mistake if you're not careful. Suppose you reach for a can of pesticide but instead mistakenly pick up a can of herbicide. If you spray that on your flowers, you'll kill the entire project. And you can do the same thing with teams. Even the best-designed teams can be destroyed by relatively common leadership mistakes.

Do No Harm

It often strikes me that there is a limited methodology for nurturing teams but an infinite number of ways to destroy them. Just ask around and you'll find this to be true. Some leaders have a personal theory about how to create teamwork, but almost all leaders can cite an example of how to destroy a team—and there is a huge variety of mechanisms to accomplish this.

At a leadership summit sponsored by the El Pomar Foundation— a Colorado philanthropy that supports nonprofit organizations working in the arts and humanities, education, health and human services, and civic and community initiatives—I was asked to work with student leaders from around the state on two subjects. A three-hour session in the morning was devoted to helping leaders enhance team success. This session was similar to ones I do for CCL with business leaders from around the world. As was predictable, those students who had experienced a successful team situation could talk about it but, in the absence of an underlying theory, recognized that their experiences could not be easily generalized.

In the afternoon I facilitated two sessions on why teams fail. These were interesting but unusual for me. I have never been asked by business leaders to provide a seminar on why teams fail. Presumably, business leaders have enough experience with this concept already. But it turned out that students too have had a plethora of team failures. Not only had everyone had an experience of team failure but in most cases the students also agreed that methods of killing a team were much easier to define than methods of helping a team succeed.

Here is their list: lack of a clear goal, vision, or dream; too many yes-people on the team; leaders who reject the input of team members; leaders who want to do everything; hidden agendas; apathy; the assumption that team members are incompetent; lack of structure; communication failures; failure to learn from mistakes and successes; rewards solely for individual performance; and dispersed leadership. Not a bad list.

I once participated in a conference with other scholars who, like me, had been studying teams and teamwork. We had hoped to produce a checklist for leaders to follow that would guarantee their success in working with teams. Unfortunately, we were unable to achieve that objective. It seems that there are many coexisting paths that will get you to successful teamwork.

Amazingly, though, we were able to agree on ways to destroy a team. Here are a few critical ones, as noted in the book *Groups That Work (and Those That Don't): Creating Conditions for Effective Teamwork,* edited by J. Richard Hackman, a psychology professor at Harvard University.

Fall off the Authority Balance Beam

Arguably the most damaging error once the team has started work is what Hackman has labeled *falling off the authority balance beam*. Few leadership decisions are more consequential for the long-term well-being of teams than those that address the partitioning of authority between leaders and teams. It takes skill to accomplish this well, and it is a skill that has emotional and behavioral as well as cognitive components. Just knowing the rules for partitioning authority is insufficient; one also needs practice in applying those rules in situations where anxieties, including one's own, are likely to be high. Especially challenging for leaders are the early stages in the life of a team, when new leaders are often tempted to give away too much authority, and the rough stretches, when the temptation is to take authority back. This inappropriate giving and taking of authority upsets the balance.

I once worked with an urban police chief who wanted the benefits of participation and teamwork from his force but who was unwilling or unable to relinquish any authority to his teams. After months of working with him, I finally persuaded him to allow some input from his officers on the question of which weapon they should choose to replace their outdated revolvers. I was so excited by the possibility of even a slight shift in authority that I neglected to coach him on the rules of effective participation. One of these critical rules is that if there are constraints on the decision, they need to be made clear up front—not after people have made an input without considering these limits. As it turned out, the police officers voted for a powerful handgun with tremendous penetrating ability but only limited capacity for ammunition. According to the experts, whose inputs were not given additional weight initially (a second error), that was a terrible choice for an urban police weapon, and the chief lost his composure. He withdrew all authority for input from the teams, and it took months to recover from that situation.

Research shows that effective leaders use much of the continuum of the authority dimension without upsetting the balance.

The management of authority relations takes a good measure of knowledge, skill, and perseverance; managed inappropriately, these relations can destroy a team.

Call People a Team but Treat Them Like Individuals

One way to set up work is to assign specific responsibilities to specific individuals and then choreograph the individuals' activities so their products coalesce into a group product. (This, incidentally, is the way my high school football coach built a "team.") A contrasting strategy is to assign the group responsibility and accountability for an entire piece of work and let members decide among themselves how they will proceed to accomplish the work. Either of these strategies can be effective at accomplishing the work, but a choice must be made between them. When people are *told* they are a team but are *treated* as a group of individual performers with their own specific jobs to do, mixed signals are sent, confusion is created, and in the long run, these individuals will not become an effective team.

To reap the benefits of teamwork, one must build an actual team. Calling a set of people a team or exhorting them to work together is insufficient. Instead, action must be taken to establish the team's boundaries, to define the task as one for which members are collectively responsible and accountable, and to give members the authority to manage both the team's internal processes and its relations with external entities such as clients and co-workers. Once this is done, leadership behavior and organizational systems can be gradually changed as necessary to support teamwork.

This leads to a final team destroyer.

Assume That Members Are Competent in a Team Setting

Once a team is launched and operating under its own steam, leaders sometimes assume their work is done. As we have seen, there are some good reasons for giving a team ample room to go about its business in its own way: inappropriate or poorly timed leadership interventions have impaired the work of more than one team. However, a pure hands-off style also can limit a team's effectiveness, particularly when members are not already skilled and experienced in teamwork.

It is not wise to assume that just because employees have clamored for the opportunity to work as a team they have the requisite skills to do so. Often employees' only prior experience in teamwork came years ago when they were members of a high school sports team—often with coaches who gave them bad team advice.

Even after initial team training is accomplished for the members, the leader's work is not done. Teams need ongoing maintenance and development. Not only will the context and environment likely change over time but, if the organization is truly committed to team effectiveness, the organizational systems in which team members operate should be expected to change over time as well.

A flower garden, like a team, requires good preparation and regular maintenance. If that is done effectively, enduring beauty can be created, and perhaps some awards will even be won.

Chapter Ten

The Long View
for Organizational Success

Your organization can best gain an advantage over your competitors by practicing strategic leadership. But how is strategic leadership accomplished, and who in an organization should be responsible for it? This chapter presents strategic leadership as a complex process of thinking, acting, and influencing that can be exercised not just by individuals but also by teams.

◆ ◆ ◆

Strategic Command: Taking the Long View
for Organizational Success

Katherine Beatty and Laura Quinn

If you were to ask a group of executives to define *strategic leadership*, you'd likely get as many different answers as there were people in the room. One executive might describe it as *creating a shared vision of the future*. Another might view it as *linking the efforts of everyone in the organization to the organization's goals,* and still another might interpret it as *not just accomplishing objectives but also steadily improving the organization*.

The difficulty of arriving at a simple, cut-and-dried definition of strategic leadership is underscored in the literature on the subject. In their 1995 book *Strategic Management: Competitiveness and Globalization*, Michael A. Hitt, R. Duane Ireland, and Robert E.

Hoskisson developed a model of strategic leadership that has six critical components. In a study based on that model and reported in a 1998 article in *SAM Advanced Management Journal*, Abdalla F. Hagen, Morsheda T. Hassan, and Sammy G. Amin found that U.S. CEOs ranked these six components in the following order of importance: determining strategic direction, developing human capital, exploiting and maintaining core competencies, sustaining an effective corporate culture, emphasizing ethical practices, and establishing strategic control.

What these various definitions and concepts make clear is that strategic leadership is extremely complex and multifaceted. Yet it is for that very reason that strategic leadership is critical to achieving individual and organizational effectiveness and success in a rapidly changing, increasingly globalized business environment that grows more complicated by the day.

Leaders who want to develop strategic abilities need to gain an understanding of the three parts of strategic leadership: *what* strategic leadership achieves, *how* strategic leadership is accomplished, and *who* in an organization has the main responsibility for leading strategically.

CCL's program Developing the Strategic Leader, designed to help senior managers gain a better understanding of the complexity of strategic leadership as it relates to themselves, their teams, and their organizations, examines all three elements of strategic leadership. To this end the program uses as a starting point this model: individuals and teams (the *who*) exert strategic leadership when they think, act, and influence (the *how*) in ways that enhance the organization's sustainable competitive advantage (the *what*).

Going Long

If strategy is defined as the patterns of choices made to achieve a sustainable competitive advantage, then strategic leadership involves focusing on the choices that enhance the health and well-being of an organization over the long term. Those last two words are key.

Nearly half a millennium ago, the Japanese military leader Miyamoto Musashi said, "In strategy it is important to see distant things as if they were close and to take a distanced view of close things." That may be easier to fathom in theory than it is to achieve in practice, because operating from a perspective that emphasizes the long term does not always come naturally or easily to leaders. This is especially true in today's business environment, in which short-term results are increasingly exalted, frequently with little consideration and to the detriment of the big picture.

As a result, leading strategically often demands courage and a willingness to swim against the tide of conventional wisdom. A case in point is Darwin Smith, who was CEO of Kimberly-Clark from 1971 to 1991. As related in Jim Collins's book *Good to Great: Why Some Companies Make the Leap . . . and Others Don't*, Smith, soon after becoming CEO, concluded that the potential of the company's core papermaking business paled in comparison to what could be achieved by branching out into a wider range of consumer products. His strategy included selling the pulp and paper mills that were an integral part of the company's tradition. Business analysts were shocked and predicted that Smith was making a huge mistake. But Smith stuck to his guns and his strategy, and today Kimberly-Clark is a global manufacturer with annual revenues of $14.5 billion. *Fortune* magazine this year pronounced it the most admired company in the forest and paper products industry.

Coming Up Short

The lack of attention that some leaders pay to thinking and acting strategically for long-term organizational success was perhaps never so evident as during the late 1990s—the now faded glory days of the dot-coms. For the leaders of many of these companies, the overriding interest was building to the point of an initial public offering of stock. There was little concern about or planning for what would happen after the IPO. The focus was on short-term objectives rather than strategic goals such as establishing and maintaining profitability, and the decisions made reflected this limited focus.

This is not to say that strategic leaders shouldn't be concerned with the short-term health of their companies. The important thing is that actions they take to address those short-term concerns also support and enhance the long-term viability of their organizations.

Strategic leadership requires leaders to focus on the far-reaching implications of their ideas, decisions, and actions for the entire enterprise, not just one or two business units or functions. Strategic leaders need to understand how the various parts of the organization's system work together, and they must integrate perspectives from across the organization. If they don't, they're likely to be frustrated in their attempts to create and accomplish organizational goals, because individuals in the organization won't have a clear perception or understanding of their roles in supporting and achieving those goals.

In addition to having a firm grasp of what's happening in their own companies, strategic leaders need to stay on top of and react to the rapid and constant changes occurring in the marketplace environment. Failing to do so can seriously hinder an organization's ability to arrive at the *what* of strategic leadership—a sustainable competitive advantage.

Gathering Information

The *how* of strategic leadership is a complicated combination of *thinking, acting,* and *influencing*—and each of these three processes is complex in and of itself.

Today's organizations and leaders often operate under ambiguous or even contradictory circumstances. Anticipating and effectively reacting to these circumstances is a key to success.

To do this, strategic leaders must not only develop the organization's vision and mission but also continually think about and review the organization's direction to ensure the organization is staying on the right course as the competitive environment changes. Strategic thinking, then, involves gathering information, making connections among the various pieces of information, and filtering the information to form ideas and strategies that are focused, relevant, and sound.

Effective strategic thinkers constantly scan the internal and external environments for factors, trends, and patterns that may have an effect on the organization's business.

In the internal environment, strategic leaders pay attention to whether the organization is fulfilling its mission, the ways in which the organizational culture and values do or don't support the organization's work, employees' capabilities and talents, budgetary issues, and how the organization's various units and systems function and interrelate.

Information must be gathered from every corner of the organization. The best way to ensure this is to build networks, which in turn requires the ability to foster trusting relationships with people in all areas and at all levels of the organization and to encourage and accept their input and feedback.

Establishing such relationships can't be done in a day; it also requires thinking and acting strategically—planting seeds and nurturing them over the long term.

Perhaps the best example of how leaders can form and stay plugged into networks that yield rich and relevant information is *management by wandering around*. Spending time among and genuinely communicating with employees throughout the organization enables strategic leaders to win those workers' trust and see the business through their eyes. And as Yogi Berra said, "You can observe a lot by watching."

As strategic leaders scan the external environment, they should pay attention to market conditions, global economies, changing technology, industry innovations, and shifting supplies of resources. But perhaps most important, they must keep a keen eye on their customers and what drives those customers' purchases.

An example of a leader who tuned in to customers and took a cue from them to set a successful organizational strategy is Louis

Gerstner, who was CEO of IBM from 1993 until March 2002. When Gerstner took over as CEO, Big Blue was singing the blues: profit margins were down in its core businesses as other technology companies successfully applied competitive pressures. Gerstner decided that IBM couldn't continue on the same course and maintain its competitive edge. As he gauged the needs of customers, he concluded that their number one problem was their burgeoning information technology systems. Few companies had people with a thorough understanding of how their various IT products combined into a system, let alone an ability to solve system problems. Gerstner shifted IBM's strategic focus from providing products to providing services that most of IBM's competitors were incapable of—helping companies troubleshoot and get the most out of their IT systems. In doing so he created a business model that other technology companies are still trying to emulate.

Linking Up

It's not enough for strategic leaders to capture information from a wide range of networks inside and outside the organization. Once they have gathered the information, they need to examine it to discover interdependencies and see how various pieces of information are linked to different parts of the organization. Doing so is a monumental information-processing challenge. A crucial part of meeting this challenge is comprehending the systemic nature of organizations—a dynamic involving individuals, teams, groups, the industry, and the marketplace.

Strategic leaders also need to take into account the relationship between the organization's history and its vision for the future. If there are conflicts between the two, they may be a hindrance to achieving long-term goals—a hindrance that needs to be addressed and resolved. For example, if a company's top management decides that the strategic focus should be on enhancing the use of new technology but the organization's culture has traditionally been averse to risk, the likelihood is high that there will be problems in keeping the strategy on track.

Strategic leaders should focus on linking all the information they gather so they can give their organizations the best chance of gaining or maintaining a competitive advantage.

Data Overload

One of the biggest problems strategic leaders encounter after they become proficient at gathering information is dealing with the sheer volume of information collected. They need to differentiate the information, and filter and distill it down to what is essential for setting the organization's strategic direction.

However, deciding which information—out of an often overwhelming amount—deserves attention and which should be passed over is easier said than done. Sometimes strategic leaders simply don't have the resources to sift through it all. Sometimes they feel an urgency to act and just don't have the time. Whatever the case, strategic leaders who are unable or unwilling to separate out the crucial information and establish a sense of order can find themselves paralyzed.

There is no simple prescription for filtering the information that is most relevant and crucial to setting an effective strategic direction. But to make sound choices, strategic leaders should be aware of their own career connections and biases and not let them sway decisions. For example, a strategic leader with a background in customer service may look at the available information and conclude—and convince others—that the organization should invest heavily in customer service, when in fact the organization's strategic goals depend more heavily on other needs.

Carrying It Out

The second part of the *how* of strategic leadership is acting. All the good strategic thinking in the world isn't worth much if leaders don't act on it (or, as is sometimes the more prudent course, if they don't withhold action, based on their strategic thinking). When a leader fails, it's usually not because of a flaw in his or her vision for the organization. Rather, the fatal error generally lies in an inability to take action on and effectively implement that vision.

Although strategic leadership is focused on an organization's long-term well-being, it should be balanced with attention to tactical day-to-day operations. The two perspectives need to be integrated. Leaders often struggle with this balancing act. They're often inclined to concentrate on the problems that arise during the day's work—issues and details that seem immediately important, straightforward, and easily resolved. In other words their instinct is to go around putting out fires. But in every decision that leaders make, it's critical that they ask themselves how that decision will affect the organization in the long term. Tactical efforts need to be aligned with and supportive of the long-term strategy.

It's also critical for strategic leaders to lead by example. Their own consistent behavior in carrying out their strategic vision has a trickle-down effect on others in the organization; it sets a standard by which others can establish priorities that are in consonance with the strategy.

A large part of the acting of strategic leadership is making decisions about whether and when to act. If opportunities arise in day-to-day operations that bolster the long-term vision, effective strategic leaders recognize and run with them. Conversely, opportunities that promise short-term benefits but may be detrimental to overall strategy are shunned. Two of the most important qualities for strategic leaders are confidence and patience—they need to steadily take actions toward the strategic goal, even in the midst of an ever-changing and often chaotic business environment. Yet strategic leaders also need to be flexible, to view strategy as emergent and all their decisions as temporary ones that can be modified as new information from strategic thinking becomes available.

Making Your Mark

Although strategic leaders must take action based on their strategic thinking to enable the organization to achieve its long-term objectives, it is not enough for them to act alone. They also need to *influence* others in the organization to work toward the strategic goals.

The first step of the process of influencing is to help people in all areas and at all levels of the organization gain a clear sense of the strategy and how it applies to their specific jobs and roles. But strategic leaders can't stop there—they then need to connect the needs and aspirations of the employees to the possibilities presented by the strategic vision, creating a commitment to, passion for, and excitement about the cause. Exercising this level of influence on everyone in the organization might seem to be a daunting task, especially when the inevitable difficulties and setbacks in advancing the strategy occur, and disenchantment and frustration loom. But leaders can instill a dedication to and zeal for the strategic vision by communicating effectively, telling powerful stories, and sharing their own sense of enthusiasm for and allegiance to the organization and its goals.

Strategic leaders can further influence the organization by aligning their systems, culture, and organizational structure to ensure consistency with the strategy. For example, CCL is working with a small company in the tool industry that has the strategic imperatives of innovation, speed, and quality. The company has made a structural change—people now report to process directors rather than functional vice presidents. The company is changing from a command-and-control culture to one that emphasizes collaboration and focusing on individual initiative. The reward system encourages both individual and company performance. The resulting synergy is powerful: people receive consistent messages about the importance of innovation, speed, and quality and are influenced to behave in ways that support the strategy.

Who's Responsible?

Now that the *what* and the *how* of strategic leadership have been established, the final question is *who* in an organization should have responsibility for the tasks of strategic leadership? The obvious answer is the people at the top—presidents, CEOs, and other senior officers. Certainly, when an organization fails, it is the people at the top who are held accountable—witness Enron.

But it would be a mistake to think that only senior officers can be strategic leaders. Individuals whose decisions have effects beyond their own functional areas often have opportunities to think, act, and influence as strategic leaders. For instance, a purchasing manager who is considering switching suppliers can anticipate the impact the move will have on the engineering and manufacturing divisions, or a human resource director in charge of crafting reward systems can do so in a way that encourages cooperation across key business units.

But because strategic leadership inherently involves multiple perspectives and a gathering of information from many sources, some organizations are beginning to see the responsibility for strategic leadership as lying not with one or a few individuals but with teams. The diversity of perspectives and opinions that naturally arises from a group can provide a clear advantage in what should be a collaborative process of strategic leadership.

But there are challenges in the team approach as well. Everyone has seen a team that is made up of talented, resourceful, and committed individuals but performs way below expectations and is less than the sum of its parts. Strategic leadership teams can avert this outcome by ensuring the presence of a number of factors and being aware of potential problems as they go through the strategic processes of thinking, acting, and influencing.

First, a team must have access to and stay attuned to all the information it needs to do its work—information from each individual on the team, from within the organization, and from the external environment, such as technological, cultural, and market trends. It is critical that all this information be shared with each member of the team and brought to bear on the task of strategic thinking.

Second, a team must be empowered to act strategically. Each member needs to have a clear idea of what the team can and can't do, and the team needs to take timely actions within those boundaries. Two of the biggest problems that strategic leadership teams run into are not having a strategic vision that is shared by each member and failing to balance near-term tactics with long-term strategy, so the team must establish and focus on these critical prerequisites for effective strategic action.

Finally, team members must trust and respect one another so they can engage in the final part of the *how* of strategic leadership—influencing. The team needs to be careful to send out a uniform message about its mission and strategy so that others in the organization become energized by and committed to—rather than confused about—the long-term goals and understand how their roles and their work are related to and support those goals.

Working Together

It's important to remember that the three processes of strategic leadership—thinking, acting, and influencing—are not independent but interdependent. No part of the process occurs in a vacuum, and each relies on the others. Nor is strategic leadership a linear process—strategic leaders should be thinking, acting, and influencing each day. And perhaps most important, strategic leaders must be proficient at each part of the process to be effective, for leaders who come up with brilliant strategic ideas but are unable to champion them and see them through will not find much success.

Index

About the Center for Creative Leadership

The Center for Creative Leadership (CCL®) is an international educational institution devoted to leadership research and training. Its mission is to advance the understanding, practice, and development of leadership for the benefit of society worldwide.

Since its founding as a nonprofit educational institution in 1970, CCL has grown to become one of the world's largest and most respected organizations devoted to leadership. Over the course of three decades, more than four hundred thousand individuals from thousands of private corporations, nonprofits, and governmental agencies have participated in CCL open-enrollment and custom programs. CCL's five campuses are located on three continents: Greensboro, North Carolina; Colorado Springs, Colorado; and San Diego, California, in North America; Brussels, Belgium, in Europe; and Singapore in Asia. In addition, nearly two dozen Network Associates around the world offer selected CCL programs and assessments.

CCL draws strength from its nonprofit status and educational mission, which provide unusual flexibility in a world where quarterly profits often drive thinking and direction. It has the freedom to be objective, wary of short-term trends, and motivated foremost by our mission—hence its substantial and sustained investment in leadership research. Although CCL's work is always grounded in a strong foundation of research, it focuses on achieving a beneficial impact in the real world. CCL's efforts are geared to be practical and action-oriented, helping leaders and their organizations more effectively achieve their goals and vision. The desire to transform learning and ideas into action provides the impetus for CCL's programs, assessments, publications, and services.

Capabilities

CCL's activities encompass leadership education, knowledge generation and dissemination, and building a community centered on leadership. CCL is broadly recognized for excellence in executive education, leadership development, and innovation by sources such as *BusinessWeek*, the *Financial Times*, the *New York Times*, and *The Wall Street Journal*.

Open-Enrollment Programs

CCL's fourteen open-enrollment courses are designed for leaders at all levels, as well as people responsible for leadership development and training at their organizations. This portfolio offers distinct choices for participants seeking a particular learning environment or type of experience. Some programs are structured specifically around small-group activities, discussion, and personal reflection, while others offer hands-on opportunities through business simulations, artistic exploration, team-building exercises, and new-skills practice. Many of these programs offer private one-on-one sessions with a feedback coach.

Visit http://www.ccl.org/programs for a complete listing of programs.

Customized Programs

CCL develops tailored educational solutions for more than two hundred client organizations around the world each year. Through this applied practice, CCL structures and delivers programs focused on specific leadership development needs within the context of defined organizational challenges, including innovation, the merging of cultures, and the development of a broader pool of leaders. The objective is to help organizations develop, within their own cultures, the leadership capacity they need to address challenges as they emerge.

Program details are available online at http://www.ccl.org/custom.

Coaching

CCL's suite of coaching services is designed to help leaders maintain a sustained focus and generate increased momentum toward achieving their goals. These coaching alternatives vary in depth and duration and serve a variety of needs, from helping an executive sort through career and life issues to working with an organization to integrate coaching into its internal development process. CCL's coaching offerings, which can supplement program attendance or be customized for specific individual or team needs, are based on its model of assessment, challenge, and support.

Learn more about CCL's coaching services on the Web at http://www.ccl.org/coaching.

Assessment and Development Resources

CCL pioneered 360-degree feedback and believes that assessment provides a solid foundation for learning, growth, and transformation and that development truly happens when an individual recognizes the need to change. CCL offers a broad selection of assessment tools, online resources, and simulations that can help individuals, teams, and organizations increase self-awareness, facilitate learning, enable development, and enhance effectiveness.

CCL's assessments are profiled at http://www.ccl.org/assessments.

Publications

The theoretical foundation for many of our programs, as well as the results of CCL's extensive and often groundbreaking research, can be found in the scores of publications issued by CCL Press and through CCL's alliance with Jossey-Bass, a Wiley imprint. Among these are landmark works, such as *Breaking the Glass Ceiling* and *The*

Lessons of Experience, as well as quick-read guidebooks focused on core aspects of leadership. CCL publications provide insights and practical advice to help individuals become more effective leaders, develop leadership training within organizations, address issues of change and diversity, and build the systems and strategies that advance leadership collectively at the institutional level.

A complete listing of CCL publications is available at http://www.ccl.org/publications.

Leadership Community

To ensure that the Center's work remains focused, relevant, and important to the individuals and organizations it serves, CCL maintains a host of networks, councils, and learning and virtual communities that bring together alumni, donors, faculty, practicing leaders, and thought leaders from around the globe. CCL also forges relationships and alliances with individuals, organizations, and associations that share its values and mission. The energy, insights, and support from these relationships help shape and sustain CCL's educational and research practices and provide its clients with an added measure of motivation and inspiration as they continue their lifelong commitment to leadership and learning.

To learn more, visit http://www.ccl.org/connected.

Research

CCL's portfolio of programs, products, and services is built on a solid foundation of behavioral science research. The role of research at CCL is to advance the understanding of leadership and to transform learning into practical tools for participants and clients. CCL's research is the hub of a cycle that transforms knowledge into practical application and practice into knowledge, thereby illuminating the way organizations think about and enact leadership and leader development.

Find out more about current research initiatives on the Web at http://www.ccl.org/research.

For additional information about CCL, please visit its Web site at http://www.ccl.org or call Client Services at (336) 545-2810.

More titles from the Center for Creative Leadership and Jossey-Bass

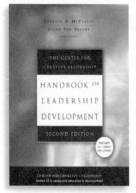
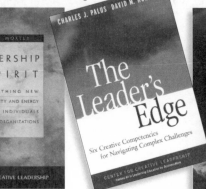

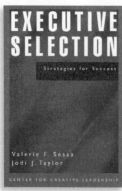

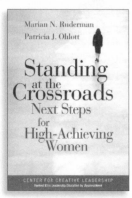

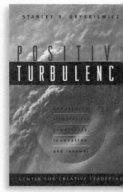
Visit us at www.josseybass.com/go/ccl

JOSSEY-BASS
An Imprint of WILEY
Now you know.